GCSE AQA

French

Like the *Tour de France*, revising for GCSE French can feel like a hard slog. Luckily, this brilliant CGP book is packed with all the study notes and practice questions you'll need for the AQA Grade 9-1 exams in 2018 and beyond!

We've also included **free audio files** to go with the listening questions. You'll find them on the CD-ROM — or you can download them from this page:

www.cgpbooks.co.uk/GCSEFrenchAudio

Complete
Revision & Practice
Everything you need to pass the exams!

Contents

Section One — General Stuff

Numbers 1
Times and Dates 2
Questions 4
Being Polite 6
Opinions 8
Putting it All Together 10
Listening Questions 11
Speaking Question 12
Reading Questions 13
Writing Questions 14
Revision Summary for Section One 15

Section Two — Me, My Family and Friends

About Yourself 16
My Family 17
Describing People 18
Personalities 19
Relationships 20
Partnership 21
Listening Questions 22
Speaking Question 23
Reading Questions 24
Writing Questions 25
Revision Summary for Section Two 26

Section Three — Free-Time Activities

Music 27
Cinema 28
TV 29
Food 30
Eating Out 31
Sport 32
Listening Questions 34
Speaking Question 35
Reading Questions 36
Writing Questions 37
Revision Summary for Section Three 38

Section Four — Technology in Everyday Life

Technology 39
Social Media 41
The Problems with Social Media 42
Listening Questions 43
Speaking Question 44
Reading Questions 45
Writing Questions 46
Revision Summary for Section Four 47

Section Five — Customs and Festivals

Festivals in French-Speaking Countries 48
Religious Festivals and Customs 50
Listening Questions 51
Speaking Question 52
Reading Questions 53
Writing Questions 54
Revision Summary for Section Five 55

Section Six — Where You Live

Talking About Where You Live 56
The Home 57
What You Do at Home 58
Clothes Shopping 59
More Shopping 61
Giving and Asking for Directions 62
Weather 63
Listening Questions 64
Speaking Question 65
Reading Questions 66
Writing Questions 67
Revision Summary for Section Six 68

Section Seven — Lifestyle

Healthy Living 69
Unhealthy Living 70
Illnesses 71
Listening Questions 72
Speaking Question 73
Reading Questions 74
Writing Questions 75
Revision Summary for Section Seven 76

Contents

Section Eight — Social and Global Issues

Environmental Problems.. 77
Problems in Society 79
Contributing to Society 81
Listening Questions 82
Speaking Question 83
Reading Questions 84
Writing Questions 85
Revision Summary for Section Eight........................... 86

Section Nine — Travel and Tourism

Where to Go 87
Accommodation 88
Getting Ready to Go... 89
How to Get There 90
What to Do 91
Listening Questions 92
Speaking Question 93
Reading Questions 94
Writing Questions 95
Revision Summary for Section Nine............................ 96

Section Ten — Current and Future Study and Employment

School Subjects 97
School Routine 98
School Life 99
School Pressures.. 100
Education Post-16... 101
Career Choices and Ambitions 102
Listening Questions 103
Speaking Question 104
Reading Questions 105
Writing Questions 106
Revision Summary for Section Ten.............................. 107

Section Eleven — Grammar

Words for People and Objects 108
'The', 'A' and 'Some'.. 109
Words to Describe Things 110
Words to Compare Things.. 113
Quick Questions.. 114
Words to Describe Actions 116
Words to Compare Actions 118
Words to Say How Much.. 119
Quick Questions.. 120
I, Me, You, We, Them... 121
Something, There, Any.. 122
Position and Order of Object Pronouns 123
Relative and Interrogative Pronouns............................. 124
Possessive and Demonstrative Pronouns 125
Quick Questions.. 126
Joining Words 127
Prepositions... 128
Quick Questions.. 130
Verbs in the Present Tense... 131
Irregular Verbs in the Present Tense............................. 132
More About the Present Tense..................................... 133
Quick Questions.. 134
Talking About the Future... 135
Talking About the Past.. 136
Quick Questions.. 140
Reflexive Verbs and Pronouns 142
Negative Forms... 143
Would, Could and Should 144
Giving Orders... 145
Quick Questions.. 146
'Had done' and '-ing' 147
The Passive 148
Impersonal Verbs and the Subjunctive 149
Quick Questions.. 150
Revision Summary for Section Eleven 151

Section Twelve — Exam Advice

The Listening Exam 152
The Speaking Exam... 153
The Reading Exam.. 154
The Writing Exam 155
The Translation Tasks.. 156

Practice Exam

Listening Paper 157
Speaking Paper 167
Reading Paper 172
Writing Paper 188

Vocabulary Lists 190
Answers... 203
Transcripts 214
Index 219

Published by CGP

Editors:
Lucy Forsyth
Cathy Lear
Hannah Roscoe
Louise Taylor
Matt Topping

Contributors:
Marie-Laure Delvallée
Sophie Desgland
Jackie Shaw
Sarah Sweeney

With thanks to Christine Bodin, Sharon Knight, Lucy Loveluck, Sam Norman and Karen Wells for the proofreading.
With thanks to Jan Greenway for the copyright research.

Acknowledgements:

Audio produced by Naomi Laredo of Small Print.

Recorded, edited and mastered by Graham Williams of The Speech Recording Studio,
with the assistance of Andy Le Vien at RMS Studios.

Voice Artists:

Daniéle Bourdais
François Darriet
Jason Grangier
Perle Solvés

CD-ROM edited and mastered by Neil Hastings.

AQA material is reproduced by permission of AQA.

With thanks to iStock.com for permission to use the images on pages 35, 52, 65, 81, 83, 93, 169 & 176.

Abridged and adapted extract from 'Madame Bovary', on page 21, by Gustave Flaubert.

Abridged and adapted extract from 'Les Misérables', on page 56, by Victor Hugo.

Abridged and adapted extract from 'Un Mariage', on page 179, by Ernest Laut.

Abridged and adapted extract from 'Les trois mousquetaires', on page 186, by Alexandre Dumas.

Abridged and adapted extract from 'Le tour du monde en quatre-vingts jours', on page 216 and audio tracks, by Jules Verne.

Abridged and adapted extract from 'La Terre', on page 218 and audio track, by Émile Zola.

ISBN: 978 1 78294 539 0
Printed by Elanders Ltd, Newcastle upon Tyne.
Clipart from Corel®

Based on the classic CGP style created by Richard Parsons.

Numbers

Understanding how numbers work in French is really important — they're not as simple as they are in English.

Un, deux, trois — One, two, three

0	zéro
1	un
2	deux
3	trois
4	quatre
5	cinq
6	six
7	sept
8	huit
9	neuf
10	dix

① 11 to 16 all end in 'ze'. But 17, 18 and 19 are 'ten-seven' etc.

11	onze
12	douze
13	treize
14	quatorze
15	quinze
16	seize
17	dix-sept
18	dix-huit
19	dix-neuf

20	vingt
30	trente
40	quarante
50	cinquante
60	soixante
70	soixante-dix
80	quatre-vingts
90	quatre-vingt-dix

② Except 'vingt', most of the 'tens' end in 'nte'. Also, '70' is 'sixty-ten', '80' is 'four-20s', and '90' is 'four-20-ten'.

Grammar — 'un' / 'une'

For feminine nouns, use '<u>une</u>' and '<u>et une</u>' instead of '<u>un</u>' and '<u>et un</u>':

Il y a **<u>vingt et une</u>** filles et **<u>vingt et un</u>** garçons.
There are <u>21</u> girls and <u>21</u> boys.

③ In-between numbers are formed like English ones, but add 'et un' for numbers ending in '1'.

21	vingt et un
22	vingt-deux

④ For the 70s and 90s, add 11-19 to 'soixante' and 'quatre-vingt' (like 'quatre-vingts' (80) but without the 's'). '81' and '91' bend the rule explained in point 3 — they miss out the 'et', e.g. **quatre-vingt-un** (81).

71	soixante et onze	91	quatre-vingt-onze	100	cent
72	soixante-douze	98	quatre-vingt-dix-huit	1000	mille

10.000	dix mille
1.000.000	un million

⑤ For hundreds and thousands, put cent, deux cent, mille (etc.) before the number.

623	six cent vingt-trois	1947	mille neuf cent quarante-sept

In French, long numbers are broken up by full stops instead of commas. Also, French decimals use commas instead of decimal points

Add '-ième' to the number to say second, third etc.

Here are a few more handy words to <u>spice up</u> your French. Watch out for 'first' — it doesn't follow the rule.

Use 'premier' for masculine nouns and 'première' for feminine ones.

1st	premier / première	5th	cinquième	10th	dixième
2nd	deuxième	6th	sixième	99th	quatre-vingt-dix-neuvième
3rd	troisième	7th	septième		
4th	quatrième	8th	huitième		
		9th	neuvième		

A 'u' is added to 'cinq'.

une douzaine	*a dozen*
une dizaine	*about ten*
une vingtaine	*about twenty*
un nombre de	*a number of*
des dizaines	*lots / dozens*

Numbers ending in 'e' lose the e.

The 'f' in 'neuf' changes to a 'v'.

READING Read, write, repeat — you simply have to know these numbers...

Read Mathieu's social media profile, and answer the questions in **French**. Write the numbers in full.

Salut ! Je m'appelle Mathieu, et j'ai dix-sept ans. Je suis le quatrième enfant de la famille — j'ai trois sœurs aînées. Nous habitons dans la première maison de la rue Phillipe — c'est la troisième rue après le parc. Il y a une vingtaine de maisons dans la rue.

e.g. Quel âge a Mathieu ? **Il a dix-sept ans.**
1. Il a combien de frères et de sœurs ? [1]
2. Quelle est sa maison ? [1]
3. Où se trouve la rue où Mathieu habite ? [1]
4. Combien de maisons y-a-t-il dans la rue ? [1]

Times and Dates

Times and dates are essential for your exam — make sure you know how to use both in French.

Quelle heure est-il? — What time is it?

1) There are different ways to tell the time in French. Make sure you <u>learn</u> all of them. To say 'it's...o'clock' use '<u>il est...heure(s)</u>'.

| Il est une heure. | *It's 1 o'clock.* |

| Il est vingt heures. | *It's 8 pm.* |

> To say 'in the evening' without referring to a specific hour of the day, just say 'le soir'. E.g. 'Le soir, j'ai dormi.' (*In the evening, I slept.*) The same rule applies for 'in the morning' and 'in the afternoon'.

2) Use this vocab to say '<u>quarter past</u>', '<u>half past</u>' and '<u>quarter to</u>'.

et quart	*quarter past*
et demie	*half past*
moins le quart	*quarter to*
du matin	*in the morning*
de l'après-midi	*in the afternoon*
du soir	*in the evening*

Il est deux heures et quart.	*It's quarter past two.*
Il est deux heures et demie.	*It's half past two.*
Il est trois heures moins le quart.	*It's quarter to three.*
Il est cinq heures du soir.	*It's five in the evening.*

Être à l'heure — To be on time

1) To say '<u>...minutes past</u>', you say the hour, then the number of minutes. You don't need any <u>extra</u> words.

| Il est trois heures douze. | *It's 03:12.* |
| Il est vingt heures trente-trois. | *It's 20:33.* |

The French use the 24-hour clock a lot — so make sure you can use it.

> **Grammar** — 'à' with times
> You use 'à' with times to say '<u>at</u>'.
> **à dix heures** — *at ten o'clock*

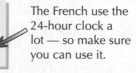

2) Use '<u>moins...</u>' *(less)* to say '<u>...to</u>'.

| Il est onze heures moins dix. | *It's ten to eleven.* |

Les jours de la semaine — The days of the week

In French, the days of the week are always <u>lower case</u>. They're also all <u>masculine</u>.

lundi	*Monday*
mardi	*Tuesday*
mercredi	*Wednesday*
jeudi	*Thursday*
vendredi	*Friday*
samedi	*Saturday*
dimanche	*Sunday*

> **Grammar** — 'le lundi' (Mondays)
> To say something happens regularly on a certain day, use the <u>masculine definite article</u> ('le') with the day — <u>not a plural</u>.
> **Le lundi, je fais du sport.**
> ***On Mondays, I do sport.***

aujourd'hui	*today*
demain	*tomorrow*
hier	*yesterday*
après-demain	*the day after tomorrow*
avant-hier	*the day before yesterday*
la semaine	*the week*
le week-end	*the weekend*

Je pars mardi.	*I'm leaving on Tuesday.*
Le week-end, j'aime faire la grasse matinée.	*At the weekend, I like to have a lie-in.*
Elle voit son père le dimanche.	*She sees her father on Sundays.*

the next day — le lendemain

During the week — Pendant la semaine

every day — tous les jours

Times and Dates

Here's some more vocab and phrases you can use to talk about times and dates.

Les mois de l'année — The months of the year

Months and seasons are <u>masculine</u> and <u>don't</u> begin with <u>capital letters</u>.

janvier	*January*	juillet	*July*	(en) hiver	*(in) winter*
février	*February*	août	*August*	**(au)** printemps	*(in) spring*
mars	*March*	septembre	*September*	(en) été	*(in) summer*
avril	*April*	octobre	*October*	(en) automne	*(in) autumn*
mai	*May*	novembre	*November*		
juin	*June*	décembre	*December*		

Watch out — 'in spring' is 'au printemps'.
All of the other seasons use 'en'.

Quelle est la date? — What's the date?

In French, you say '<u>the nine April</u>' or '<u>the seventeen November</u>'. The exception to this rule is the <u>first day</u> of a month, where you use '<u>le premier</u>' (*the first*), like you would in English.

Aujourd'hui c'est le quinze mai.   *Today is the 15th of May.*

Mon frère est né le vingt-cinq février mille neuf cent quatre-vingt-dix-huit.   *My brother was born on the 25th of February 1998.*

the first of August — le premier août

in the 90s — dans les années quatre-vingt-dix
in the year 2000 — en l'an deux mille

Ce matin / ce soir — This morning / this evening

These time phrases are really useful for <u>making arrangements</u>... and for your <u>exams</u>.

ce matin	*this morning*	la semaine prochaine	*next week*
cet après-midi	*this afternoon*	la semaine dernière	*last week*
ce soir	*this evening / tonight*	toujours	*always*
demain matin	*tomorrow morning*	quelquefois	*sometimes*
cette semaine	*this week*	(assez) souvent	*(quite) often*
ce week-end	*this weekend*	(assez) rarement	*(quite) rarely*

Qu'est-ce que tu fais ce soir?   *What are you doing this evening?*

Le soir, je vais souvent au cinéma.   *In the evening, I often go to the cinema.*

La semaine prochaine, je vais danser.   *Next week, I'm going to dance.*

this weekend — ce week-end

rarely — rarement

This afternoon — Cet après-midi

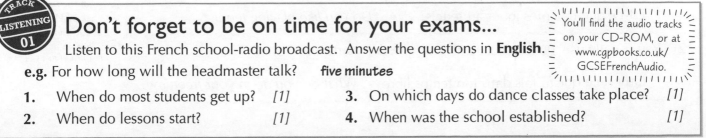

TRACK LISTENING 01

Don't forget to be on time for your exams...

You'll find the audio tracks on your CD-ROM, or at www.cgpbooks.co.uk/ GCSEFrenchAudio.

Listen to this French school-radio broadcast. Answer the questions in **English**.

e.g. For how long will the headmaster talk?   **five minutes**

1. When do most students get up?   *[1]*
2. When do lessons start?   *[1]*
3. On which days do dance classes take place?   *[1]*
4. When was the school established?   *[1]*

Questions

Knowing how to ask questions is key in any language. And it's not just the words that matter...

Les mots interrogatifs — Question words

quand?	*when?*
pourquoi?	*why?*
où?	*where?*
comment?	*how?*
combien?	*how much / many?*
qui?	*who?*
quoi?	*what?*
que?	*what?*
quel?	*which?*

These are known as interrogatives.

Grammar — quel, quelle, quels, quelles

'Quel' means 'which' or 'what'. It's an interrogative adjective, so it agrees with the noun it refers to. It has masculine, feminine, singular and plural forms:

quel (masc. singular)	quels (masc. plural)
quelle (fem. singular)	quelles (fem. plural)

Quelles filles aiment chanter?
Which girls like singing?
'Filles' (*girls*) is feminine and plural, so 'quelles' is used.

Pourquoi es-tu en retard?   *Why are you late?*

Qui vient avec moi?   *Who's coming with me?*

Où est la plage?   *Where is the beach?*

Ask questions by changing your tone of voice

1) The easiest way to ask a question in French is to say a normal sentence, but make your voice go up at the end. This works well for questions that are answered yes or no.

Tu as faim?   *Are you hungry?*

C'est loin?   *Is it far?*

In writing, the only difference between this question and the statement 'C'est loin.' (*It's far.*) is the question mark.

Tu travailles le week-end?   *Do you work at the weekend?*

2) To answer 'yes' to a question containing a negative, use 'si'.

Est-ce que tu n'as pas faim? — Si, j'ai faim.   *Aren't you hungry? — Yes, I'm hungry.*

Use 'est-ce que' or 'qu'est-ce que' for questions

1) You can also turn a statement into a yes or no question by using 'est-ce que'.

Est-ce que tu as des frères ou des sœurs?   *Do you have any brothers or sisters?*

Est-ce que tu aimes jouer au tennis?   *Do you like playing tennis?*

You can use 'qu'est-ce qui' to ask 'what' when it's the subject of the sentence. See p.124 for more about using 'qui' and 'que' in questions.

2) You usually use 'qu'est-ce que' if your question starts with 'what'.

Qu'est-ce que tu fais dans ton temps libre?   *What do you do in your free time?*

Questions

Now you've learnt the basics, you can start developing your questions.

Put the verb first to form a question

You can ask questions in French by <u>swapping</u> the <u>verb</u> (see p.131) and the <u>subject</u> (the person or thing doing the action) around. Don't forget to add the <u>hyphen</u>, though.

Fais-tu du sport?	*Do you do any sport?*
Pouvez-vous m'aider?	*Can you help me?*
Aimes-tu le hip-hop?	*Do you like hip-hop?*

If the verb ends in a <u>vowel</u> and is followed by <u>il</u>, <u>elle</u> or <u>on</u>, you add a '<u>t</u>' to make it <u>easier to say</u>:

A-t-il fini ses devoirs?
Has he finished his homework?

Qu'est-ce que c'est? — What is it?

Here are some useful <u>questions</u> that you might want to ask:

À quelle heure?	*At what time?*		C'est de quelle couleur?	*What colour is it?*
Quelle heure est-il?	*What time is it?*		D'où?	*From where?*
C'est combien?	*How much is it?*		Pour combien de temps?	*For how long?*
C'est quelle date?	*What is the date?*		Que veut dire...?	*What does...mean?*
C'est quel jour?	*What day is it?*		Ça s'écrit comment?	*How is that written?*

Question	Simple Answer	Extended Answer
D'où viens-tu?	Je viens de Millom.	Je viens de Millom, dans le nord-ouest de l'Angleterre. C'est une petite ville rurale.
Where are you from?	*I'm from Millom.*	*I'm from Millom, in north-west England. It's a small, rural town.*

SPEAKING — You'll have to ask a question in the role-play part of the exam...

Here's a role-play that Marie did with her teacher.

Teacher: Est-ce que tu fais du sport ?   *(Grade 8-9)*

Marie: Oui, je fais du ski. Normalement je vais à **la piste de ski**[1] le lundi et le mercredi soir.

Teacher: Où est la piste de ski ?

Marie: La piste de ski **se trouve**[2] en centre-ville, à côté de la piscine.

Teacher: C'est loin de ta maison ?

Marie: Non, au contraire, c'est à quinze minutes à pied. C'est très pratique.

Teacher: C'est bien.

Marie: Et vous, qu'est-ce que vous faites pendant votre temps libre ?

Teacher: J'adore faire des promenades à la campagne.

[1] ski slope
[2] is (literally 'finds itself')

'!' means you'll need to answer a question you haven't prepared.
When you see '?' you need to ask a question.

There's more info about role-plays on p.153.

Tick list:
✓ correctly formed question
✓ time phrases
✓ present tense

To improve:
+ use an opinion phrase e.g. 'à mon avis...'

Use the instructions below to prepare your own role-play. Address your friend as 'tu' and speak for about two minutes. [15 marks]

Tu parles du sport avec un(e) ami(e) français(e).
- *la natation — l'heure*
- *quand — jour(s)*
- *la natation — le prix*
- *!*
- *? sport préféré*

Being Polite

Politeness makes a big difference — not everyone you talk to will be a friend. Here's a run-down of how to adjust your speech in different situations.

Bonjour...au revoir — Hello...goodbye

<u>Learn</u> these phrases — they're <u>crucial</u>.

bonjour	*hello*	au revoir	*goodbye*
salut	*hi*	à bientôt	*see you soon*
allô	*hello (on phone)*	à tout à l'heure	*see you soon / later*
bienvenue	*welcome*	à demain	*see you tomorrow*
bonsoir	*good evening*	Bon voyage!	*Have a good trip!*
bonne nuit	*good night*	Bonne chance!	*Good luck!*

Comment ça va? — How are you?

Make your conversation <u>sparkle</u> by using these little <u>gems</u>.

Comment ça va?	*How are you?*
Comment allez-vous?	*How are you? (formal)*
Et toi?	*And you? (informal)*
Et vous?	*And you? (formal)*
Ça va bien, merci.	*(I am) fine, thanks.*
Ça ne va pas bien.	*(I am) not well.*
Pas mal.	*Not bad.*
Je ne sais pas.	*I don't know.*
Super!	*Great!*
Je me sens...	*I feel...*
Comme ci, comme ça.	*OK.*

Grammar — using 'tu' and 'vous'

There are two ways of saying '<u>you</u>' in French. '<u>Tu</u>' is <u>singular</u> and <u>informal</u>. You should use it with a <u>friend</u> or <u>family member</u>. '<u>Vous</u>' is for <u>more than one person</u>, or for one person in a <u>formal</u> situation, e.g. a <u>stranger</u> or <u>someone older</u> than you.

Comment ça va?	*How are you? (informal)*	*How are you? (formal) —* Comment allez-vous?
Je me sens fantastique.	*I feel fantastic.*	*awful —* affreux / affreuse
Pas mal.	*Not bad.*	*well —* bien

Puis-je vous présenter...? — May I introduce...?

Puis-je vous présenter Dave?	*May I introduce Dave?*
Voici Dave.	*This is Dave.*
enchanté(e)	*pleased to meet you*

'Enchanté' agrees with the gender of the speaker. It needs an extra 'e' ('enchantée') if the person saying it is female.

The <u>conversation</u> below shows how these phrases are used:

Madame Rollet:	Salut Delphine, comment ça va?	*Hi Delphine, how are you?*
Delphine:	Ça va bien. Comment allez-vous?	*I'm fine. How are you?*
Madame Rollet:	Comme ci, comme ça.	*O.K.*
Delphine:	Puis-je vous présenter Bruno?	*May I introduce Bruno?*
Madame Rollet:	Enchantée.	*Pleased to meet you.*

Delphine uses the polite 'vous' form — Madame Rollet is older than her.

If you're talking to someone you call 'tu', you say 'Puis-je te présenter...?' — it's informal.

Being Polite

This page is about asking politely. These handy words and phrases will help you avoid causing offence.

Je voudrais — I would like

1) 'Je voudrais' (I would like) is more polite than 'je veux' (I want). 'J'aimerais' also means 'I would like'.

'Je voudrais' and 'j'aimerais' are in the conditional tense — see p.144 for more.

Je voudrais une tasse de thé.	*I would like a cup of tea.*
Je voudrais du pain.	*I would like some bread.*
J'aimerais de l'eau.	*I would like some water.*

We would like — Nous voudrions

She would like — Elle voudrait

He would like — Il aimerait

2) 'Puis-je...' and 'Est-ce que je peux...' both mean 'May I...'.

See p.4-5 for more about forming questions.

Puis-je avoir un café? *May I have a coffee?*

Est-ce que je peux m'asseoir? *May I sit down?*

S'il vous plaît — Please

Don't forget these useful polite words — they could make all the difference...

s'il vous plaît	*please (formal)*	d'accord	*OK / fine*
s'il te plaît	*please (informal)*	pardon	*excuse me (informal)*
merci	*thank you*	excusez-moi	*excuse me (polite)*
merci beaucoup	*thank you very much*	quel dommage	*what a shame*
de rien	*you're welcome*	Je suis désolé(e).	*I'm sorry.*

Don't forget to say 's'il te plaît' instead of 's'il vous plaît' if you're talking to someone you call 'tu.'

Grammar — désolé or désolée?

Like 'enchanté', 'désolé' has to agree with the subject. You add an extra 'e' if you're female:
Je suis désolé. *I'm sorry.* (male)   **Je suis désolée. *I'm sorry.* (female)**

WRITING — Knowing how to use 'tu' and 'vous' correctly is important...

Here's a script for you. Jean is introducing his friend, Michel, to his girlfriend, Aurélie.

Jean : Salut Michel ! Comment ça va ? *(Grade 4-5)*

Michel : Oui, ça va bien merci — c'est le week-end ! Et toi ?

Jean : Pas trop mal. Puis-je te présenter Aurélie, ma **petite-amie**[1] ?

Michel : Enchanté.

Aurélie : Enchantée.

Michel : Comment allez-vous, Aurélie ?

Aurélie : Super, merci, mais **j'ai faim**[2].

Jean : Allons **chercher**[3] un sandwich. À tout à l'heure, Michel.

Michel : A bientôt !

[1]girlfriend
[2]I'm hungry
[3]to get

Tick list:
✓ variety of polite phrases
✓ gender agreement of enchanté(e)

To improve:
+ more detail to develop the ideas
+ different tenses (add a past or future)

Now it's your turn:

Écrivez un script au sujet de deux personnes qui se présentent pour la première fois.
*Écrivez environ **40** mots en **français**. [8 marks]*

To get more tenses in your answer, you could make plans to meet in the future, or one person could say where they used to live. Try to include as many of the phrases you learnt on p.6 and 7 as you can.

Opinions

Having an opinion is a great way to pick up lots of marks in the exam, so don't hold back on giving your views. Just make sure that you use a cracking variety of phrases and vocab to really impress the examiner.

Qu'est-ce que tu penses de...? — What do you think of...?

There are <u>lots of ways</u> to ask someone their <u>opinion</u> in French... and to give your own.

Qu'est-ce que tu penses de...?	*What do you think of...?*
Quel est ton avis sur...?	*What's your opinion of...?*
Qu'est-ce que tu penses?	*What do you think?*
Comment trouves-tu...?	*How do you find...?*
Est-ce que tu le / la trouves sympa?	*Do you think he / she is nice?*

Je pense que...	*I think that...*
À mon avis...	*In my opinion...*
Je trouve que...	*I find that...*
Je crois que...	*I believe that...*
Personnellement...	*Personally...*

Qu'est-ce que tu penses de mon frère?
What do you think of my brother? →

Je pense qu'il est très sympa.
I think that he's very nice.

Speak your mind — it'll sound impressive

Here's how to say what you <u>like</u> and <u>dislike</u>.

J'adore...	*I love...*
J'aime...	*I like / love...*
J'aime bien...	*I like...*
Ça me plaît.	*I like it.*
Je m'intéresse à...	*I'm interested in...*
Je trouve...chouette	*I find...great*

Je n'aime pas...	*I don't like...*
Ça ne me plaît pas.	*I don't like it.*
Ça ne m'intéresse pas.	*It doesn't interest me.*
Je trouve...affreux / affreuse	*I find...awful*
Je déteste...	*I hate...*
Ça ne me dit rien.	*It means nothing to me.*

Be careful — 'j'aime Pierre' can mean 'I like Pierre' OR 'I love Pierre'. If you only like him, it's safer to say 'je trouve Pierre sympathique' ('*I think Pierre is nice*') or 'j'aime bien Pierre' ('*I like Pierre*'). Otherwise you might be giving out the wrong message...

J'adore jouer au basket.	*I love playing basketball.*	*I like* — J'aime bien
Je m'intéresse à la musique.	*I'm interested in music.*	*I'm not interested in* — Je ne m'intéresse pas à
Je déteste les films d'horreur.	*I hate horror films.*	*I find... awful.* — Je trouve... affreux.

Es-tu d'accord? — Do you agree?

absolument	*absolutely*	bien sûr	*of course*	moi non plus	*me neither*
bien entendu	*of course*	ça dépend	*it depends*	ça m'est égal	*I don't care*

Es-tu d'accord avec moi?	*Do you agree with me?*	*with that* — avec ça
Bien sûr.	*Of course.*	*It depends.* — Ça dépend.

Opinions

Don't forget to back up your opinions — it's not enough just to say what you think.
Being able to justify and develop those opinions is crucial for earning extra marks.

Parce que — Because

The best way to justify your opinion is to give a reason. 'Parce que' and 'car' both mean because.

J'aime ce film parce que les acteurs sont formidables.	*I like this film because the actors are great.*
Je trouve ce film affreux car l'histoire est ennuyeuse.	*I think this film is awful because the story is boring.*

Use describing words to explain your opinions

Here are some describing words that you can use to explain your opinion.

affreux / affreuse	*awful*
amical(e)	*friendly*
amusant(e)	*funny*
barbant(e)	*boring*
beau / belle	*handsome / beautiful*
bon(ne)	*good*
doué(e)	*gifted / talented*
ennuyeux / ennuyeuse	*boring*
fantastique	*fantastic*
formidable	*great*
génial(e)	*brilliant*
mauvais(e)	*bad*
super, chouette	*great*
sympa, sympathique	*nice (person)*

Ce film me plaît parce que les acteurs sont doués.

I like this film because the actors are talented.

Remember, adjectives (describing words) need to agree with the noun they refer to — see p.110 for more.

These phrases might come in handy, too.

Ça m'énerve.	*It gets on my nerves.*
Ça me fait rire.	*It makes me laugh.*

Je n'aime pas ce film car ça m'énerve.	*I don't like this film because it gets on my nerves.*

READING Always make sure you can justify your opinions...

Sophie and Mayeul are talking about a French actor, Maurice le Pain.
Have a look at the text, then answer the questions in **English**.

Sophie : Quel est ton avis sur Maurice le Pain ?

Mayeul : Ça dépend. Je pense qu'il est assez bon dans les films d'action, mais je ne l'aime pas dans les comédies. Il n'est pas très amusant.

Sophie : Je ne suis pas d'accord ! C'est mon acteur préféré parce qu'il est vraiment doué. Ses films sont toujours formidables.

Mayeul : Il te plaît car il est beau. Moi, je préfère les acteurs qui ont du vrai talent.

Sophie : Tu es envieux ! Toutes mes amies adorent Maurice aussi. Nous le trouvons chouette.

e.g. What does Mayeul think about Maurice le Pain in action films?
He thinks he's quite good.

1. Why doesn't Mayeul like Maurice le Pain in comedies? [1]

2. Why is Maurice Sophie's favourite actor? [1]

3. What does Sophie say about Maurice le Pain's films? [1]

4. Why does Mayeul think that Sophie likes Maurice le Pain? [1]

5. What do Sophie's friends think of Maurice? [1]

Putting it All Together

You could get asked your opinion on any of the GCSE topics, so make sure you can bring all the stuff on these pages together. You won't get top marks if you make a statement that you can't back up properly.

Talking about books, films, music...

In the exam, you might get asked if you <u>like</u> or <u>dislike</u> a band, film, book etc. If you don't have an opinion, just make one up. There aren't any marks available for <u>shrugging</u>...

ce film	*this film*	ce groupe	*this band*
ce journal	*this newspaper*	cette équipe	*this team*
ce livre	*this book*	cet acteur	*this actor*
ce roman	*this novel*	cette actrice	*this actress*
ce magazine	*this magazine*	ce chanteur	*this singer (male)*
cette émission	*this programme*	cette chanteuse	*this singer (female)*
cette chanson	*this song*	cette vedette	*this star / celebrity*

Quel est ton avis sur cette équipe?

What's your opinion of this team?

J'aime bien cette équipe. À mon avis, les joueurs sont doués.

I like this team. In my opinion, the players are gifted.

'Ce' ('this' / 'that') becomes 'cette' in front of feminine nouns. For masculine nouns starting with a vowel, use 'cet'. See p.112 for more info.

À mon avis — In my opinion

Question	**Simple Answer**	**Extended Answer**
Qu'est-ce que tu penses de la musique classique? *What do you think of classical music?*	C'est ennuyeux. *It's boring.*	À mon avis, la musique classique est ennuyeuse. *In my opinion, classical music is boring.*

Qu'est-ce que tu penses de ce magazine?

What do you think of this magazine? — this actor — cet acteur

J'adore cette émission parce que ça me fait rire.

I love this programme because it makes me laugh. — it makes me cry — ça me fait pleurer

Je trouve ce chanteur affreux car sa musique est ennuyeuse.

I find this singer awful because his music is boring. — he is arrogant — il est arrogant

---

TRACK LISTENING 02

Show the examiner that you can express your opinions...

Listen to this podcast from your French partner school. Blandine and Marc are talking about what they do at the weekend. Decide whether the statements below are true or false.

e.g. Blandine always likes doing sport at the weekend. **false**

1. A. Blandine has fun with her football team. *[1]*

B. Marc hates all sports. *[1]*

2. A. The book Marc is reading is boring. *[1]*

B. Blandine often reads novels. *[1]*

3. A. Blandine likes different kinds of films. *[1]*

B. Marc enjoys watching comedies. *[1]*

Listening Questions

Practice exam questions are a brilliant way to prepare for the real things. We've got four pages coming up that give you some realistic tasks to tackle for each of the four GCSE French papers. Good luck!

1   You overhear Paul talking on the phone about his weekend.
     Answer the questions in **English**.

TRACK LISTENING 03

1 a   How many T-shirts did Paul buy? ....   *[1 mark]*

1 b   Roughly how many DVDs did he buy? ....   *[1 mark]*

1 c   How much did his shopping cost in total? ....   *[1 mark]*

1 d   How many friends did Paul see on Saturday evening? ....   *[1 mark]*

1 e   Roughly how many presents did his best friend receive? ....   *[1 mark]*

2   While on a bus in Paris, you overhear two people talking about a singer.
     Decide whether the statements are **true** or **false**.

TRACK LISTENING 04

2 a   Lilette Laurent is Claire's favourite singer. ....   *[1 mark]*

2 b   Claire and Georges both think Lilette is very talented. ....   *[1 mark]*

2 c   According to Claire, Lilette loves making money. ....   *[1 mark]*

2 d   Georges likes Lilette's music. ....   *[1 mark]*

2 e   Claire says Lilette's songs make people happy. ....   *[1 mark]*

2 f   Georges doesn't like rock music. ....   *[1 mark]*

Speaking Question

For the Speaking Question pages, you'll need to get a friend or a parent to read the teacher's role, so you can pretend it's a real assessment. Before the conversation starts, give yourself a couple minutes to read through the candidate's role, and think about what you're going to say.

Candidate's Role

- Your teacher will play the role of your French friend. They will speak first.

- You should use *tu* to address your friend.

- – ! – means you will have to respond to something you have not prepared.

- – ? – means you will have to ask your friend a question.

> Tu organises une excursion au cinéma avec un(e) ami(e).
>
> - Genre de film que tu préfères (**deux** raisons).
>
> - ? Transport au cinéma.
>
> - Heure de rencontre.
>
> - !
>
> - Activité après le film (**un** détail).

Teacher's Role

- You begin the role-play using the introductory text below.

- You should address the candidate as *tu*.

- You may alter the wording of the questions in response to the candidate's previous answers.

- Do not supply the candidate with key vocabulary.

> Introductory text: *Tu organises une excursion au cinéma avec un(e) ami(e).*
> *Moi, je suis ton ami(e).*
>
> - Quel genre de film préfères-tu ?
>
> - ? Allow the candidate to ask you a question.
>
> - On se retrouve à quelle heure ?
>
> - ! Est-ce que tu veux inviter quelqu'un d'autre ?
>
> - Qu'est ce que tu voudrais faire après le film ?

Section One — General Stuff

Reading Questions

1 Read this chatroom conversation three teenagers had about their families.

Marie	J'habite avec mes grand-parents. Ma grand-mère a soixante-dix ans et mon grand-père a soixante-treize ans. Ils sont très sympathiques.
Claude	J'ai une assez grande famille. D'abord il y a mon frère aîné, qui a vingt ans. Puis il y a moi, et j'ai dix-sept ans. J'ai aussi une petite sœur, qui a quatorze ans, et un petit frère, qui a douze ans.
Ahmed	Je n'ai ni frères ni sœurs. J'habite avec ma mère, qui a quarante-sept ans. Moi, j'ai quinze ans. Nous avons un vieux chat, qui est plus âgé que moi — il a seize ans. Notre petite famille est harmonieuse.

How old are the following people / animals? Write the numbers in digits.

Example: Marie's grandmother ....70....

1 a Marie's grandfather ....63....   1 d Claude's sister ....

1 b Claude's older brother ....20....   1 e Ahmed's mother ....

1 c Claude ....17....   1 f Ahmed's cat .... [6 marks]

2 Lisez ce que ces personnes ont écrit dans un forum sur leurs passe-temps. Répondez aux questions en **français**.

Je fais souvent du sport. Le mardi soir, je fais de la natation. Ça commence à sept heures. Ce week-end, il y a un concours et je vais y participer. — **Aurélie**

Moi, j'aime la musique. Le lundi soir et le samedi matin, je joue de la trompette dans un orchestre. La semaine prochaine il y aura un grand concert. — **Damien**

2 a Quand est-ce qu'Aurélie fait de la natation ? ....Le mardi soir........ [2 marks]

2 b Qu'est-ce qu'elle fait ce week-end ? ....un concours....... [1 mark]

2 c Quand est-ce que Damien joue dans l'orchestre ? ...Le lundi soir et le samedi.... [2 marks]

2 d Quand est le concert ? ....La semaine prochaine........ [1 mark]

Section One — General Stuff

Writing Questions

1   Translate the following passage into French.

> On Mondays, I see my friends. Last week, we watched an action film.
> This weekend, I am going to go shopping with my cousins.

La semaine   *nous avons regardé*
Le lundi Je vois mes copains. ~~l'année dernière~~, ~~on regarde~~ un film d'action

ce weekend   *faire*   *les*   *mes*
Cette le weeked Je vais ~~aller-à aux~~ magasins avec ~~ma~~ cousins

[6 marks]

2   Translate the following passage into French.

> My favourite sport is rugby because it is very exciting. I have been playing rugby for seven
> years. At the weekend I like to watch sport on television with my friends, but I'm not interested
> in football. I think that the players are arrogant. In the future, I would like to be a teacher.

passionnant   *je*   *au*
mon sport préféré c'est le rugby car c'est très amusante. J'ai joue le rugby
depuis
~~pour~~ sept ans. Sur le weekend j'aime regarder le sport à la television

m'interesse   *au*
avec mes amies. mais je ne ~~interessant~~ pas dans le foot. Je pense que
le joueurs sont arrogants
c'est ~~arroga les paresseux~~ A l'avenir Je voudrais être prof.

[12 marks]

Revision Summary for Section One

These questions are here to help you find out what you know well, and what might need some more work. Once you've had a go at all of them, have another look through the section and revise the bits you found tricky. Tick off the questions you can answer, then put a tick by the page title when you've finished all the questions in that section.

Numbers (p.1) ☑

1) Count out loud from 1–20 in French. ☑
2) How do you say these numbers in French?
   a) 35   b) 71   c) 86   d) 112   e) 2000 ☑
3) How would you say 'ninth' in French? ☑

Times and Dates (p.2-3) ☑

4) Your friend says: 'Je vais aller au parc à huit heures du soir.' Translate her sentence into English. ☑
5) Using the 24-hour clock, say 'it's four forty-five pm' in French. ☑
6) State all of the days of the week in French, from Monday to Sunday. ☑
7) How do you say the following time expressions in French?
   a) yesterday   b) tomorrow   c) the weekend ☑
8) If something happened 'avant-hier', when did it happen? ☑
9) Say all of the months of the year in French, from January to December. ☑
10) Quelle est la date de ton anniversaire? Répondez en français. ☑

Questions (p.4-5) ☑

11) To ask a question just by changing the tone of your voice, what do you need to do? ☑
12) 'Tu joues' means 'you play' or 'you are playing'. What do these questions mean in English?
   a) Pourquoi tu joues?   c) Où est-ce que tu joues?   e) Est-ce que tu joues?
   b) Quand est-ce que tu joues?   d) Joues-tu bien?   f) De quoi joues-tu? ☑

Being Polite (p.6-7) ☑

13) What's the French for...? a) see you soon   b) see you tomorrow   c) good luck ☑
14) You're speaking to your head teacher. Which of the following questions would be most appropriate?
   a) Comment ça va?   b) Comment allez-vous? ☑
15) What's the English for...? a) Je voudrais...   b) Est-ce que je peux...?   c) s'il vous plaît ☑

Opinions (p.8-10) ☑

16) How would you ask someone, in French, what they think of rap music ('la musique rap')?
   Give as many different ways as you can think of. ☑
17) Translate these phrases into English:
   a) je pense que   b) à mon avis   c) je crois que   d) personnellement ☑
18) Translate these opinions about pop music ('la musique pop') into French.
   a) I love pop music.   c) I'm interested in pop music.   e) I find pop music great.
   b) I don't like pop music.   d) I find pop music awful.   f) It means nothing to me. ☑
19) Your friend says: 'Moi, je préfère la musique rock car c'est formidable.' What's he saying? ☑
20) Think of an actor or singer you like, and explain why you like them (in French). ☑
21) Answer this question in French: 'Quel est ton avis sur les films d'action?' ☑

About Yourself

Learning to tell the examiner about yourself is really important. Don't worry if you don't have much to say — just make stuff up so you can show off your knowledge of French vocab and grammar.

Je m'appelle... — My name is...

s'appeler	to be called
avoir... ans	to be... years old
le nom	surname
le prénom	first name
né(e) le...	born on the...
l'anniversaire (m)	birthday

Grammar — saying your age

In French, you don't say how old you <u>are</u> — you say how many years you <u>have</u>. This means you need to use the verb '<u>avoir</u>' (*to have*).

Quel âge <u>as</u>-tu?   ⟹   **J'<u>ai</u> seize ans.**

How old <u>are</u> you?   ⟹   *I <u>am</u> sixteen years old.*

> For more on numbers and dates see p.1-3.

Je m'appelle Sara et j'habite à Natland.   *I'm called Sara and I live in Natland.* ← near to Kendal — près de Kendal

J'ai quinze ans, et je suis né(e) le neuf juin 2001.   *I'm fifteen years old, and I was born on the ninth of June 2001.* ← 'Né(e)' needs an extra 'e' on the end if you're female (see p.110).

Mon anniversaire, c'est le deux février.   *My birthday is on the second of February.*

Je suis britannique mais je suis d'origine asiatique.   *I'm British but I'm of Asian origin.*

> See p.200 for a list of more nationalities.

English — anglais(e)
Welsh — gallois(e)
Scottish — écossais(e)
Irish — irlandais(e)

Ça s'écrit... — That's spelt...

You might be asked to <u>spell out</u> your <u>name</u>, or another piece of information you've given. Generally, the French alphabet is <u>very similar</u> to English, but there are a few <u>tricky letters</u> to watch out for:

A — 'aah'	H — 'ash'	O — 'oh'	V — 'vay'
B — 'beh'	I — 'ee'	P — 'pay'	W — 'doobluh vay'
C — 'seh'	J — 'djee'	Q — 'koo'	X — 'eex'
D — 'deh'	K — 'kah'	R — 'air'	Y — 'eegrek'
E — 'euh'	L — 'ell'	S — 'ess'	Z — 'zed'
F — 'eff'	M — 'em'	T — 'tay'	
G — 'djay'	N — 'en'	U — 'oo'	

> In French, it's 'double V', not 'double U'.

Grammar — accents

For letters with accents, say the <u>letter</u> followed by the <u>accent</u>:

è — 'euh accent <u>grave</u>'
é — 'euh accent <u>aigu</u>'
ê — 'euh accent <u>circonflexe</u>'
ë — 'euh <u>tréma</u>'
ç — 'seh <u>cédille</u>'

SPEAKING

French letters can be tricky, so learn how to say them...

Read the question and Sophie's response below.
Parle-moi un peu de toi-même.

Je m'appelle Sophie. Ça s'écrit S-O-P-H-I-E. Je suis née le trois mars deux mille un et j'ai presque quinze ans. Je suis anglaise et j'habite actuellement à Manchester, en Angleterre. Pourtant, je suis d'origine asiatique et mes parents sont nés à Hong Kong.

 Grade 6-7

Tick list:
✓ tenses: present, perfect
✓ dates formed correctly
✓ conjunctions to link phrases
✓ adjective agreements

Now try to answer the same question. Aim to talk for about two minutes. **[10 marks]**

You could say things like your name, age and where you're from.

To improve:
+ more varied conjunctions

My Family

You need to be able to describe your family as well as yourself. This topic is a favourite with the examiners — so learn it well and keep coming back to test yourself on the vocab on this page.

La famille proche — Close relatives

le père	*father*	la nièce	*niece*
la mère	*mother*	le beau-père	*step-father*
le frère	*brother*	la belle-mère	*step-mother*
la sœur	*sister*	le demi-frère	*half-brother*
le fils / la fille unique	*only child*	la demi-sœur	*half-sister*
le grand-père	*grandfather*	le jumeau	*twin brother*
la grand-mère	*grandmother*	la jumelle	*twin sister*
le / la petit(e) ami(e)	*boyfriend / girlfriend*	le / la partenaire	*partner*
le neveu	*nephew*	aîné(e)	*elder*

To say 'I'm an only child' in French, you don't need an article, e.g. 'je suis fils unique'.

When you're talking about something or someone that belongs to you, e.g. 'my sister', you need to use a possessive adjective (see p.112).

Parle-moi de ta famille — Tell me about your family

Question

As-tu une grande famille?
Have you got a big family?

Simple Answer

J'ai une petite famille — nous sommes quatre.

I've got a small family — there are four of us.

Extended Answer

J'ai une petite famille car ma mère est fille unique. J'ai un petit frère et une cousine. J'ai aussi une petite amie qui s'appelle Amy.

I've got a small family because my mum is an only child. I have a little brother and one cousin (female). I've also got a girlfriend called Amy.

Dans ma famille, il y a neuf personnes.

In my family, there are nine people.

J'ai une grande famille car mes parents sont séparés et ils se sont tous les deux remariés.

I have a big family because my parents are separated and they have both remarried.

don't live together — ne vivent pas ensemble

are divorced — sont divorcés

J'ai deux frères qui sont plus âgés que moi.

I've got two brothers who are older than me.

younger — plus jeunes

Le partenaire de ma mère vient d'Italie, donc j'ai de la famille à l'étranger.

My mum's partner comes from Italy, so I have some family abroad.

isn't British — n'est pas britannique

Grammar — comparisons

To <u>compare</u> one person or thing to another, use '<u>plus</u> / <u>moins...que</u>' (*more* / *less...than*) with an <u>adjective</u> in the middle.

Elle est plus <u>âgée</u> / <u>jeune</u> que moi.
She is <u>older</u> / <u>younger</u> than me.

Don't just list your family members — add in details as well...

A French friend has written a blog post and wants you to translate it into **English**. *[9 marks]*

Dans ma famille, il y a trois personnes — ma mère, mon père et moi. Malheureusement, je n'ai ni frères ni sœurs donc je suis fils unique. Par contre, j'ai beaucoup de cousins et je les vois souvent. Le week-end dernier, par exemple, nous sommes allés au cinéma ensemble et nous nous sommes très bien amusés.

Look out for any changes in tense.

Describing People

Now you know how to name people in French, you can begin to describe them. This page will help you to gain marks by describing people accurately with lots of fancy vocab. Read on for more...

On décrit les autres — Describing others

It's really likely that you'll have to <u>describe</u> your family and friends, so learn these useful <u>adjectives</u>:

<u>les yeux (m):</u>	<u>eyes:</u>
marron / noisette	brown / hazel
<u>les cheveux (m):</u>	<u>hair:</u>
roux / bruns / blonds	ginger / brown / blond
longs / mi-longs / courts	long / medium-length / short
ondulés / bouclés / frisés / raides	wavy / curly / curly / straight
la barbe	beard
joli(e)	pretty
beau / belle	handsome / beautiful
laid(e)	ugly
grand(e)	tall
petit(e)	short
clair(e) / foncé(e)	light / dark
de taille (f) moyenne	average height

Grammar — agreements

Adjectives <u>agree</u> with the <u>person or thing</u> they're describing — if it's <u>feminine</u>, you need to add an '<u>e</u>' onto the <u>end of the adjective</u>. If it's <u>plural</u>, add an '<u>s</u>'. If it's <u>feminine and plural</u>, add '<u>es</u>'.

Ma copine est très petite.
My girlfriend is very short.

Elle a les cheveux longs.
She has long hair.

'Marron' (*brown*) and 'noisette' (*hazel*) never agree with the noun they're describing.

Ils sont comment? — What are they like?

'Gros' (*fat*) becomes 'grosse' when it agrees with a feminine noun.

Ma sœur est assez grande et jolie. Elle a les yeux noisette et les cheveux longs et raides.

My sister is quite tall and pretty. She has hazel eyes and long straight hair.

fat — grosse
slim — mince

Ma meilleure copine a les yeux marron et les cheveux bruns. Elle porte des lunettes.

My best friend has brown eyes and brown hair. She wears glasses.

jewellery — des bijoux (m)

Mon frère aîné a beaucoup de boutons sur le visage.

My older brother has lots of spots on his face.

a scar — une cicatrice
a mole — un grain de beauté

Elles sont toutes les deux de taille moyenne.

They're both average height.

very beautiful — très belles

Remember — you need to make all the adjectives agree...

In this extract from a podcast, Fabien is being interviewed about his family.

Find the true statement from the pair below.

e.g. A. Fabien lives with his parents.   **B.** Fabien lives by himself.   **A**

There are two true statements in each list below. Choose the correct statements from each list.

1. **A.** It's never quiet at Fabien's house.
    B. Fabien is the youngest child at home.
    C. His sisters have blue eyes.
    D. Fabien's half-brother is older than him.
    E. His half-brother lives at home.   [2]

2. **A.** Fabien's mother has long hair.
    B. His mother has curly hair.
    C. Fabien's father is tall.
    D. His father has a beard.
    E. Fabien looks like his father.   [2]

Personalities

It's what's on the inside that counts, so it's probably a good idea to learn how to describe your personality. It isn't always easy to sum up your wonderful self in a few words, but use this page as a starting point.

Les personnalités (f) — Personalities

Adjectives need to agree with the nouns they're describing. See p.110 for more.

gentil / gentille	*nice*	bavard(e)	*chatty / talkative*	égoïste	*selfish*
vif / vive	*lively*	aimable	*kind*	jaloux / jalouse	*jealous*
heureux /		compréhensif /		bête	*stupid / silly*
heureuse	*happy*	compréhensive	*understanding*	fou / folle	*mad / crazy*

Question

Tu as quel genre de caractère?
What kind of personality do you have?

Simple Answer

Je suis gentil(le) et un peu bavard(e).
I'm nice and a bit chatty.

Extended Answer

Je suis assez vif / vive et bavard(e). Mes amis me disent que je suis vraiment généreux / généreuse, mais je sais que je suis parfois égoïste.
I'm quite lively and talkative. My friends tell me that I'm really generous, but I know that I'm sometimes selfish.

Grammar — imperfect tense

To describe someone in the past, use the imperfect tense (see p.138).
Elle était vive et bavarde.
She was lively and talkative.

Grammar — false friends

Some French words sound like English words, but have a different meaning.

sensible	*sensitive (not sensible)*
le caractère	*personality (not a fictional character)*
grand(e)	*big / tall (not grand)*

Parler des autres — To talk about others

It's useful to be able to say what other people are like too.

Mon frère est égoïste et il ne pense jamais aux autres. Pourtant, je suis très fier / fière de ma famille.

My brother is selfish and he never thinks about others. However, I'm very proud of my family.

Ma meilleure copine, Ann, est vraiment aimable et elle est toujours là pour moi quand j'ai un problème.

My best friend, Ann, is really kind and she is always there for me when I have a problem.

WRITING — Say how people have changed so you can use different tenses...

Pierre has written a blog entry about his best friend.

Mon meilleur ami s'appelle Marc. Il est sportif, intelligent et toujours heureux. Pourtant, au collège, il est un peu bavard et bête. Cependant il n'est jamais égoïste, et il veut toujours aider les autres. Le week-end, on va souvent au cinéma et on joue au foot ensemble dans le parc.

Grade 6-7

Tick list:
✓ good use of connectives
✓ wide range of adjectives

To improve:
+ use at least two tenses

Vous décrivez votre meilleur(e) ami(e) pour votre blog. Décrivez :
* *l'apparence et la personnalité de votre ami(e)*
* *pourquoi il / elle est votre meilleur(e) ami(e)*
* *ce que vous faites ensemble le week-end*
* *ce que vous ferez ensemble dans l'avenir*

*Écrivez environ **90** mots en **français**, et répondez à chaque aspect de la question.* [16 marks]

Connectives can help you to express an opinion.
cependant / pourtant	*however*
de plus	*moreover*
donc	*so / therefore*

Relationships

The examiners are also pretty interested in your relationships with other people. Luckily, this page will give you the chance to practise some of those pesky reflexive verbs you know and love. Get reading...

On se fait des amis — Making friends

se disputer	*to argue*
s'entendre (avec)	*to get on (with)*
connaître	*to know (a person)*
être fâché(e)	*to be angry*
se faire des amis	*to make friends*
casse-pieds	*a pain in the neck*
séparé(e)	*separated*
gâté(e)	*spoilt*
le sens de l'humour	*sense of humour*

Grammar — reflexive verbs

Reflexive verbs (see p.142) have an extra part — a reflexive pronoun.

Je m'entends bien avec...   ***I get on well with...***
Nous nous disputons souvent.   ***We often argue.***

In the perfect tense (see p.136-137), the pronoun goes before the present tense part of 'être' (*to be*).

Il s'est fait facilement des amis.   ***He made friends easily.***

Je connais plein de gens dans ma ville.

Je sors avec mon petit ami depuis un an, mais parfois il est casse-pieds.

I know lots of people in my town.

I've been going out with my boyfriend for a year, but sometimes he's a pain in the neck.

I've made friends — Je me suis fait des amis

I get annoyed with him — il m'énerve

Tu t'entends bien avec...? — Do you get on well with...?

Tu t'entends bien avec ta famille?

Je m'entends bien avec mes parents.

Quelquefois je me dispute avec ma sœur aînée parce qu'elle est vraiment gâtée.

Do you get on well with your family?

I get on well with my parents.

Sometimes I argue with my older sister because she is really spoilt.

I have a good relationship — J'ai un bon rapport

doesn't have a sense of humour — n'a pas le sens de l'humour

Use 'être' with reflexives in the perfect tense...

SPEAKING

Read these questions and Sandrine's response below.

Qu'est-ce qu'il y a sur la photo ? La famille, semble-t-elle comme la tienne ?

Sur la photo, il y a une famille de cinq personnes — trois femmes et deux enfants. **Parmi**[1] les enfants, il y a un garçon et une fille. Le garçon **a l'air**[2] plus jeune que la fille. Ils ont l'air heureux et on dirait qu'ils s'entendent bien ensemble.

Moi, je m'entends très bien avec ma famille aussi. Mon père est plus strict que ma mère, mais il est raisonnable **quand même**[3]. Ma sœur est **mignonne**[4], mais elle m'énerve quelquefois.

Grade 8-9

[1]Amongst
[2]looks
[3]even so
[4]cute

Tick list:
✓ good use of comparatives like 'plus que'
✓ accurate use of reflexive verbs

To improve:
+ include a past tense

Now, answer the following questions. Try to talk for about two minutes.

- *Comment-est ta famille ?*
- *Est-ce que tu t'entends bien avec ta famille ? Pourquoi / pourquoi pas ?*
- *La famille sur la photo, semble-t-elle comme la tienne ?*   [10 marks]

You'll always be asked what you can see in the photo. Use 'Sur la photo, il y a...' to get started. Include as much detail as you can — look at the example for inspiration.

Partnership

Seeing as Paris is the city of love, we couldn't let this topic slip by. Plus, you might have to talk about your views on love and marriage in the exam, so you need to know this stuff inside out and back to front.

Le mariage — Marriage

l'amour (m)	*love*	les fiançailles (f)	*engagement*	la femme	*wife*
célibataire	*single*	les noces (f)	*wedding*	épouser	*to marry*
la confiance	*trust*	le mari	*husband*	se marier	*to get married*

Le mariage montre au monde qu'on s'aime. Cependant, à mon avis, le mariage commence à devenir démodé.

Marriage shows the world that you love each other. However, in my opinion, marriage is starting to become old-fashioned.

these days / today — de nos jours

Les noces sont trop chères. Avec l'argent, je préférerais acheter une maison.

Weddings are too expensive. With the money, I would prefer to buy a house.

I think that — Je pense que

Je crois que le mariage est important, il donne de la structure à la vie de famille.

I believe that marriage is important, it gives structure to family life.

In my opinion — Selon moi

Question

Tu voudrais te marier un jour?

Do you want to get married one day?

Simple Answer

Oui, à l'avenir je voudrais me marier et avoir des enfants.

Yes, in the future I'd like to get married and have children.

Extended Answers

Oui, pour moi le mariage est très important, et à l'avenir j'espère rencontrer l'homme / la femme de mes rêves et rester avec lui / elle pour toujours. Franchement, je ne comprends pas ceux qui ne veulent pas se marier.

Yes, marriage is very important for me, and in the future I hope to meet the man / woman of my dreams and stay with him / her forever. Frankly, I don't understand those people who don't want to get married.

Moi, je ne veux pas du tout me marier. Par contre, pour moi, ce qui est plus important c'est l'amour et la confiance. On peut être avec quelqu'un et avoir des enfants sans l'épouser.

I really don't want to get married. On the other hand, for me, what's more important is love and trust. You can be with someone and have children without marrying them.

Grammar — talking about the future

There are lots of different ways to talk about your <u>future plans</u>. You can use:

- The <u>future tense</u> (see p.135):
  je serai   *I will be*
- Or the <u>conditional tense</u> (see p.144):
  je voudrais   *I would like*
- Or use '<u>j'espère</u>' (*I hope*) + infinitive:
  J'espère me marier un jour.
  I hope to get married one day.

READING This is the perfect opportunity for you to use the future tense...

Read this extract from 'Madame Bovary' by Gustave Flaubert and answer the questions.

Emma a, au contraire, désiré se marier à minuit, **aux flambeaux**[1]; mais le père Rouault n'a rien compris à cette idée. Il y avait donc des noces, où quarante-trois personnes sont venues, où l'on est resté seize heures à table, qui a recommencé le lendemain et quelque peu les jours suivants.

[1] in torchlight

1. When did Emma want to get married?
   A. the next day
   B. in sixteen hours
   C. at midnight   [1]

2. Choose the sentence that best summarises the passage.
   A. Emma got the wedding that she wanted.
   B. Emma had a long wedding that suited her father's wishes.
   C. Emma's father didn't attend her wedding.   [1]

Listening Questions

Time to put what you've learnt to the test. Have a go at answering these practice questions — if you struggle with something, read through the section again and then have another stab at it.

1   Albert and Patricia are trying to describe a burglary suspect to a police officer. Describe whether the statements are **true** or **false**.

TRACK
LISTENING
06

1 a   Patricia thinks that the man was short. ....

[1 mark]

1 b   Albert thinks that the man was fat. ....

[1 mark]

1 c   Patricia believes that the man was ugly. ....

[1 mark]

1 d   According to Albert, the man had short hair. ....

[1 mark]

2   Écoutez cette émission de radio sur le mariage. Complétez les phrases suivantes en **français**.

TRACK
LISTENING
07

2 a   Armand est capable de

....
[1 mark]

2 b   Armand pense que la vie est plus simple quand on est

....
[1 mark]

2 c   Le copain de Zoé croit qu'il est trop tôt de

....
[2 marks]

Speaking Question

Candidate's Role

- Your teacher will play the role of your French friend. They will speak first.

- You should use *tu* to address your friend.

- – ! – means you will have to respond to something you have not prepared.

- – ? – means you will have to ask your friend a question.

> Tu parles de ta famille avec un(e) ami(e) français(e).
>
> - Ta famille (**deux** détails).
>
> - !
>
> - Activité récente avec ta famille.
>
> - Enfants dans le futur.
>
> - ? Frères et sœurs.

Teacher's Role

- You begin the role-play using the introductory text below.

- You should address the candidate as *tu*.

- You may alter the wording of the questions in response to the candidate's previous answers.

- Do not supply the candidate with key vocabulary.

> Introductory text: *Tu parles de ta famille avec un(e) ami(e) français(e).*
> *Moi, je suis ton ami(e).*
>
> - Comment est ta famille ?
>
> - ! Est-ce que tu t'entends bien avec ta famille ?
>
> - Parle-moi d'une activité que tu as faite récemment avec ta famille.
>
> - Est-ce que tu voudrais avoir des enfants dans le futur ?
>
> - ? Allow the candidate to ask you a question.

Reading Questions

1   Lisez l'email de Tania qui parle d'elle-même. Répondez aux questions en **français**.

> Je m'appelle Tania, j'ai seize ans et je suis française. J'habite dans une petite ville près de La Rochelle avec ma famille. Je suis assez grande, mais je ne suis pas aussi grande que mon frère. Il aime toujours me rappeler qu'il est déjà plus grand que notre père même s'il n'a que quatorze ans. Mes cheveux sont blonds et courts, et j'ai les yeux verts. Je suis sportive et j'aime nager et jouer au football. Je joue au football tous les samedis depuis trois ans.

1 a   Comment est Tania ? Donnez **un** détail.

Elle est sportive. ~~Elle est a les yeux~~ ....   *[1 mark]*

1 b   Son frère est très fier. Pourquoi ?

....   *[1 mark]*

1 c   Qu'est-ce qu'elle dit sur le football ? Donnez **un** détail.

....   *[1 mark]*

2   Lisez les commentaires sur un site de rencontres et identifiez la bonne personne.

> Je m'appelle Étienne, je viens de Nantes et j'ai trente-deux ans. Je suis gentil et généreux et mes amis disent que je suis très compréhensif. J'aimerais rencontrer quelqu'un qui soit travailleur et honnête.

> Je suis Sylvie et j'habite à Rouen. J'ai un bon sens de l'humour et je suis toujours vive. Quelquefois je suis un peu folle mais je crois que la plupart du temps je suis amusante. Je cherche un homme qui soit plein de vie et qui ne soit jamais ennuyeux.

> Je m'appelle Louis et je viens de Marseille. Je voudrais rencontrer quelqu'un qui ne soit ni méchant ni égoïste. Je suis sportif et mon partenaire idéal ne devrait pas être paresseux.

2 a   .... cherche un partenaire qui peut l'amuser.   *[1 mark]*

2 b   .... cherche un partenaire qui est très actif.   *[1 mark]*

2 c   .... cherche un partenaire qui ne ment pas.   *[1 mark]*

Writing Questions

1 Vous écrivez un email à votre correspondant(e) au sujet d'un mariage récent dans votre famille.

Décrivez:

• les personnes qui se sont mariées

• vos sentiments pendant la cérémonie

• votre opinion au sujet du mariage

• votre partenaire idéal(e).

Écrivez environ **90** mots en **français**. Répondez à chaque aspect de la question.

[16 marks]

2 Translate the following passage into **French**.

> I met my two best friends at a youth club. Edith is very funny and chatty, like me.
> Delphine is shy but kind and generous. They are very different but they are very nice and
> we spend lots of time together. We get on well. Sometimes it is difficult to make friends.

....

....

....

....

....

....

[12 marks]

Revision Summary for Section Two

These questions bring together everything you've learnt in this section, so they're good at highlighting any bits you still need to brush up on. Don't worry if some questions are a little hard — have a go at them and then flick back through the section to revisit anything you're not sure about.

About Yourself (p.16) ☑

1) How would you say your name, age and birthday to a French person you've just met? ☑
2) Now tell them where you live, and what nationality you are. ☑
3) Élodie says: 'Je suis française mais je suis d'origine algérienne.' What does this mean in English? ☑
4) Spell your first name and surname out loud using the French alphabet. ☑
5) How would you say the following letters in French? a) é b) à c) ç ☑

My Family (p.17) ☑

6) As-tu une grande famille? Répondez en français. Utilisez des phrases complètes. ☑
7) If Jonty is 'ton petit ami', what is he? ☑
8) Your penfriend tells you: 'Mes parents ne vivent pas ensemble, donc j'habite avec ma mère. Mon frère n'habite pas à la maison car il est plus âgé que moi.' What's she saying? ☑

Describing People (p.18) ☑

9) Your best friend has light, curly hair and hazel eyes. She's quite tall and wears lots of jewellery. How would you describe her in French? ☑
10) How would you say the following words in French? a) short b) ugly c) average height ☑
11) 'Est-ce que tu ressembles à tes parents?' Translate this question into English and then answer it in French. ☑

Personalities (p.19) ☑

12) Write three sentences in French describing your personality. ☑
13) Anna has written: 'Ma sœur est vive et heureuse, mais parfois elle est trop sensible. Elle est différente de moi car je suis timide et réservée. Nous nous entendons bien.' Translate what Anna has said into English. ☑

Relationships (p.20) ☑

14) You don't get on with your brother. Out of the sentences below, which one would best describe your relationship?
   a) J'ai un bon rapport avec lui.   c) Il se fait facilement des amis.
   b) Nous nous disputons souvent.   d) Il est fou. ☑
15) Est-ce que tu t'entends bien avec tes parents? Répondez en deux phrases en français. ☑
16) How would you say that your nephew is very spoilt? ☑

Partnership (p.21) ☑

17) Describe your ideal partner. Think about their personality as well as their appearance. ☑
18) How would you say the words below in French?
   a) to get married b) trust c) family life d) to be angry ☑
19) In French, jot down two reasons for marriage and two reasons against it. ☑
20) 'J'espère me marier un jour, mais je vais attendre jusqu'à l'âge de trente ans. Je veux être sûr de trouver la femme de mes rêves.' What does Jean think about marriage? ☑

Music

Free-time activities are a common topic in the exam. Music's a good one to talk about, but there's lots of vocabulary to get your head around, so take your time learning the stuff on this page.

La musique — Music

jouer	to play
(d'un instrument)	(an instrument)
la chanson	song
le musicien / la musicienne	musician
le chanteur / la chanteuse	singer
le genre	genre
le concert	concert
apprendre à	to learn to
faire partie de	to be part of
le groupe	band
la chorale	choir
l'orchestre (m)	orchestra
répéter	to rehearse

Grammar — jouer de

'Jouer' is followed by 'de', 'du', 'de la' or 'des' when you're talking about playing a musical instrument.
For more on how 'de' changes see p.109.

Je joue du violon et de la flûte.
I play the violin and the flute.

Grammar — imperfect tense

To talk about what you 'used to' do, use the imperfect tense. See p.138 for more.

Je chantais. *I used to sing*.

Question

Est-ce que tu joues d'un instrument de musique?

Do you play a musical instrument?

Simple Answer

Oui, je joue de la guitare et du piano.

Yes, I play the guitar and the piano.

Extended Answer

Oui, maintenant je joue de la batterie. Quand j'étais petit(e), je jouais de la trompette et je chantais dans une chorale.

Yes, now I play the drums. When I was younger, I used to play the trumpet and sing in a choir.

Écouter de la musique — To listen to music

It's worth thinking about how to express your opinions about music.

Je préfère le rap à la musique classique.	*I prefer rap to classical music.*
Mon grand-père détestait écouter de la musique classique quand il avait mon âge, mais maintenant c'est son genre de musique préféré.	*My grandad hated listening to classical music when he was my age, but now it is his favourite music genre.*
À mon avis, les chansons techno sont quelquefois trop bizarres.	*In my opinion, techno songs are sometimes too weird.*

dance music — la dance
rock music — la musique rock
pop music — la musique pop

⟋⎮⎮⎮⎮⎮⎮⎮⎮⎮⎮⎮⎮⎮⎮⎮⎮⎮⎮⎮⎮⎮⎮⎮⎮⟍
See p.8-9 for more on opinions.
⟍⎮⎮⎮⎮⎮⎮⎮⎮⎮⎮⎮⎮⎮⎮⎮⎮⎮⎮⎮⎮⎮⎮⎮⎮⟋

music videos — les clips (m)

Practice makes perfect — have a go at this exam question...

*Écoutez cet interview avec le musicien Joël Lejoueur. Complétez les phrases suivantes en **français**.*

e.g. Joël a commencé à jouer d'un instrument quand il avait ......**cinq ans**.............

1. Joël n'aimait pas son .... [1]
2. Il a beaucoup aimé l'............................... de son premier concert. [1]
3. Selon Joël, pour devenir un bon musicien, il faut .... régulièrement. [1]

Cinema

Everyone loves a good film — and they're great to talk about in the exam. Make sure you know the names for different types of film and that you can give and justify your opinions.

Allons au cinéma — Let's go to the cinema

le film d'action	*action film*	l'acteur (m) / l'actrice (f)	*actor / actress*
le film d'horreur	*horror film*	le personnage	*character*
le film d'amour	*romantic film*	les effets (m) spéciaux	*special effects*
le film comique	*comedy*	la bande-annonce	*trailer*
le dessin animé	*cartoon*	le billet de cinéma	*cinema ticket*
le film d'animation	*animated film*	le tarif réduit	*reduced price*

Question

Quel est ton genre de film préféré?

What is your favourite type of film?

Simple Answer

J'aime les films d'action mais je n'aime pas les dessins animés.

I like action films but I don't like cartoons.

Extended Answer

Je trouve que les films comiques sont plus divertissants que les films d'horreur. Les films d'horreur me font peur.

I find comedies more entertaining than horror films. Horror films scare me.

J'aime aller au cinéma pour voir des films sur grand écran.

I like going to the cinema to see films on the big screen.

Pourtant, les bandes-annonces m'énervent.

However, the trailers annoy me.

the tickets are expensive — les billets sont chers

Grammar — film genres

For <u>genres</u> with an <u>adjective</u>, e.g. 'un film <u>comique</u>', the adjective agrees if it's plural — 'les film<u>s</u> comique<u>s</u>'.

But for genres made up of '<u>de</u>' and a <u>noun</u>, e.g. 'un film <u>d'amour</u>', the noun doesn't agree — 'les film<u>s</u> d'amour'.

As-tu aimé le film? — Did you like the film?

You can use <u>interesting descriptions</u> as well as <u>adjectives</u> to express your <u>opinion</u>.

Le film était ennuyeux parce qu'il n'y avait pas d'action. C'était tellement ennuyeux que je me suis endormi(e) avant la fin. ☆

The film was boring because there wasn't any action. It was so boring I fell asleep before the end. ☆

the plot wasn't exciting — l'intrigue n'était pas passionnante

the storyline wasn't believable — l'histoire n'était pas croyable

L'intrigue était intéressante et la musique était entraînante. J'ai réussi à oublier tous mes problèmes en regardant le film. ☆☆☆

The plot was interesting and the music was catchy. I managed to forget all my problems as I watched the film. ☆☆☆

The special effects were brilliant — Les effets spéciaux étaient géniaux

The main actor was talented — L'acteur / L'actrice principal(e) était doué(e)

WRITING

Make sure you give reasons to support your opinions...

Translate the following passage into **French**. *[12 marks]*

My friend and I went to the cinema last weekend. We watched a horror film. I wasn't scared, but my friend screamed during the film. I like going to the cinema. It is always entertaining. Next month, I will go and see the new action film.

Read each sentence fully before you decide which tense you need.

TV

From the big screen to the small screen... make sure you learn the TV-related vocab below, including different types of programme. You'll need to be able to give your opinion on them as well...

Qu'est-ce qu'il y a à la télé? — What's on TV?

'On' is usually translated as 'sur' in French, but remember, it's 'à la télé'.

à la télé	*on TV*	l'émission (f)	*programme*	le documentaire	*documentary*
la publicité	*advert*	le feuilleton	*soap opera*	le jeu télévisé	*game show*
regarder	*to watch*	la télé réalité	*reality TV*	la chaîne de télé	*TV channel*
diffuser	*to broadcast*	les informations (f)	*the news*	célèbre	*famous*

Mon passe-temps préféré est... — My favourite hobby is...

Mon passe-temps préféré est regarder la télévision — c'est divertissant.

My favourite hobby is watching television — it's entertaining.

relaxing — relaxant

J'aime regarder les documentaires car on apprend beaucoup quand on les regarde.

I like watching documentaries because you learn a lot when you watch them.

crime shows — les séries (f) policières

Je préfère regarder les chaînes de télé qui ne diffusent pas de publicités.

I prefer watching the TV channels that don't broadcast adverts.

period dramas — les séries (f) historiques

Grammar — 'qui' and 'que'

'Qui' refers to the <u>subject</u> of the sentence. 'Que' refers to the <u>object</u>. See p.124 for more.

La personne <u>qui</u> regarde la télévision. ***The person <u>who</u> watches television.***

La télévision <u>que</u> la personne regarde. ***The television <u>that</u> the person watches.***

Hier soir, j'ai regardé... — Last night, I watched...

Question

Qu'est-ce que tu as regardé à la télé hier soir?

What did you watch on TV last night?

Simple Answer

J'ai regardé un jeu télévisé et un feuilleton.

I watched a game show and a soap.

Extended Answer

J'ai regardé une émission de télé-réalité. Je trouve ce genre d'émission intéressant parce qu'on peut suivre la vie quotidienne des personnes célèbres.

I watched a reality TV show. I find this type of programme interesting because you can follow celebrities' daily lives.

Vary your language — don't just use 'j'aime' all the time...

Read about what Julie watches on TV. Then decide if each sentence is true or false.

Je regarde souvent la télévision. Je regarde les informations tous les jours, et j'aime aussi regarder les feuilletons. Mes parents ont l'impression que je passe trop de temps devant la télé au lieu de faire mes devoirs. Ils pensent aussi que les feuilletons sont stupides. Moi, je pense que j'ai besoin de regarder la télé pour me reposer après une journée de cours fatigante.

e.g. Julie only watches soap operas. **false**
1. Julie's parents are happy with her watching TV. [1]
2. They don't approve of her watching soap operas. [1]
3. Julie thinks she needs to watch TV. [1]
4. She watches TV to relax. [1]

Food

Food... my favourite topic. There's lots of vocab to learn — very useful for avoiding shocks in restaurants...

Qu'est-ce qu'on mange ce soir? — What are we eating tonight?

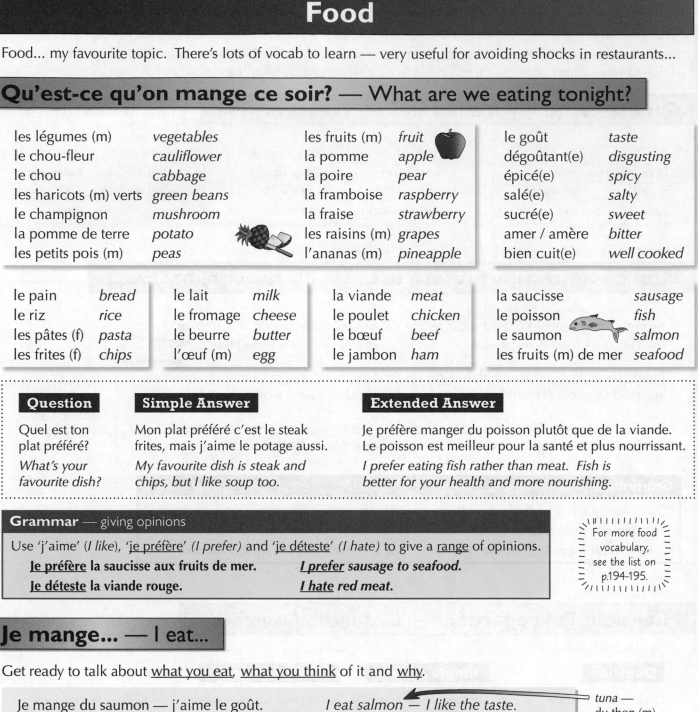

les légumes (m)	*vegetables*	les fruits (m)	*fruit*	le goût	*taste*
le chou-fleur	*cauliflower*	la pomme	*apple*	dégoûtant(e)	*disgusting*
le chou	*cabbage*	la poire	*pear*	épicé(e)	*spicy*
les haricots (m) verts	*green beans*	la framboise	*raspberry*	salé(e)	*salty*
le champignon	*mushroom*	la fraise	*strawberry*	sucré(e)	*sweet*
la pomme de terre	*potato*	les raisins (m)	*grapes*	amer / amère	*bitter*
les petits pois (m)	*peas*	l'ananas (m)	*pineapple*	bien cuit(e)	*well cooked*

le pain	*bread*	le lait	*milk*	la viande	*meat*	la saucisse	*sausage*
le riz	*rice*	le fromage	*cheese*	le poulet	*chicken*	le poisson	*fish*
les pâtes (f)	*pasta*	le beurre	*butter*	le bœuf	*beef*	le saumon	*salmon*
les frites (f)	*chips*	l'œuf (m)	*egg*	le jambon	*ham*	les fruits (m) de mer	*seafood*

Question	**Simple Answer**	**Extended Answer**
Quel est ton plat préféré?	Mon plat préféré c'est le steak frites, mais j'aime le potage aussi.	Je préfère manger du poisson plutôt que de la viande. Le poisson est meilleur pour la santé et plus nourrissant.
What's your favourite dish?	*My favourite dish is steak and chips, but I like soup too.*	*I prefer eating fish rather than meat. Fish is better for your health and more nourishing.*

Grammar — giving opinions

Use 'j'aime' (*I like*), 'je préfère' (*I prefer*) and 'je déteste' (*I hate*) to give a range of opinions.

Je préfère la saucisse aux fruits de mer.   ***I prefer** sausage to seafood.*

Je déteste la viande rouge.   ***I hate** red meat.*

For more food vocabulary, see the list on p.194-195.

Je mange... — I eat...

Get ready to talk about what you eat, what you think of it and why.

Je mange du saumon — j'aime le goût.	*I eat salmon — I like the taste.*
En général, je ne mange pas de poisson parce que je le trouve dégoûtant.	*In general, I don't eat fish because I find it disgusting.*
Je devrais manger moins de nourriture sucrée parce que cela serait meilleur pour ma santé.	*I should eat less sugary food because that would be better for my health.*

tuna — du thon (m)

lamb — de l'agneau (m)

This is in the conditional — see p.144 for more.

There's a lot of vocab here — you need to know all of it...

Listen to Selina, Ahmed and Élodie. Choose the correct answer to complete each statement.

e.g. Selina never eats...	**A.** lamb	**B.** fish	**C.** pork	*C*
1. Ahmed particularly likes...	**A.** raspberries	**B.** mushrooms	**C.** cauliflower	*[1]*
2. Élodie's sister eats...	**A.** sweet food	**B.** spicy food	**C.** healthy food	*[1]*
3. Ahmed doesn't eat...	**A.** ham	**B.** peas	**C.** vegetables	*[1]*
4. Selina hates...	**A.** bananas	**B.** pineapple	**C.** strawberries	*[1]*

Eating Out

More on food... this time it's eating out. Make sure you can give opinions on which foods you like and why.

Qu'est-ce que vous voudriez? — What would you like?

la boisson	*drink*	le thé	*tea*
avoir soif / faim	*to be thirsty / hungry*	le café	*coffee*
un verre de	*a glass of*	le vin	*wine*
l'eau (f) plate / gazeuse	*still / fizzy water*	la bière	*beer*

There's more vocab on p.194-195.

le hors d'œuvre	*starter*	la carte	*menu*	le serveur	*waiter*
le plat principal	*main meal*	commander	*to order*	la serveuse	*waitress*
le dessert	*dessert*	végétarien(ne)	*vegetarian*	l'addition (f)	*the bill*

J'ai soif. Je voudrais une bouteille d'eau et un thé, s'il vous plaît. Je voudrais les emporter.

I'm thirsty. I would like a bottle of water and a tea, please. I'd like them to take away.

Allons au restaurant — Let's go to the restaurant

J'aime manger au restaurant parce qu'on peut goûter des plats qu'on ne cuisinerait jamais chez soi. J'ai essayé la cuisine chinoise, par exemple.

I like eating in restaurants because you can try food that you would never cook at home. I tried Chinese food, for example.

Je suis végétarien(ne) donc c'est difficile de trouver des restaurants où je peux manger.

I'm vegetarian so it's hard to find restaurants where I can eat.

J'ai commandé des escargots au restaurant français. Comme dessert, j'ai mangé une glace à la fraise.

I ordered snails in the French restaurant. For dessert, I ate a strawberry ice cream.

Indian — indienne
Mexican — mexicaine

vegan — végétalien(ne)
allergic to... — allergique à...

a pancake — une crêpe
a toasted ham and cheese sandwich — un croque-monsieur

SPEAKING — This topic often comes up in the role-play, so get learning it...

Here's an example role-play — Yann is talking to Fatima about a visit to a restaurant.

Fatima : Qu'est-ce que tu as commandé au restaurant ?

Grade 8-9

Yann : J'ai commandé du potage comme hors d'œuvre et du poulet avec du riz comme plat principal.

Fatima : Tout s'est bien passé ?

Yann : **Je me suis plaint**[1] du poulet parce qu'il était froid.

Fatima : Qu'est-ce que tu as aimé le plus ?

Yann : J'ai aimé le riz car il était bien cuisiné.

Fatima : Quel est ton repas préféré ?

Yann : Le poulet avec les petits pois et les pommes de terre. Et toi, quel est ton repas préféré ?

Fatima : Mon repas préféré est les fruits de mer. Qu'est-ce que tu mangeras ce soir ?

Yann : Je mangerai des pâtes avec des petits pois et des champignons. J'aime manger ça avec du fromage.

Tick list:
- ✓ tenses: perfect, imperfect, present, future
- ✓ opinion phrases
- ✓ correctly formed question

To improve:
- + use adjectives, e.g. 'délicieux', to avoid repeating 'aimer'

Prepare the role-play card below. Use 'tu' and speak for about two minutes. [15 marks]

[1] I complained

Tu parles avec ton ami(e) d'une visite au restaurant.
- *les plats commandés*
- *problème*
- *!*
- *? repas préféré*
- *ce soir — votre dîner*

Sport

Ah, sport... Whether you're sporty or not, you need to learn the names of different sports and be able to give your opinion on them. The next two pages should guide you through nicely.

Faire du sport — To do sport

le foot / football	*football*	le hockey	*hockey*	l'aviron (m)	*rowing*
le rugby	*rugby*	le netball	*netball*	la voile	*sailing*
le tennis	*tennis*	le basket	*basketball*	le ski	*skiing*
le badminton	*badminton*	la natation	*swimming*	l'équitation (f)	*horse riding*

pratiquer un sport	*to do a sport*	courir	*to run*	tricher	*to cheat*
faire une randonnée	*to go on a walk*	gagner	*to win*	s'entraîner	*to train*
faire du vélo	*to cycle*	perdre	*to lose*	marquer un but	*to score a goal*

Je joue au badminton deux fois par semaine, et je fais de la voile régulièrement aussi.

I play badminton twice a week, and I also go sailing regularly.

Je n'aime pas faire des randonnées avec mes parents.

I don't like going on walks with my parents.

Mon sport préféré c'est... — My favourite sport is...

It helps to <u>vary</u> your language — have a look at the grammar box for <u>different</u> ways of saying you do sport.

Grammar — faire, jouer and pratiquer

faire — *to do*
Use <u>faire</u> with '<u>de</u>' to talk about sport <u>in general</u>, e.g. Je fais du sport régulièrement. *I do sport regularly.*

You can use it for <u>specific</u> sports, e.g. Je fais <u>du</u> rugby. *I do rugby.*

jouer — *to play*
Use <u>jouer</u> with '<u>à</u>', e.g. Je joue <u>au</u> rugby. *I play rugby.*

pratiquer — *to practise / do*
Use <u>pratiquer</u> with '<u>le</u>' or '<u>la</u>'. Je pratique <u>le</u> rugby. *I practise rugby.*

l'équipe (f)	*team*
fana de	*a fan of*
le stade	*stadium*
le centre sportif	*sports centre*
le terrain de sport	*sports field*
la piscine	*swimming pool*
l'entraînement (m)	*sports practice*
la course	*race*
le tournoi	*tournament*

Je préfère les sports individuels aux sports d'équipe. Ils sont plus compétitifs parce qu'on joue seulement pour soi-même.

I prefer individual sports to team sports. They're more competitive because you're playing just for yourself.

Moi, je joue au tennis. Cependant, je préfère m'entraîner avec d'autres personnes donc je fais de l'aviron aussi.

I play tennis. However, I prefer to train with other people so I do rowing as well.

Je suis fana de basket et j'ai regardé le match de basket à la télé hier.

I am a basketball fan and I watched the basketball match on TV yesterday.

À mon avis, regarder un match de basket est plus divertissant que regarder une course automobile parce qu'on peut toujours voir les expressions des joueurs.

In my opinion, watching a basketball match is more entertaining than watching a car race because you can always see the players' expressions.

exciting
— passionnant

engaging
— captivant

Sport

It's a good idea to practise using the sport vocab on p.32 in context. And this page just so happens to be full of useful examples of things you could say — it's almost as if we planned it...

Je suis sportif / sportive — I'm sporty

It's likely you'll be asked about sport in the exam, so think about how you'd answer the question below.

Question

Est-ce que tu pratiques un sport régulièrement?

Do you do a sport on a regular basis?

Simple Answer

Oui, j'aime le sport et je joue au rugby le mercredi. Je regarde des matchs de tennis à la télé aussi.

Yes, I like sport and I play rugby on Wednesdays. I watch tennis matches on TV as well.

Extended Answer

Oui, je suis très sportif / sportive. Je fais partie d'une équipe de football et nous nous entraînons trois fois par semaine. La semaine dernière, nous avons perdu le match, mais j'ai marqué un but.

Yes, I'm very sporty. I'm part of a football team and we train three times a week. Last week, we lost the game, but I scored a goal.

Grammar — adverbs of time

Use the definite article '<u>le</u>' + the name of a <u>day</u> to say you do something on the <u>same day each week</u>.

Je fais de la voile <u>le jeudi</u>.   *I sail <u>on Thursdays</u>.*

Grammar — s'entraîner

'<u>S'entraîner</u>' is a <u>reflexive</u> verb (see p.142). The '<u>se</u>' part changes depending on the <u>person</u> it refers to. Because it's reflexive, it takes '<u>être</u>' in the <u>perfect</u> tense.

J'essaie de faire du sport régulièrement.

I try to do sport regularly.

Je m'entraîne au centre sportif.

I train at the sports centre.

Quelquefois c'est difficile de me motiver, particulièrement quand je suis déjà fatigué(e), ce qui est souvent le cas.

Sometimes it's difficult to motivate myself, especially when I'm already tired, which is often the case.

Nous jouons les matchs au stade. Je ne les aime pas parce qu'ils me rendent toujours nerveux / nerveuse.

We play matches at the stadium. I don't like them because they always make me nervous.

every Friday — chaque vendredi

at the weekend — le week-end

because they're too competitive — car ils sont trop compétitifs

because we often lose them — car nous les perdons souvent

 WRITING

Don't just say which sport you do — add in when, where, why...

Nadiya has written an article promoting a new sports centre.

Le nouveau centre sportif est ouvert tous les jours. Vous pouvez y pratiquer beaucoup de sports différents. On peut jouer au tennis et nager tous les jours dans la piscine **chauffée**[1]. Il y a aussi trois terrains de badminton. Le centre organise des tournois régulièrement — hier, il y a eu un tournoi de **tennis de table**[2]. C'était très compétitif. Nous espérons que vous viendrez **nous rejoindre**[3] au centre sportif bientôt !

Grade 6-7

[1]heated
[2]table tennis
[3]join us

Tick list:
✓ tenses: present, perfect, imperfect, future
✓ adverbs of frequency
✓ pouvoir + infinitive
✓ pronouns (y, nous)

To improve:
+ tenses: use the conditional
+ complex structures, e.g. 'si' clauses

Vous écrivez un article sur la qualité des centres sportifs dans votre région pour un site-web français. Décrivez :
- *pourquoi le centre sportif dans votre ville est bon*
- *un événement récent au centre sportif*

*Écrivez environ **150** mots en **français**.*
Répondez aux deux aspects de la question.

[32 marks]

Try to use a variety of tenses. Use the conditional and future tenses to say why people should join and what they will be able to do there.

Listening Questions

Another section, another set of exam-style questions. Don't be tempted to flick past these pages — practising the skills you'll need in the exams is time well spent.

1 Listen to this radio report about the Lumière brothers.
Answer the questions in **English**.

TRACK LISTENING 10

1 a What does the cinematograph device do?

.... *[1 mark]*

1 b How long was the Lumière brothers' first film?

.... *[1 mark]*

1 c Give **two** details about the first paying public film screening.

1. ....

2. .... *[2 marks]*

2 Listen to this phone conversation about eating out.
Answer the questions in **English**.

TRACK LISTENING 11

2 a What kind of food is particularly good at the restaurant?

.... *[1 mark]*

2 b What did Juliette used to like eating?

.... *[1 mark]*

2 c What **two** excuses does Juliette give for not going to eat pancakes with Leo?

1. ....

2. .... *[2 marks]*

Speaking Question

Candidate's Material

- Spend a couple of minutes looking at the photo and the questions below it.

- You can make notes on a separate piece of paper.

© iStock.com/fiphoto

You will be asked the following **three** questions, and **two** questions you haven't prepared:

- Qu'est-ce qu'il y a sur la photo ?

- Quelle est ta cuisine préférée ? Pourquoi ?

- Préfères-tu manger chez toi ou manger au restaurant ? Pourquoi ?

Teacher's Material

- Allow the student to develop his / her answers as much as possible.

- You need to ask the student the following questions **in order**:

  - Qu'est-ce qu'il y a sur la photo ?

  - Quelle est ta cuisine préférée ? Pourquoi ?

  - Préfères-tu manger chez toi ou manger au restaurant ? Pourquoi ?

  - Quel était ton plat préféré quand tu étais enfant ?

  - Quel restaurant voudrais-tu visiter dans le futur ? Pourquoi ?

Reading Questions

1   Read these responses to an online questionnaire about TV and identify the people.
Write **A** (Annabelle), **B** (Bastien) or **A+B** (Annabelle and Bastien) in the boxes.

Qu'est-ce que tu aimes regarder à la télé?			
Annabelle 	J'aime regarder les émissions informatives comme les documentaires et les actualités, mais je ne peux pas supporter les jeux télévisés.	Bastien 	Je suis très sportif et j'adore regarder les émissions de sport. Je regarde un match de football tous les soirs, même si ce n'est pas mon équipe préférée.

1 a   Who likes to watch the news? ☐   **1 b**   Who watches TV every night? ☐

Est-ce que tu penses qu'on regarde trop de télé?			
Annabelle 	Je pense qu'il y a beaucoup d'émissions intéressantes à la télé, et on peut profiter de toute cette variété pour s'instruire et s'informer. Pourtant je trouve qu'il y a trop de publicités.	Bastien 	Selon moi, ce qui est important, c'est la qualité de ce qu'on regarde. La télévision peut nous aider à comprendre les gens et le monde. Même les feuilletons peuvent nous faire apprendre quelque chose de la vie.

1 c   Who thinks that television can help educate us? ☐

[3 marks]

2   Translate this post from a forum about music into **English**.

> J'adore la musique. J'aime tous les genres de musique. J'écoute de la musique tout le temps, normalement sur mon portable. Hier, j'écoutais de la musique en marchant au collège quand j'ai commencé à chanter avec la musique. Mes amis me regardaient mais je ne savais pas pourquoi !

....

....

....

....

....

....

[9 marks]

Writing Questions

1 Vous écrivez un article pour un magazine de musique afin d'encourager plus de jeunes à jouer d'un instrument.

Décrivez:

• l'instrument dont vous jouez

• les raisons pour lesquelles vous avez commencé à jouer d'un instrument

• les avantages de jouer d'un instrument

• l'instrument dont vous voudriez apprendre à jouer.

Écrivez environ **90** mots en **français**. Répondez à chaque aspect de la question.

[16 marks]

2 Translate the following passage into **French**.

> My favourite sport is basketball. I have been playing basketball for three years. I train twice a week after school and sometimes there is a tournament at the weekend. Last week my team won. I also play tennis on Saturdays. In the future, I would like to learn how to ski.

....

....

....

....

....

....

....

[12 marks]

Revision Summary for Section Three

Now you've been through the section, it's time to bring all those fun free-time activities together — you could say it's the most enjoyable page in the book... Make sure you have a go at all of the questions, and don't forget to use the tick boxes to help you keep track of your progress.

Music (p.27) ☑

1) 'Est-ce que tu joues d'un instrument de musique?' Translate this question into English and then answer it in French. ☑

2) A French musician has given an interview: 'Je joue de beaucoup d'instruments de musique, mais j'adore surtout la flûte. Dans l'avenir, je veux apprendre à jouer de la batterie pour que je puisse jouer dans les concerts de rock.' What's he saying? ☑

3) You love pop music, but when you were little you liked dance music. How would you say this in French? ☑

Cinema (p.28) ☑

4) What do these phrases mean in English?
a) le dessin animé   b) le personnage   c) la bande-annonce   d) l'actrice ☑

5) Quels genres de film aimes-tu? Pourquoi? Répondez en français. ☑

6) Your friend is telling you about a film she saw last week: 'L'intrigue n'était pas croyable et j'avais du mal à comprendre ce qui s'était passé.' Did she like it? Why / Why not? (Answer in English). ☑

7) Think about the last film you watched. Did you enjoy it? Why / Why not? (Answer in French). ☑

TV (p.29) ☑

8) You're on holiday in France and are watching television in your hotel. The channels are divided into different categories — what are their English translations?
a) les feuilletons   b) la télé-réalité   c) les informations   d) les jeux télévisés ☑

9) You like watching crime shows, but you don't like watching adverts on television. Say this in French. ☑

10) 'La télé-réalité est ennuyeuse et elle encourage les jeunes à avoir une perception fausse de la vie normale.' Do you agree with this statement? Explain your answer in French. ☑

Food and Eating Out (p.30-31) ☑

11) You're going to the supermarket to buy ingredients for a meal. In French, write down five items you might buy. ☑

12) 'Quel est ton plat préféré?' Translate this question into English and then answer it in French. ☑

13) You're at a restaurant in France. Say that you'd like to see the menu, and order a glass of fizzy water. ☑

14) How would you tell a waiter that you're allergic to nuts in French? ☑

15) You're a vegetarian. Which of these dishes are you able to eat?
a) le bœuf bourguignon   b) le poulet rôti   c) le potage aux légumes   d) la tourte à la viande ☑

Sport (p.32-33) ☑

16) Write three sentences about your favourite sport (make it up if you don't like sport). Think about why you like it and when / how regularly you play it. ☑

17) Olivier tells you: 'Je fais de l'aviron régulièrement et j'ai un tournoi la semaine prochaine. Si je gagne toutes mes courses, je ferai partie de l'équipe nationale française.' Translate his sentences into English. ☑

18) Est-ce que tu préfères les sports individuels ou d'équipe? Pourquoi / Pourquoi pas? Répondez en français. ☑

Technology

Technology is a hot topic nowadays — it's difficult to imagine life without it. The examiners love asking questions that delve into its advantages and disadvantages, so it's worth going over this section carefully.

Accro à mon ordinateur — Addicted to my computer

l'ordinateur (m) portable	*laptop*		l'email (m) /	
la tablette	*tablet*		le courrier électronique	*email*
le portable	*(mobile) phone*		le mot de passe	*password*
le texto	*text message*		l'écran (m) tactile	*touch screen*

envoyer	*to send*	télécharger	*to download*
recevoir	*to receive*	faire des achats (en ligne)	*to shop (online)*
tchatter	*to talk online*	être accro à	*to be addicted to*

Grammar — pouvoir / vouloir / devoir / il faut + infinitive

Some verbs can be followed directly by an <u>infinitive</u> (see p.133):

Je <u>peux acheter</u> de la musique en ligne.
I <u>can buy</u> music online.

Je <u>veux avoir</u> la dernière technologie.
I <u>want to have</u> the latest technology.

Les jeunes <u>doivent être</u> prudents en ligne.
Young people <u>must be</u> careful online.

Il <u>faut faire</u> attention sur les forums.
You <u>must be</u> careful on chat rooms.

Question	**Simple Answer**	**Extended Answer**
Utilises-tu souvent la technologie dans ta vie quotidienne?	Oui, j'utilise mon portable tous les jours et j'ai un ordinateur portable.	Oui, je suis accro à mon portable et j'envoie des messages à mes amis tout le temps. Par contre, je n'ai pas d'ordinateur portable.
Do you often use technology in your everyday life?	*Yes, I use my mobile phone every day and I have a laptop.*	*Yes, I'm addicted to my mobile phone and I send messages to my friends all the time. On the other hand, I don't have a laptop.*

Jamais sans mon portable — Never without my mobile phone

J'ai eu mon premier portable à dix ans.	*I got my first mobile phone at age ten.*
J'envoie et je reçois des dizaines de textos par jour.	*I send and receive dozens of texts a day.*
Je ne pourrais pas vivre sans mon portable.	*I couldn't live without my mobile phone.*

Dans la vie quotidienne, les textos ont remplacé la conversation.	*In everyday life, text messages have replaced conversation.* ←	*we're constantly in contact with others* — on est toujours en contact avec d'autres
On passe trop de temps sur nos portables.	*We spend too much time on our mobile phones.* ←	*lots of* — beaucoup de *little* — peu de
Si je suis en retard, mes parents peuvent me téléphoner pour savoir où je suis. Je me sens en sécurité.	*If I'm late, my parents can phone me to find out where I am. I feel safe.* ←	*They find it very useful.* — Ils le trouvent très utile.

Technology

Of course, technology isn't just about phones — the Internet practically runs the world, so it probably deserves a mention. It could come up in any one of your French exams, so learn it well.

Parlons d'Internet — Let's talk about the Internet

Views about the <u>Internet</u> vary massively, so it's worth considering its <u>advantages</u> and <u>disadvantages</u>.

Je peux faire des recherches pour mes projets scolaires en ligne. Les sites web factuels sont très utiles.	*I can do research for my school projects online. Factual websites are very useful.*
On peut trouver toutes les informations que l'on recherche rapidement.	*You can find all the pieces of information that you're looking for quickly.*
Je peux jouer à des jeux en ligne avec mes copains sans sortir de ma chambre.	*I can play online games with my friends without leaving my bedroom.*
Mon frère achète des billets de concert et de cinéma en ligne. C'est plus facile et pratique que de faire la queue au guichet.	*My brother buys concert and cinema tickets online. It's easier and more convenient than queuing at the box office.*

Grammar — direct object pronouns (me, te, le, la, nous, vous, les)

A <u>direct object</u> is the <u>person or thing</u> (noun) that an action is <u>being done to</u>.

Elle joue <u>le jeu</u> en ligne. *She plays <u>the game</u> online.*

<u>Direct object pronouns</u> (see p.121) <u>replace</u> that noun. In French, they come <u>before</u> the verb and are used to <u>avoid repetition</u>.

Elle <u>le</u> joue en ligne. *She plays <u>it</u> online.*

> The direct object pronouns 'me', 'te', 'le' and 'la' drop their final letter and replace it with an apostrophe when they come directly before a word beginning with a vowel. E.g. 'Je peux t'aider.' (*I can help you.*)

Question	**Simple Answer**	**Extended Answer**
Selon vous, quels sont les dangers d'Internet? *In your opinion, what are the dangers associated with the Internet?*	Il faut faire attention à ce qu'on écrit sur Internet, surtout quand on met ses détails personnels en ligne. *You need to be careful with what you write on the Internet, especially when you put personal details online.*	Le problème principal, c'est de rester en sécurité. Il ne faut pas mettre de photos en ligne, ni afficher de détails personnels car tout le monde peut les voir. De plus, il faut faire attention en faisant des achats en ligne car il y a de la fraude. Il faut protéger tes détails personnels avec un mot de passe. *The main problem is staying safe. You mustn't put photos online, nor post personal details because everyone can see them. Furthermore, you need to be careful when shopping online because of fraud. You must protect your personal details with a password.*

WRITING Use 'on' to talk about what people do in general...

Translate the following passage into **French**. *[12 marks]*

I got a new mobile phone for my birthday. My mum bought it for me. It's very useful because I can contact my parents and my friends when I want. I can also download music and games from the Internet. Tomorrow, I will use it to buy a book online.

> Make sure you think about whether the nouns are masculine or feminine — you'll get marks for accurate grammar.

Social Media

And on to social media... chances are you know a fair bit about social media, so hopefully revising this page will be nice and straightforward. You just need to learn the terminology in French, and off you go...

Les réseaux sociaux — Social networks

le jeu	game
cliquer	to click
taper	to type
mettre en ligne	to upload
naviguer (sur)	to browse
l'écran (m)	screen
le forum	chat room

Grammar — irregular verb — 'envoyer' (to send)

'Envoyer' is an irregular verb. Learn how to conjugate it properly — it's useful for talking about online communication.

j'envoie	I send	nous envoyons	we send
tu envoies	you send	vous envoyez	you send
	(informal, singular)		(formal, plural)
il / elle / on envoie	he / she / one sends	ils / elles envoient	they send

Question

Utilises-tu souvent les réseaux sociaux?

Do you often use social networks?

Simple Answer

Oui, j'utilise les réseaux sociaux chaque jour.

Yes, I use social networks every day.

Extended Answer

Oui, je suis un bloggeur. J'aime partager mes recettes et photos. Je passe en moyenne deux heures par jour sur les réseaux sociaux.

Yes, I am a blogger. I love to share my recipes and photos. On average, I spend two hours a day on social networks.

Je l'utilise parce que... — I use it because...

It's worth thinking about the different ways that people use social media and learning how to discuss them.

J'aime bien mettre mes vidéos en ligne pour les montrer à mes amis.	*I like uploading my videos to show them to my friends.*	my photos — mes photos my blog posts — mes articles de blog
J'utilise les réseaux sociaux pour rencontrer ceux qui partagent les mêmes intérêts que moi.	*I use social networks to meet those who share the same interests as me.*	organise social events — organiser des événements sociaux
Les sites sociaux me permettent d'être à jour avec des nouvelles importantes.	*Social media sites allow me to keep up to date with important news.*	to stay in contact with my family — de rester en contact avec ma famille

READING

Learn how to conjugate 'envoyer' — it's a bit tricky...

Lisez le texte d'Anaïs, puis répondez aux questions en **français**.

En tout, je passe au moins trois heures par jour sur les réseaux sociaux. Je tchatte avec mes amis sur les sites sociaux **tout en faisant**[1] mes devoirs.

Je pense que, de nos jours, les réseaux sociaux sont indispensables. Par exemple, ils me permettent de savoir ce que fait mon cousin qui voyage en Amérique du Sud. Il met ses photos en ligne et je peux les regarder sur mon ordinateur. [1] while doing

e.g. Combien de temps par jour passe Anaïs sur les réseaux sociaux ?
au moins trois heures

1. Qu'est-ce qu'Anaïs fait pendant qu'elle complète ses devoirs ? [1]

2. Qu'est-ce qu'Anaïs pense des réseaux sociaux ? [1]

3. Comment est-ce que les sites sociaux l'aide à savoir ce que fait son cousin ? [1]

The Problems with Social Media

Of course, social media does have its drawbacks — even if you think it's great, you still need to be able to talk about its disadvantages and give a balanced argument in the exam. Use this page to get some ideas.

Les inconvénients — Disadvantages

l'avantage (m)	advantage
l'inconvénient (m)	disadvantage / drawback
la cyber-intimidation	cyber-bullying
la vie privée	private life
à cause de	as a result of
au lieu de	instead of
grâce à	thanks to

Grammar — 'de' (preposition)

'à cause de' and 'au lieu de' both use the preposition 'de'. Remember, if 'de' is followed by 'le' or 'les', they combine:

de + le = du   de + les = des

À cause des réseaux sociaux...

As a result of social networks...

À mon avis — In my opinion

You might have to discuss the <u>advantages</u> and <u>disadvantages</u> of social media.

Moi, j'adore utiliser les réseaux sociaux — grâce à eux, je sais ce que font mes amis, même quand on ne s'est pas vu depuis longtemps.

I love using social networks — thanks to them, I know what my friends are doing, even when we haven't seen each other for a long time.

Cependant, je reconnais qu'il y a aussi des inconvénients. Par exemple, la vie privée n'est plus privée du tout — dès qu'on a mis une photo en ligne, tout le monde peut la voir.

However, I recognise that there are also drawbacks. For example, your private life is no longer private at all — as soon as you've put a photo online, everybody can see it.

De plus, la cyber-intimidation est un grand problème. Il y a des personnes qui écrivent des choses fausses et méchantes sur les sites sociaux.

Furthermore, cyber-bullying is a big problem. There are people who write fake and cruel things on social media sites.

SPEAKING ## Giving a balanced opinion will really impress the examiner...

Have a look at Paul's answer to this question.

À ton avis, quels sont les avantages et inconvénients des réseaux sociaux ?

À mon avis, l'avantage le plus important des réseaux sociaux est que **n'importe qui**[1] peut être **écrivain**[2]. Moi, j'aimerais être journaliste un jour, et avec mon blog, j'ai l'opportunité d'écrire pour mes deux cents **abonnés**[3] — et c'est complètement gratuit !

Néanmoins[4], je les trouve parfois effrayants. Actuellement on est préoccupé des **centaines**[5] d'amis sur Internet, donc on abandonne souvent les rapports réels.

Grade 6-7

[1] anybody
[2] author
[3] subscribers
[4] nevertheless / however
[5] hundreds

Tick list:
✓ tenses: present, conditional
✓ superlative

To improve:
+ complex structures, e.g. pour + inf.
+ use quantifiers e.g. 'très' or 'vraiment'
+ more tenses: perfect, imperfect, future

Now answer the following questions.
Try to speak for about two minutes. [10 marks]

- *Comment utilises-tu les réseaux sociaux ?*
- *À ton avis, quels sont les avantages des réseaux sociaux ?*
- *À ton avis, quels sont les inconvénients des réseaux sociaux ?*

Knowing a range of conjunctions will come in handy when giving both sides of an argument:

pourtant	however
néanmoins	nevertheless
par contre	on the other hand

Listening Questions

We're on a roll with these practice questions — get to it, and have a crack at the next four pages.

1   Listen to this radio debate about technology.
Complete the sentences in **English**.

(TRACK LISTENING 12)

Example: This boy thinks that technology is a bit dangerous because

you never know what you're going to find on the internet.
....

1 a   This girl uses her smartphone to

....   *[1 mark]*

1 b   This girl uses technology to

....   *[1 mark]*

1 c   This boy thinks that young people

....   *[1 mark]*

2   Écoutez ces interviews au sujet des réseaux sociaux.
Choisissez **deux** phrases qui sont **vraies** et écrivez les bonnes lettres dans les cases.

(TRACK LISTENING 13)

2 a   Cho:

A	Elle n'utilise jamais les réseaux sociaux.
B	Elle échange tous ses détails personnels en ligne.
C	Elle connaît quelqu'un qui a eu des problèmes graves.
D	Son collège donne des conseils à propos des réseaux sociaux.

☐ ☐   *[2 marks]*

2 b   Jules:

A	Il préfère que ses vidéos restent privées.
B	Il aime montrer à tout le monde qu'il s'amuse.
C	Il envoie des messages constamment.
D	Il aime voir ce que font les autres.

☐ ☐   *[2 marks]*

2 c   Clara:

A	Elle met toujours toutes ses photos en ligne.
B	Elle demande la permission avant de partager des photos.
C	Tout le monde peut voir les photos qu'on poste.
D	Il est facile de supprimer les choses qu'on a mises en ligne.

☐ ☐   *[2 marks]*

Speaking Question

Candidate's Role

- Your teacher will play the role of your French friend's grandparent. They will speak first.

- You should use *vous* to address your friend's grandparent.

- – ! – means you will have to respond to something you have not prepared.

- – ? – means you will have to ask your friend's grandparent a question.

> Vous parlez de la technologie avec le grand-père / la grand-mère de votre ami(e) français(e).
>
> - Les smartphones (le plus grand avantage).
>
> - Comment vous vous en servez.
>
> - ? Utiliser un smartphone.
>
> - Nouvelles technologies dans votre collège.
>
> - !

Teacher's Role

- You begin the role-play using the introductory text below.

- You should address the candidate as *vous*.

- You may alter the wording of the questions in response to the candidate's previous answers.

- Do not supply the candidate with key vocabulary.

> Introductory text: *Vous parlez de la technologie avec le grand-père / la grand-mère de votre ami(e) français(e). Moi, je suis le grand-père / la grand-mère.*
>
> - Quel est le plus grand avantage des smartphones ?
>
> - Comment vous vous en servez ?
>
> - ? Allow the candidate to ask you a question.
>
> - Est-ce que vous utilisez les nouvelles technologies au collège ?
>
> - ! Est-ce que vous pensez que c'est facile d'apprendre à utiliser les technologies modernes ?

Reading Questions

1 Lisez ce que ces personnes ont écrit dans un forum sur l'utilisation d'Internet.
Identifiez la bonne personne. Écrivez **L** (Laure), **M** (Marc) ou **A** (Alex).

	J'adore Internet. Je parle souvent avec mes amis et je passe des heures devant l'écran. Pour moi, c'est important de pouvoir communiquer avec les autres sans quitter la maison. On peut toujours faire de nouvelles connaissances. C'est très sociable donc on ne se sent jamais seul. — **Laure**
	Je suis un vrai internaute. Je surfe sur Internet tous les jours. Par contre, je pense qu'il faut faire attention en utilisant Internet parce que les gens peuvent voler des renseignements personnels. On doit se protéger contre le crime en ligne. Moi, je ne partage jamais mes détails personnels. — **Marc**
	Personnellement, je n'aime pas Internet. Les jeunes s'en servent pour télécharger des films et de la musique illégalement. Cela a des effets négatifs pour les artistes. En plus, beaucoup de magasins de disques ont fermé car on peut trouver les mêmes produits en ligne sans payer. — **Alex**

1 a Il y a des dangers en ligne. ☐ *[1 mark]*

1 b Je ne suis pas fana d'Internet. ☐ *[1 mark]*

1 c Internet est utile pour la vie sociale. ☐ *[1 mark]*

1 d On peut écouter de la musique gratuitement. ☐ *[1 mark]*

2 Translate the following passage into **English**.

> Je suis accro aux réseaux sociaux. Je veux savoir ce que font mes amis et je pense que c'est un bon moyen de communiquer et de rencontrer les autres. L'année dernière, par exemple, j'ai fait la connaissance d'un garçon au Canada et nous tchattons en ligne chaque semaine.

....

....

....

....

....

....

[9 marks]

Writing Questions

1   Vous écrivez un article pour le journal scolaire sur les dangers des réseaux sociaux.

Décrivez:

• les problèmes concernant les réseaux sociaux

• comment on pourrait éviter ces problèmes.

Écrivez environ **150** mots en **français**. Répondez à chaque aspect de la question.

[32 marks]

2   Translate the following passage into **French**.

My parents don't want me to use social networks. They think that it can be very dangerous, but I don't agree. I don't upload my photos and I never share my videos. We discuss the problems like bullying at school. However, I think that the teachers should give us more information.

....

....

....

....

....

....

....

....

[12 marks]

Revision Summary for Section Four

These questions really do check what you know and what you don't know, so they're pretty handy as far as revision goes. If you need to flick back through and revise a couple of things, don't forget to come back to these questions and have another go — after all, practice makes perfect...

Technology (p.39-40) ☑

1) Your bag has been stolen whilst you're on holiday in Belgium, and the police want a list of any valuables that were inside it. How would you say the following phrases in French?
   a) my laptop   b) my tablet   c) my mobile phone ☑

2) Karim says: 'Les ordinateurs sont démodés. De nos jours, tous les jeunes ont des ordinateurs portables.' What does this mean in English? ☑

3) 'I want to send an email, but I've forgotten my password.' How would you say this in French? ☑

4) Your teacher explains: 'Il y a toujours de la pression pour avoir la dernière technologie.' Translate this into English. ☑

5) Utilises-tu souvent ton portable dans la vie quotidienne? Répondez en français. Utilisez des phrases complètes. ☑

6) Say, in French, that you got your first phone when you were eight years old. ☑

7) Aurélie says: 'Il n'est pas du tout nécessaire d'avoir un portable avant l'âge de onze ans. Quand on est petit, il suffit de voir les amis à l'école.' What does this mean in English? ☑

8) In French, write down two advantages and two disadvantages of having a mobile phone. ☑

9) 'Qu'est-ce que tu fais sur Internet en général?' Répondez en français. ☑

10) In French, say that your mum does her shopping online because it's more practical. ☑

11) You're reading a leaflet about internet safety: 'Il ne faut pas afficher des photos de soi-même dans les forums, ni organiser un rendez-vous avec quelqu'un que vous ne connaissez pas.' What advice is the leaflet giving? Answer in English. ☑

12) Céline says: 'De nos jours, c'est impossible de rester en sécurité sur Internet. N'importe qui peut accéder à vos détails personnels.' Do you agree? Explain your answer in French. ☑

Social Media (p.41-42) ☑

13) Do you use social networks? Why / Why not? Give at least three reasons (in French). ☑

14) À ton avis, est-ce que c'est possible de devenir accro aux réseaux sociaux? Répondez en français. Utilisez des phrases complètes. ☑

15) Say in French that you have a blog and you like to share your opinions on important events. ☑

16) Marie is giving her views on social media sites: 'À cause des sites sociaux, la vie privée n'existe plus.' Translate her sentence into English. ☑

17) Qu'est-ce que c'est la cyber-intimidation? ☑

18) 'Yann uses social networks from time to time, but he prefers to send texts to his friends.' How would you say this in French? ☑

Festivals in French-Speaking Countries

These pages are on festivals that are traditional in French-speaking countries. Some are similar to British ones but it's important you know how they're celebrated differently in other countries.

Les fêtes françaises — French festivals

la fête	festival / party	Bonne année!	Happy New Year!
fêter / célébrer	to celebrate	la Saint-Sylvestre	New Year's Eve
le jour férié	bank holiday	le Jour de l'An	New Year's Day
le cadeau	present	la fête des rois	Epiphany / Twelfth Night
Bon anniversaire!	Happy birthday!	la fête des mères / pères	Mother's / Father's Day
Bonne chance!	Good luck!	la Saint Valentin	Valentine's Day
Félicitations!	Congratulations!	le poisson d'avril	April Fools' Day
la fête du travail	May Day	le défilé	procession
la fête nationale	Bastille Day	les feux (m) d'artifice	fireworks

Les écoles sont fermées les jours fériés.	Schools are closed on bank holidays.
La Saint Valentin est trop commerciale.	Valentine's Day is too commercial.
La Saint-Sylvestre, on la fête à minuit et on prend des bonnes résolutions.	People celebrate New Year's Eve at midnight and make resolutions.

sentimental —
sentimentale

La fête nationale — Bastille Day

Many events are held on <u>Bastille Day</u> to commemorate the <u>French Revolution</u>. It's the French <u>national day</u>.

Le quatorze juillet est le jour de la fête nationale. Il y a beaucoup d'événements pour la célébrer.	14th July is Bastille Day. There are many events to celebrate it.
Le quatorze juillet, beaucoup de gens s'habillent aux couleurs tricolores.	On 14th July, lots of people dress in the colours of the French flag.
J'aime regarder les feux d'artifice parce qu'ils sont toujours magnifiques.	I like watching the fireworks because they're always amazing.
J'aime la fête nationale parce qu'on peut la célébrer avec toute la famille.	I like Bastille Day because you can celebrate it with the whole family.

the processions
— les défilés (m)

the dances —
les danses (f)

impressive —
impressionnant(e)s

it's an historical
event — c'est
un événement
historique

Any of these festivals could make an appearance in the exam...

Read the results of an online survey about how French people will be spending Bastille Day.

Nous avons demandé aux français: «Qu'est ce que vous ferez le quatorze juillet ?» Voici les résultats :

- La majorité (86%) va sortir avec des amis.
- 74% des gens verront des feux d'artifice.
- 34% mangeront un repas avec leur famille.
- Seulement 16% vont voir un défilé au centre-ville.
- Un peu plus (18%) vont se maquiller aux couleurs tricolores.
- Cependant, 20% ne feront rien.

e.g. What percentage of people will be watching fireworks? **74%**

1. What percentage of people will be doing the following activities?
   A. Eating a meal. [1]
   B. Painting their faces. [1]
   C. Watching a procession. [1]
2. What percentage of people won't be celebrating? [1]

Festivals in French-Speaking Countries

Here are a couple more festivals that are celebrated in France and are worth knowing a little bit about.

La fête des rois — Epiphany

Epiphany is on 6th January — twelve days after Christmas — and celebrates the kings' visit to the baby Jesus.

le roi	*king*	la fève	*charm*	la galette des rois	*cake for Epiphany*
la reine	*queen*	la couronne	*crown*	le gâteau des rois	*cake for Epiphany*

Dans une grande partie de la France on mange une 'galette des rois', qui est un type de gâteau rond.

In most of France people eat a 'galette des rois', which is a type of round cake.

Dans le Sud de la France on fait un 'gâteau des rois', un type de brioche en forme de couronne.

In southern France people make a 'gâteau des rois', a type of brioche in the shape of a crown.

On cache une fève dans la galette. La personne qui trouve la fève devient le roi / la reine et il / elle porte une couronne pendant toute la journée.

A charm is hidden in the cake. The person who finds the charm becomes the king / the queen and he / she wears a crown for the whole day.

Question	**Simple Answer**	**Extended Answer**
Qu'est-ce que tu as fait pour la fête des rois?	J'ai fait une galette des rois pour ma famille.	Toute ma famille élargie était chez nous. Nous avons beaucoup mangé. J'ai trouvé la fève donc je suis devenu(e) le roi / la reine.
What did you do for Epiphany?	*I made a 'galette des rois' for my family.*	*All my extended family were at our house. We ate a lot. I found the charm so I became king / queen.*

Poisson d'avril! — April Fool!

On 1st April, children try to stick a picture of a fish on people's backs. When their friend finds out, the child responsible shouts 'Poisson d'avril!'

On met des poissons sur le dos de ses amis.	*People put fish on their friends' backs.*
Mon ami(e) m'a joué un tour.	*My friend played a trick on me.*
Il m'a raconté une plaisanterie.	*He told me a joke.*

Grammar — 'on'

Use 'on' to say what many people tend to do and to describe a custom:

Le 1er avril, on joue des tours aux autres.
On 1st April, people play tricks on others.

TRACK LISTENING 14 It's useful to know about French traditions and customs...

Youssou is describing his birthday celebrations. Choose the correct option to finish each sentence.

e.g. Youssou is...   *c*
A. six years old.
B. seventeen years old.
C. sixteen years old.   *[1]*

1. He opened his gifts in the evening because...
A. he didn't want to get up early to do it.
B. he starts school early in the morning.
C. he didn't want to do it at school.   *[1]*

2. His sister made him...
A. his favourite meal.
B. a cake.
C. some biscuits.   *[1]*

3. There were fireworks...
A. because it was Bastille Day.
B. because it was May Day.
C. to celebrate Youssou's birthday.   *[1]*

Religious Festivals and Customs

There are also several religious festivals and customs that you need to know about.

La foi — Faith

religieux / religieuse	*religious*	athée	*atheist*	la Hanoukka	*Hanukkah*
juif / juive	*Jewish*	la synagogue	*synagogue*	le ramadan	*Ramadan*
musulman(e)	*Muslim*	la mosquée	*mosque*	l'Aïd (f) al-Fitr	*Eid al-Fitr*
chrétien(ne)	*Christian*	l'église (f)	*church*	Pâques	*Easter*

Joyeux Noël! — Merry Christmas!

Nous mettons des cadeaux sous le sapin de Noël. Nous les ouvrons soit après la messe de minuit soit le jour de Noël.	*We put presents under the Christmas tree. We open them either after midnight mass or on Christmas Day.*
'Le réveillon' est le dîner qu'on mange après minuit la veille de Noël. Nous mangeons de l'oie pour le réveillon.	*'Le réveillon' is the dinner we eat after midnight on Christmas Eve. We eat goose for 'le réveillon'.*

turkey — de la dinde

Christmas loaf — du pain calendal

yule log — de la bûche de Noël

D'autres fêtes religieuses — Other religious festivals

La Hanoukka est une fête juive. On allume des bougies et on prie ensemble.	*Hanukkah is a Jewish festival. People light candles and pray together.*
Au cours du Ramadan, les musulmans ne devraient ni manger ni boire de l'aube au coucher du soleil.	*During Ramadan, Muslims should neither eat nor drink from dawn until sunset.*

celebrate it for eight days — on la fête pendant huit jours

exchange gifts — on échange des cadeaux

Grammar — 'ne...ni...ni' (neither...nor)

To say 'neither this nor that', use this structure: ne before the verb + ni ... ni ... .
Je ne fête ni Noël ni Pâques.   I celebrate neither Christmas nor Easter.

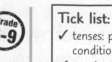
SPEAKING

Learn the French words for religions and their festivals...

Grace is speaking to her teacher about how she spent the Christmas holidays.

Teacher : Qu'est-ce que tu as fait pendant les vacances de Noël ? **Grade 8-9**

Grace :   Je suis allée à Londres pour rendre visite à mon oncle.

Teacher : Qu'est-ce que tu aimes faire à Noël ?

Grace :   J'aime acheter des cadeaux pour ma famille et mes amis. Qu'est-ce que vous aimez manger pour Noël ?

Teacher : J'aime manger de la bûche de Noël — elle est délicieuse ! Qu'est-ce que tu as fait pour fêter la Saint-Sylvestre ?

Grace :   Je suis allée au concert — c'était magnifique !

Teacher : Qu'est-ce que tu feras l'année prochaine pour Noël ?

Grace :   Je ne sais pas encore, mais je voudrais faire du ski.

Tick list:
- ✓ tenses: perfect, imperfect, conditional, present
- ✓ good variety of verbs

To improve:
- + more detail in the last two questions
- + give reasons for the opinions

Now answer the questions in the example yourself. Address your teacher as 'vous' and aim to talk for about 2 minutes. [15 marks]

Remember to use different tenses and give detailed answers by justifying your opinions.

Listening Questions

As is the tradition in this book, we'll now have some exam practice. Let's put your new-found festival knowledge to the test — grab your pen and some paper and answer these questions.

1   Listen to this podcast about Eid.
Choose the **two** statements which are **true** and write the letters in the boxes.

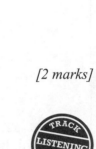

A	Early morning prayer is part of the celebrations.
B	Adults dress in simple, plain clothes.
C	Muslims in all countries eat the same thing at Eid.
D	It is forbidden to dance during Eid.
E	It is traditional for children to wear new clothes.

☐ ☐

[2 marks]

2   Listen to this radio programme about how New Year is celebrated in France.
Choose the correct answer for each question and write the letter in the box.

2 a   According to Madame Romero, what time do guests usually arrive for New Year's Eve?

A	around 8 pm
B	just before 9 pm
C	whenever they feel like it

☐

[1 mark]

2 b   When celebrating New Year's Eve, guests...

A	must finish eating before midnight.
B	start eating long before 10 pm.
C	eat around 10 pm or 11 pm.

☐

[1 mark]

2 c   What do people do after midnight?

A	They go home straight away.
B	They continue to celebrate.
C	They play games.

☐

[1 mark]

2 d   What are "les étrennes"?

A	special sweets made at New Year
B	the meals eaten on New Year's Day
C	gifts of money or sweets

☐

[1 mark]

Speaking Question

Candidate's Material

- Spend a couple of minutes looking at the photo and the questions below it.

- You can make notes on a separate piece of paper.

© iStock.com/monkeybusinessimages

You will be asked the following **three** questions, and **two** questions you haven't prepared:

- Qu'est-ce qu'il y a sur la photo ?

- Que fais-tu à Pâques ?

- Est-ce que tu as une fête préférée ? Laquelle ? Pourquoi ?

Teacher's Material

- Allow the student to develop his / her answers as much as possible.

- You need to ask the student the following questions **in order**:

- Qu'est-ce qu'il y a sur la photo ?

- Que fais-tu à Pâques ?

- Est-ce que tu as une fête préférée ? Laquelle ? Pourquoi ?

- Qu'est-ce que tu as fait l'année dernière pour fêter Noël ?

- Voudrais-tu fêter la Saint-Sylvestre à l'étranger ? Pourquoi / Pourquoi pas ?

Reading Questions

1   Read Marie's blog about festivals in French Guiana.
        Answer the questions in **English**.

> Ici en Guyane française, on fête bon nombre de festivals que l'on célèbre en France, comme la Fête nationale, Pâques et Noël. Les jours fériés sont les mêmes qu'en France, sauf qu'il y en a quelques-uns de plus. Par exemple, nous avons la commémoration de l'abolition de l'esclavage dans les colonies françaises. Cela a lieu chaque année le dix juin. Il y a de la danse, du théâtre et des conférences pour que les gens apprennent plus sur le passé du pays.
>
> Il y a aussi quelques festivals culturels, comme le festival de jazz à Cayenne, la capitale du pays. Moi, j'adore ce festival parce qu'il y a de la musique en plein air au jardin botanique, et l'ambiance est superbe. En plus, on invite des musiciens du monde entier pour y participer, donc c'est très international. Je trouve cela formidable.

1 a   List **two** festivals which are celebrated in both France and French Guiana.

....   *[2 marks]*

1 b   What is the aim of the conferences held on 10th June?

....   *[1 mark]*

1 c   Why does Marie enjoy the jazz festival? Give **one** detail.

....   *[1 mark]*

2   Complétez cet article au sujet du Carnaval avec les mots de la liste ci-dessous.

> Le Carnaval vient de la ☐ catholique du 'Mardi gras', qui est le dernier jour avant le **carême**[1]. Historiquement, les chrétiens n'avaient pas le droit de manger de la ☐ pendant les quarante jours du carême. Pour cette raison, le Mardi gras est ☐ une journée de festivités et de grands repas, et le Carnaval vient de cette tradition.
>
> On fête le Carnaval partout en France. Les rues sont pleines de gens et il y a des défilés et d'autres événements ☐. Le Carnaval de Nice est très ☐ et il attire de nombreux touristes qui ont envie d'y participer. Il y a beaucoup de musique et de danse.

[1]**Lent**

A	célèbre	D	devenu	F	viande
B	touristes	E	développé	G	tradition
C	spectaculaires				

[4 marks]

Writing Questions

1   Vous écrivez un article sur les fêtes pour un magazine français.

Décrivez:

- comment on célèbre les fêtes françaises

- une fête mémorable que vous avez célébrée.

Écrivez environ **150** mots en **français**. Répondez à chaque aspect de la question.

[32 marks]

2   Translate the following passage into **French**.

> The 14th July is Bastille Day in France. Lots of tourists go to Paris to see the processions.
> This year, I went to a park near the Eiffel Tower to watch the fireworks. It was a great
> experience. My friends would like to visit Paris next year, so we will celebrate together.

....

....

....

....

....

....

....

[12 marks]

Revision Summary for Section Five

To round off the festivities, here are some more questions for you. Try to answer them all without looking back at the section — if you can't answer a question, spend some time re-learning the relevant page and then have another go. Once you can answer everything, tick off the pages.

Festivals in French-Speaking Countries (p.48-49) ☑

1) If someone said 'Bonne année!' to you, which month of the year would it be?
   a) June   b) December   c) January ☑

2) Jot down the French for:
   a) Bastille Day   b) April Fools' Day   c) New Year's Eve   d) New Year's Day   e) Epiphany ☑

3) How would you say 'Happy birthday!' to someone in French? ☑

4) Qu'est-ce que tu fais normalement pour fêter ton anniversaire? ☑

5) 'Je n'aime pas les fêtes d'anniversaire — il faut tout organiser et en plus, les fêtes sont chères. Why doesn't Isabelle like birthday parties? Answer in English. ☑

6) Qu'est-ce que tu penses de la Saint Valentin? ☑

7) 'I've forgotten to buy a present for my mum. It's Mother's Day tomorrow.' Translate this into French. ☑

8) Your French penfriend describes her favourite festival to you: 'Moi, j'adore la Fête nationale. Je regarde les feux d'artifice avec ma famille et chaque année nous prenons part aux défilés.' What is she saying? ☑

9) Translate this into French: 'I like to celebrate New Year's Eve with my friends. I always make a New Year's resolution.' ☑

10) How would you say 'I cooked a meal for my family' in French? ☑

11) Sophia says: 'Je déteste le premier avril. La fête ne sert à rien, et parfois les gens sont cruels envers les autres.' Why doesn't she like April Fools' Day? Answer in English. ☑

12) 'On April Fools' day, I played a trick on my little brother.' Say this in French. ☑

Religious Festivals and Customs (p.50) ☑

13) What's the French for...?
    a) Easter   b) Christmas   c) Ramadan   d) religious   e) church   f) mosque ☑

14) 'On Christmas Day, my family eats a yule log.' How would you say this in French? ☑

15) Que fais-tu en général pendant les vacances de Noël? ☑

16) Kassim says: 'De nos jours, Noël est devenu trop commercial. Il ne s'agit que des cadeaux et du chocolat.' What is Kassim saying? Answer in English. ☑

17) Your friend has sent you a message saying: 'Fêtons Pâques ensemble cette année, en déjeunant chez moi.' What is your friend suggesting? ☑

18) Farid describes what he does during Ramadan. He says: 'During Ramadan, I don't eat or drink during the day, even when I'm at school.' Say this in French. ☑

Talking About Where You Live

Whether it's in the middle of nowhere or the inner city, you need to be able to describe where you live...

Où habites-tu? — Where do you live?

le centre-ville	*town centre*	la poste	*post office*	la boucherie	*butcher's*
le magasin	*shop*	le tabac	*newsagent's*	la bibliothèque	*library*
le marché	*market*	la boulangerie	*bakery*	la campagne	*countryside*

les transports (m) en commun	*public transport*
la gare (routière)	*(bus) station*
la zone piétonne	*pedestrian zone*
la circulation	*traffic*
l'embouteillage (m)	*traffic jam*

Grammar — masculine and feminine

It's worth remembering that most nouns ending in '-ie' are feminine, e.g. la bijouterie (*the jeweller's*). Have a look at p.108 for a full list of common masculine and feminine endings.

J'habite dans une ville à la campagne.   *I live in a town in the countryside.*

Je préfère habiter dans une ville.   *I prefer living in a town.*

by the sea — au bord de la mer
in the mountains — à la montagne
a city — une grande ville

Parle-moi de ta ville — Tell me about your town

Le système des transports en commun aide à réduire la circulation en ville.

The public transport system helps to reduce the traffic in the town.

À cause des embouteillages fréquents, le centre-ville deviendra une zone piétonne.

Because of regular traffic jams, the town centre will become a pedestrian zone.

Il n'y a pas beaucoup à faire dans ma ville. Il n'y a aucun cinéma, par exemple.

There isn't a lot to do in my town. There's no cinema, for example.

Dans ma ville, il y a un grand centre-ville et de nombreux magasins.

In my town, there's a big town centre and numerous shops.

the noise — le bruit
theatre — théâtre (m)
supermarket — supermarché (m)
shopping centre — centre commercial (m)

READING

Think of interesting ways to describe your town to gain marks...

Read this extract from 'Les Misérables' by Victor Hugo, and answer the questions in **English**. It describes how père Madeleine prospered in the black jet industry after moving to Montreuil-sur-mer.

Montreuil-sur-mer était devenu **un centre d'affaires**[1] considérable. L'Espagne, qui consomme beaucoup de **jais noir**[2], y commandait chaque année des grands achats. [...] L'argent que père Madeleine a gagné était tel que, dès la deuxième année, il avait pu construire une grande usine dans laquelle il y avait deux vastes **ateliers**[3], l'un pour les hommes, l'autre pour les femmes. N'importe qui avait faim pouvait s'y présenter, et était sûr de trouver là de l'emploi et du pain. [...] Le chômage et la **misère**[4] étaient inconnus.

[1] a centre of trade
[2] black jet (a gemstone)
[3] workshops
[4] poverty

e.g. Which country bought a large amount of black jet?   **Spain**

1.   When had père Madeleine earned enough money to build a factory?   [1]

2.   Why did père Madeleine build two workshops?   [1]

3.   How did père Madeleine help people who were hungry? Give **two** details.   [2]

4.   Name **two** things which were unheard of in Montreuil-sur-mer.   [2]

The Home

Home sweet home... this page will help you describe where you live using some super French sentences.

La maison — The home

le quartier	*area*	l'immeuble (m)	*block of flats*	la salle de bains	*bathroom*
la maison...	*...house*	la pièce	*room*	les meubles (m)	*furniture*
individuelle	*detached*	le salon	*living room*	le lit	*bed*
jumelée	*semi-detached*	la cuisine	*kitchen*	le placard	*cupboard*
mitoyenne	*terraced*	la chambre	*bedroom*	l'armoire (f)	*wardrobe*

J'habite dans une maison mitoyenne. Nous avons six pièces.

I live in a terraced house. We have six rooms.

Dans ma chambre, il y a une chaise bleue, un lit et un bureau.

In my bedroom, there's a blue chair, a bed and a desk.

Grammar — adjectives

Most adjectives go <u>after</u> the noun, but some go <u>in front</u>:

un <u>beau</u> quartier a <u>beautiful</u> area

See p.111 for more.

C'est comment chez toi? — What's your home like?

You need to vary which <u>adjectives</u> you use and learn some <u>descriptive phrases</u>.

J'habite dans un appartement.

I live in a flat.

J'aime habiter dans une maison jumelée.

I like living in a semi-detached house.

C'est dans un quartier calme avec vue sur la mer.

It's in a quiet area with a sea view.

La cuisine est au rez-de-chaussée.

The kitchen is on the ground floor.

Nous avons un canapé confortable qui est dans le salon.

We have a comfortable sofa which is in the living room.

in a council house — dans une habitation à loyer modéré (une HLM)

on a farm — dans une ferme

picturesque — pittoresque

on the first floor — au premier étage

dining room — la salle à manger

Use adjectives to make your descriptions more detailed...

Mahmoud has written a letter to his British exchange partner about his new flat.

Mon appartement a cinq pièces et se situe dans un immeuble **tout neuf**[1]. J'ai **emménagé**[2] il y a dix jours — j'habitais à la campagne avant cela.
Ma chambre n'est pas très grande, donc la semaine prochaine j'achèterai des meubles plus petits. La cuisine est **carrément**[3] géniale. Il y a une grande **baie vitrée**[4] alors on y voit le soleil et la mer. J'aime beaucoup le bureau aussi. J'y fais mes devoirs car il y a une bibliothèque pour ranger mes livres. Et comme c'est à côté de la cuisine, c'est l'idéal pour **grignoter**[5]. Cependant, si la cuisine était plus loin, ce serait plus facile de manger moins de chocolat !

[1]brand new
[2]moved in
[3]absolutely
[4]bay window
[5]snacking

Tick list:
✓ tenses: present, perfect, imperfect, future, conditional
✓ correct pronoun position
✓ complex vocabulary
✓ use of 'si' clause

To improve:
+ use more exciting adjectives

Vous écrivez une carte postale à un(e) ami(e) pour lui décrire votre nouvelle maison. Décrivez :
- *la maison où vous habitez maintenant*
- *pourquoi vous avez déménagé*

*Écrivez environ **150** mots en **français**. Répondez aux deux aspects de la question.* *[32 marks]*

What You Do at Home

Tidying, cleaning, cooking... I'm sure you do all those things. Here's how to talk about them in French.

Une journée typique — A typical day

se lever	*to get up*	prendre le petit-déjeuner	*to eat breakfast*
se laver	*to wash (yourself)*	faire le lit	*to make the bed*
se doucher	*to shower*	se brosser les dents	*to brush your teeth*
s'habiller	*to get dressed*	se coucher	*to go to bed*

Question

Qu'est-ce que tu fais le matin?

What do you do in the morning?

Simple Answer

Je quitte la maison à sept heures après avoir rangé la cuisine.

I leave home at seven after having tidied the kitchen.

Extended Answer

Je me lave, m'habille et prends mon petit-déjeuner en moins d'une heure. Mais l'année prochaine, j'aurai plus de temps car j'irai au lycée qui est plus proche.

I wash, get dressed and eat breakfast in less than an hour. But next year, I'll have more time because I will go to sixth form college which is closer.

Grammar — reflexive

The '<u>se</u>' part of <u>reflexive</u> verbs has to <u>change</u>:

Je	*me*
Tu	*te*
Il / elle / on	*se*
Nous	*nous*
Vous	*vous*
Ils / elles	*se*

See p.142 for more.

Gagner de l'argent de poche — To earn pocket money

les tâches (f) ménagères	*household tasks / chores*	faire du jardinage	*to do some gardening*
faire la lessive	*to do the laundry*	faire du bricolage	*to do some DIY*
faire la vaisselle	*to do the washing-up*	laver la voiture	*to wash the car*
mettre la table	*to lay the table*	garder les enfants	*to look after children / to babysit*

Je mets la table et je fais la vaisselle plusieurs fois par semaine. En plus, je range la cuisine le samedi.

I lay the table and I do the washing up several times a week. In addition, I tidy the kitchen on Saturdays.

I vacuum — je passe l'aspirateur

I clean — je nettoie (from nettoyer)

Mes parents font les courses et la lessive en rentrant du travail.

My parents do the shopping and the laundry once they get back from work.

Parfois, j'aide ma mère à faire du jardinage ou du bricolage le week-end.

Sometimes, I help my mum do some gardening or DIY at the weekend.

cook — cuisiner

bake (cakes etc.) — faire des pâtisseries

Je n'achète rien avec mon argent de poche car je veux l'économiser.

I don't buy anything with my pocket money because I want to save it.

And now for another chore — learn the phrases on this page...

Translate the blog entry about household chores into **English**. *[9 marks]*

Je reçois dix euros d'argent de poche par semaine. Mais je dois travailler pour gagner cet argent. Je participe tous les jours aux tâches ménagères pour aider mes parents. En plus, samedi dernier, j'ai gardé des enfants. J'achète beaucoup de musique en ligne, mais je vais essayer de faire des économies parce que j'aimerais partir en vacances avec mes copains.

Clothes Shopping

Whether you love fashion or you hate shopping, here's a page to help you talk about it in the exam.

Faire les magasins — To go shopping

'Faire les magasins' and 'faire des courses' refer to shopping in general. 'Faire les courses' refers to food shopping.

les vêtements (m)	*clothes*
la marque	*brand*
la mode	*fashion*
la carte bancaire	*bank card*
en espèces	*with cash*
la taille	*size*
le pantalon	*trousers*
le pull	*jumper*
la chemise	*shirt*
la robe	*dress*
les chaussettes (f)	*socks*
les chaussures (f)	*shoes*
en solde	*in the sale*
en vitrine	*in the window*

Question

Qu'est-ce que tu as acheté?
What did you buy?

Simple Answer

J'ai acheté un pull rouge et un T-shirt qui était en solde.
I bought a red jumper and a T-shirt that was in the sales.

Extended Answer

J'ai acheté une robe. Elle était chère, donc j'ai dû payer par carte bancaire. J'ai voulu acheter un pantalon aussi, mais il ne m'allait pas.
I bought a blue dress. It was expensive, so I had to pay by card. I wanted to buy some trousers too, but they didn't suit me.

Grammar — aller à (to suit)

'Ça me va' means 'it suits me'. The indirect object pronoun 'me' shows who it suits (see p.121). The pronoun usually goes directly before the verb.

Je voudrais... — I would like...

Here are some useful phrases to use when you're shopping.

Autre chose?	*Anything else?*
Avec ça?	*Anything else?*
Ce sera tout?	*Is that everything?*
Ce sera tout.	*That's all.*
J'aimerais bien...	*I would like...*

Grammar — conditional

'J'aimerais bien' *(I would like)* is in the conditional. This is formed with a verb's future stem plus the imperfect tense endings:
J'aimerai *(future)* + J'aimais *(imperfect)* = J'aimerais
See p.144 for more about the conditional.

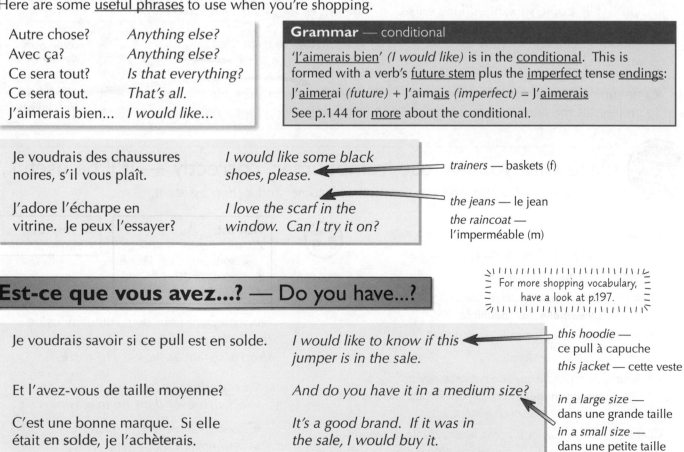

Je voudrais des chaussures noires, s'il vous plaît.

I would like some black shoes, please.

trainers — baskets (f)

J'adore l'écharpe en vitrine. Je peux l'essayer?

I love the scarf in the window. Can I try it on?

the jeans — le jean

the raincoat — l'imperméable (m)

Est-ce que vous avez...? — Do you have...?

For more shopping vocabulary, have a look at p.197.

Je voudrais savoir si ce pull est en solde.

I would like to know if this jumper is in the sale.

this hoodie — ce pull à capuche

this jacket — cette veste

Et l'avez-vous de taille moyenne?

And do you have it in a medium size?

in a large size — dans une grande taille

in a small size — dans une petite taille

C'est une bonne marque. Si elle était en solde, je l'achèterais.

It's a good brand. If it was in the sale, I would buy it.

Est-ce que vous avez cette robe en vert?

Do you have this dress in green?

this skirt — cette jupe

Je cherche un jean blanc.

I'm looking for white jeans.

pyjamas — un pyjama

Clothes Shopping

Prices are useful things to know, I've heard. Here's the nitty-gritty of shopping — labels, receipts, refunds...

Je peux vous aider? — Can I help you?

le vendeur / la vendeuse	*shop assistant*
le ticket de caisse	*receipt*
l'étiquette (f)	*label*
rembourser	*to refund*
bon marché	*good value*
je regarde	*I'm browsing*

Grammar — rembourser (to refund)

'Rembourser' means 'to refund'.

> **Je vous rembourse.**   *I refund you.*

'Se faire rembourser' means 'to get a refund'.

> **Je me fais rembourser.**   *I get a refund.*

'Faire' doesn't agree in the perfect when followed by an infinitive, e.g. 'Elle s'est fait rembourser' *(She got a refund)*, not 'faite'.

Question	**Simple Answer**	**Extended Answer**
Je peux vous aider?	Je cherche des chaussures rouges. Je les ai vues en ligne.	Je voudrais acheter cette chemise. J'ai trouvé la bonne taille, mais il n'y a aucune étiquette. C'est combien s'il vous plaît?
Can I help you?	*I'm looking for some red shoes. I saw them online.*	*I'd like to buy this shirt. I've found the right size, but there's no label. How much is it please?*

À la caisse — At the till

See p.1 for numbers in French.

La veste est réduite à cinquante pour cent du prix. Elle coûte soixante-douze euros.	*The jacket is reduced to fifty percent of the price. It costs seventy-two euros.*
Je voudrais échanger ce pull contre un chapeau.	*I would like to exchange this jumper for a hat.*
Cette jupe ne me va pas. Je préférerais me faire rembourser.	*This skirt doesn't suit me. I would prefer to get a refund.*

good value — bon marché

some gloves — des gants (m)

This coat — Ce manteau

SPEAKING

Make sure you can use 'rembourser' correctly — it'll be useful...

Have a look at this conversation between a customer and a shop assistant.

Grade 8-9

Vendeur : Bonjour. Est-ce que je peux vous aider ?

Client : Oui, je voudrais me faire rembourser.

Vendeur : Quelque chose ne va pas ?

Client : Oui, j'ai acheté ces baskets il y a trois jours. **La semelle**[1] est **déchirée**[2].

Vendeur : Vous avez le ticket de caisse ?

Client : Oui, voici le ticket.

Vendeur : Je regrette que vos baskets soient **endommagées**[3]. Vous pouvez nous donner votre avis du magasin en général ?

Client : Naturellement, après avoir acheté ce produit **défectueux**[4], je suis deçu. Cependant, les vendeurs sont aimables et je pense que je reviendrai ici.

Vendeur : Bien, merci. À bientôt alors !

Tick list:
- ✓ tenses: perfect, imperfect, present, future, conditional
- ✓ opinion phrases
- ✓ complex, relevant vocab

To improve:
+ justify opinions

Now prepare your own role-play using the bullet points below. Address the shop assistant as 'vous'. [15 marks]

Vous parlez avec un(e) vendeur(euse) dans un magasin.

- *vêtement acheté — quand*
- *problèmes (deux détails)*
- *? rembourser*
- *!*
- *le magasin — votre opinion, raison*

[1]the sole   [2]torn   [3]damaged   [4]faulty

More Shopping

More shopping, you say? Well you're in luck — here's some stuff on quantities and online shopping...

Au magasin — At the shop

les courses (f)	*shopping*	la moitié	*half*	
une tranche	*a slice*	le quart	*quarter*	
tranché(e)	*sliced*	peser	*to weigh*	
un morceau	*a piece*	un gramme	*a gram*	
une portion	*a portion*	un kilogramme	*a kilogram*	
une boîte	*a box / tin*	un paquet	*a packet*	

Grammar — encore de (more)

'De' **doesn't** change with the gender or number of the noun after quantifiers. (See p.119.)
'Encore de' is an exception — it's followed by 'de' and the definite article (du, de la, de l', des).
Je voudrais encore du pain. I'd like more bread.

Je voudrais une tranche de pain.

I would like a slice of bread.

Nous voudrions une petite portion de flan.

We would like a small portion of flan.

Je pourrais avoir un demi-kilogramme de fromage, s'il vous plaît?

Could I have half a kilogram of cheese, please?

Voulez-vous un litre de lait?

Do you want a litre of milk?

half of this tart — la moitié de cette tarte

a piece of — un morceau de

more — encore du

half a litre — un demi-litre

Faire des courses en ligne — To shop online

Question

Est-ce que vous préférez faire des courses en ligne?

Do you prefer shopping online?

Simple Answer

Oui, je trouve ça très pratique. On sait qu'on pourra trouver ce qu'on veut.

Yes, I find it very convenient. You know you will be able to find what you want.

Extended Answer

Je ne suis pas sûr. C'est vraiment pratique et les prix sont souvent moins chers en ligne. Mais j'aime pouvoir toucher et voir ce que j'achète. En plus, dans les magasins, on peut demander conseil aux vendeurs.

I'm not sure. It's really convenient and prices are often cheaper online. But I like being able to touch and see what I'm buying. In addition, in shops, you can ask for advice from the shop assistants.

J'ai acheté des légumes en ligne mais ils étaient abîmés.

I bought some vegetables online but they were damaged.

Je préfère acheter les vêtements en ligne parce qu'ils sont livrés vite et les prix sont souvent réduits.

I prefer to buy clothes online because they're delivered quickly and the prices are often reduced.

Mais c'est difficile car on ne sait pas si on a choisi la bonne taille.

But it's difficult because you don't know if you've chosen the right size.

Il est difficile pour les petits magasins de faire concurrence aux grands commerces en ligne.

It's difficult for small shops to compete with big businesses online.

Have a good think about the pros and cons of online shopping...

Listen to Sara and Pierre discussing the advantages and disadvantages of online shopping. Write **one advantage** and **one disadvantage** for each person, in **English**. The advantage for Sara is already done.

e.g. Sara — advantage: It's easy.

[3 marks]

Giving and Asking for Directions

This page has all you need to know about getting to where you want to go. So get learning it...

Où est...? — Where is...?

situé(e)	*situated*	en face de	*opposite*	environ	*about*
se trouver	*to be situated*	juste à côté de	*right next to*	jusqu'à	*until*
traverser	*to cross*	ici	*here*	le nord	*north*
à gauche	*on / to the left*	là-bas	*over there*	le sud	*south*
à droite	*on / to the right*	loin de	*far from*	l'est (m)	*east*
tout droit	*straight ahead*	près de	*near*	l'ouest (m)	*west*

La poste est située en face de l'église.
Allez tout droit pour environ deux minutes, puis prenez la première rue à droite.

The post office is situated opposite the church. Go straight ahead for about two minutes, then take the first street on the right.

Traversez la rue, puis tournez à gauche.
La boulangerie est juste à côté de l'école.

Cross the street, then turn left. The bakery is right next to the school.

Le village est au sud-ouest de la ville.
La ville est dans le sud du pays.

*The village is south-west of the town.
The town is in the south of the country.*

> Remember, if you're talking to someone you don't know, use the 'vous' form of the verb.

C'est loin d'ici? — Is it far from here?

It's useful to use <u>landmarks</u> when describing how to get somewhere.

la rue	*street*	les feux (m) (de signalisation)	*(traffic) lights*
la place	*square*	le rond-point	*roundabout*
le pont	*bridge*	le carrefour	*crossroads*
le trottoir	*pavement*	le panneau	*sign*

Grammar — imperative

The <u>imperative</u> form is used to give <u>instructions</u>:
  Traversez! *Cross!*
See p.145 for more.

Pour aller à la gare, continuez tout droit, et tournez à gauche au carrefour.

To go to the train station, keep going straight ahead, and turn left at the crossroads.

Suivez le panneau 'toutes directions', et allez jusqu'aux feux, mais ne traversez pas le pont.

Follow the sign for 'all directions', and go up to the lights, but don't cross the bridge.

La banque est située en face de l'épicerie, juste à côté de la mosquée.

The bank is opposite the grocer's, right next to the mosque.

to the bank — à la banque
to the theatre — au théâtre
to the café — au café

the toll — le péage
the hospital — l'hôpital (m)
the town hall — l'hôtel (m) de ville

on the other side of — de l'autre côté de

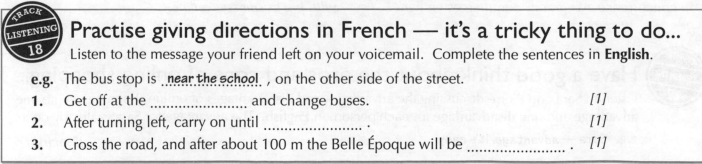

Practise giving directions in French — it's a tricky thing to do...

TRACK LISTENING 18

Listen to the message your friend left on your voicemail. Complete the sentences in **English**.

e.g. The bus stop is <u>near the school</u> , on the other side of the street.

1. Get off at the .... and change buses.   *[1]*
2. After turning left, carry on until ....   *[1]*
3. Cross the road, and after about 100 m the Belle Époque will be .... *[1]*

Weather

British people are famous for moaning about the weather. Now you get to do it in a different language...

Le temps — The weather

'Pleuvoir' and 'neiger' are impersonal verbs that can only be used with 'il' — see p.149.

le climat	*climate*	Il fait...	*It is...*	pleuvoir	*to rain*
Il y a...	*It is...*	beau	*fine*	neiger	*to snow*
du vent	*windy*	mauvais	*bad*	ensoleillé(e)	*sunny*
du soleil	*sunny*	chaud	*hot*	nuageux / nuageuse	*cloudy*
du brouillard	*foggy*	froid	*cold*	sec / sèche	*dry*

Il pleut.   *It's raining.* ← *It's snowing.* — Il neige.

Le climat là est doux.   *The climate there is mild.*

C'est nuageux et il pleut beaucoup.   *It's cloudy and it's raining a lot.* ← *stormy* — orageux   *overcast* — couvert

Grammar — il y a

'Il y a' *(there is)* is often used to discuss the weather. '<u>Il y aura</u>' is the future form and '<u>il y avait</u>' is the imperfect — both are useful for talking about <u>weather</u>.

La météo — The weather forecast

Question	**Simple Answer**	**Extended Answer**
Quel temps fera-t-il demain?	Il va faire beau et chaud, mais il va pleuvoir le soir.	Il fera beau le matin, mais au cours de la journée le temps deviendra plus nuageux et orageux. Il pleuvra en fin d'après-midi. Cela restera couvert le soir.
What will the weather be like tomorrow?	*It will be fine and hot, but it will rain in the evening.*	*It will be fine in the morning, but during the day the weather will become more cloudy and stormy. It will rain late in the afternoon. It will remain overcast in the evening.*

Demain, ça va devenir plus ensoleillé.   *Tomorrow, it's going to become sunnier.*

Le week-end, il y aura des éclaircies.   *At the weekend, there will be bright spells.*

Ce sera orageux et il va neiger.   *It will be stormy and it will snow.*

Il fera mauvais et froid.   *The weather will be bad and cold.*
Il y aura des orages.   *There will be storms.*

lightning — des éclairs (m)
thunder — du tonnerre
freeze — geler
showers — des averses (f)

To describe the weather, use 'il fait' or 'il y a' to say 'it is'...

Read the weather forecast and decide whether each sentence is true or false.

- Ce matin, le temps **reste agité**[1] dans le sud-est, et il y aura des nuages orageux. Pourtant, cet après-midi, il fera plus beau et sec.
- Un peu de neige est attendu sur les Pyrénées au-dessus de 2000 m. Des averses orageuses et des coups de tonnerres se produiront dans le sud-ouest.
- En revanche, pour les régions au nord de Bordeaux, il y aura du brouillard le matin, et **un ciel**[2] ensoleillé l'après-midi.

[1]remains turbulent   [2]a sky

e.g. In the south-east, it will be cloudy and stormy all day.   **false**

1. It will snow in the Pyrenees above 2000 m.   [1]

2. There will be showers and thunder in the south-west.   [1]

3. It will be foggy all day in the regions north of Bordeaux.   [1]

Listening Questions

Time to navigate your way through some exam practice. Remember that doing practice questions is a great way to revise — you're less likely to get caught out if you keep going over everything.

1 Listen to these people talking about what they do to help at home. Complete the table to show what they like and dislike doing.

TRACK LISTENING 19

	Likes...	Dislikes...
Example: Fatima	walking the dog	gardening

		Likes...	Dislikes...
1 a	Ousmane		
1 b	Mai		

[2 marks]

[2 marks]

2 Some shoppers were interviewed as part of a competition in a shopping centre. Answer the questions in **English**.

TRACK LISTENING 20

2 a Which **two** extra items did Frédéric buy?

1. ....

2. .... *[2 marks]*

2 b Why didn't Manon buy anything?

.... *[1 mark]*

2 c What does Abdoul say he prefers to do?

.... *[1 mark]*

Speaking Question

Candidate's Material

- Spend a couple of minutes looking at the photo and the questions below it.

- You can make notes on a separate piece of paper.

© iStock.com/johnnorth

You will be asked the following **three** questions, and **two** questions you haven't prepared:

- Qu'est-ce qu'il y a sur la photo ?

- Quel temps a-t-il fait hier ?

- Préfères-tu le temps froid ou chaud ? Pourquoi ?

Teacher's Material

- Allow the student to develop his / her answers as much as possible.

- You need to ask the student the following questions **in order**:

  - Qu'est-ce qu'il y a sur la photo ?

  - Quel temps a-t-il fait hier ?

  - Préfères-tu le temps froid ou chaud ? Pourquoi ?

  - Est-ce que tu regardes la météo ? Pourquoi / pourquoi pas ?

  - Que feras-tu s'il fait beau ce week-end ?

Reading Questions

1 Read Mattéo's post on a website and Chantelle's reply. Answer the questions in **English**.

Mattéo	Je viens de visiter Paris, et vraiment je ne voudrais jamais revenir dans cette ville affreuse. La circulation était vraiment effrayante, je n'avais jamais vu autant de voitures au centre d'une ville. Il y avait un embouteillage dans chaque rue et par conséquent, la pollution de l'air et le bruit étaient insupportables.
Chantelle	Comment peux-tu écrire une telle chose, Mattéo ? Paris est la ville la plus belle du monde ! Oui, c'est vrai qu'il y a beaucoup de circulation mais on ne peut pas trouver une autre ville avec autant d'histoire et de culture. Viens voir la ville avec une parisienne et je te montrerai les merveilles de Paris ! Il te reste beaucoup à découvrir.

1 a Why doesn't Mattéo like Paris? Give **one** detail.

.... *[1 mark]*

1 b How does Chantelle describe Paris?

.... *[1 mark]*

1 c What does Chantelle offer to do?

.... *[1 mark]*

2 Translate the following passage into **English**.

> J'habite avec mes parents, mon frère et ma sœur. Quand j'étais plus jeune, nous habitions dans un appartement au centre-ville. Maintenant, nous habitons dans une grande maison qui se trouve près du parc. J'aime ma maison parce qu'il y a beaucoup d'espace pour toute la famille. Pourtant, la maison est très vieille.

....

....

....

....

....

....

[9 marks]

Writing Questions

1   Vous décrivez les tâches ménagères que vous faites pour votre blog.

Décrivez:

- les tâches que vous avez faites récemment

- pourquoi vous aidez à la maison

- les tâches que font vos parents

- les tâches ménagères que vous donneriez à vos enfants.

Écrivez environ **90** mots en **français**. Répondez à chaque aspect de la question.

[16 marks]

2   Translate the following passage into **French**.

> It is my girlfriend's birthday this week, so I must buy a present. Yesterday I went to the department store. I found a pretty dress but the shop did not have her size. I also saw a hat, but it was too expensive. I will buy flowers for my girlfriend, but I think that is boring.

....

....

....

....

....

....

....

[12 marks]

Revision Summary for Section Six

Another section, another revision summary. There was a lot packed into this section, so don't worry if some of it passed you by — once you've finished, just revisit anything you struggled with.

Talking About Where You Live (p.56) ☑

1) You've arrived in Boulogne and are writing to your penfriend Matthieu about the town. Tell him: 'In the town centre, there's a post office, a newsagent's, a library, a bakery and a bus station.' ☑

2) A friendly policeman warns you about "un embouteillage". What is he warning you about? ☑

The Home (p.57-58) ☑

3) Choose a room in your house and describe it in detail in French. ☑

4) Leyla says: 'J'habite dans une habitation à loyer modéré, et ma chambre est au premier étage. Je préférerais habiter dans une maison à la campagne, mais ce serait trop cher.' What's she saying? ☑

5) Est-ce que tu aimes habiter dans ta région? Pourquoi / Pourquoi pas? ☑

6) What's the French for...?
   a) to get up   b) to shower   c) to brush your teeth   d) to go to bed ☑

7) Qu'est-ce que tu fais pour aider tes parents à la maison? ☑

8) Nadim is putting up some shelves this weekend. Which of these phrases best describes his plans?
   a) Il va faire du bricolage.   b) Il va faire du jardinage.   c) Il va faire la lessive. ☑

Shopping (p.59-61) ☑

9) Renée wants to buy: some socks, some trousers, a jumper and a dress. Translate her shopping list into French. ☑

10) You're talking to an assistant in a clothes shop. In French, tell them: 'I would like to know if these shoes are in the sale. Can I try them on?' ☑

11) Your friend is telling you about his weekend. He says: 'Samedi, j'ai acheté un jean mais le vendeur ne m'a pas donné la bonne taille. J'ai perdu le ticket de caisse donc c'est impossible de me faire rembourser. Quel désastre!' What happened? Answer in English. ☑

12) You're in a French food shop. In French, tell the assistant that you want a slice of ham and a kilogram of sausage. ☑

13) Est-ce que tu fais des courses en ligne? Pourquoi / Pourquoi pas? ☑

Giving and Asking for Directions (p.62) ☑

14) In French, how would you say...?
    a) on the left   b) on the right   c) opposite   d) over there   e) until ☑

15) A tourist comes up to you and asks: 'Excusez-moi, où est l'église?' What does she want to know? ☑

16) In French, tell the tourist: 'It's right next to the swimming pool. Go straight ahead for about 5 minutes, then turn left.' ☑

17) 'La banque se trouve près du rond-point, en face de la mairie. Pour y aller, suivez le panneau indiquant l'autoroute.' Translate this into English. ☑

Weather (p.63) ☑

18) What is 'la météo'? ☑

19) In French, say: 'It's rainy, but tomorrow it's going to be fine.' ☑

20) 'Demain, au cours de la journée, le temps deviendra orageux.' What's the best way to describe this weather?   a) cold   b) stormy   c) windy ☑

Healthy Living

A healthy lifestyle is something that many people aspire to — if only delicious pizza and great TV didn't get in the way. For this topic, try to think about the choices you make on a daily basis and why — deep stuff.

Vivre sainement — Living healthily

For more about sports and exercise, see p.32-33.

faire un régime	*to be on a diet*	faire de l'exercice	*to exercise*	sain(e)	*healthy*
garder la forme	*to stay in shape*	la nourriture bio	*organic food*	la forme	*fitness*
en bonne santé	*in good health*	se détendre	*to relax*	équilibré(e)	*balanced*

Question

Qu'est-ce que tu fais pour te détendre?
What do you do to relax?

Simple Answer

Je regarde la télé et je me couche tôt.
I watch TV and go to bed early.

Extended Answer

Normalement, je me détends en sortant avec mes amis le soir. Mais parfois, je reste chez moi en pyjama.
Normally, I relax by going out with my friends in the evenings. But sometimes, I stay at home in my pyjamas.

Grammar — en + present participle

You can use 'en' plus a present participle (see p.147) to say 'by / while doing something'.

Je garde la forme en mangeant des repas équilibrés.
I stay in shape by eating balanced meals.

Je fais du yoga en regardant la télé.
I do yoga while watching the television.

Pour rester en bonne santé — To stay healthy

For more about food, see p.30.

The type of diet you have and the amount of exercise you do can both affect your health.

Je mange au moins cinq fruits et légumes par jour pour rester en bonne santé.
I eat at least five fruits and vegetables a day to stay healthy.

little fat — peu de gras
little sugar — peu de sucre

J'ai décidé de prendre les escaliers au lieu de l'ascenseur pour faire plus d'exercice.
I've decided to take the stairs instead of the lift to do more exercise.

to walk there — d'y aller à pied
to go there by bike — d'y aller en vélo

Ce mois-ci, j'ai réussi à manger de la nourriture bio tous les jours.
This month, I've succeeded in eating organic food every day.

WRITING — The vocab for this topic is quite complex, so learn it carefully...

Adèle wrote a post on her blog about her healthy lifestyle.

Pour rester en forme, je prends un bon petit-déjeuner. Je bois un jus de fruit et je mange un yaourt et du pain avec du beurre et de la confiture. Je déjeune au lycée. C'est très équilibré. Quand j'étais plus jeune, je mangeais **plein de**[1] bonbons. Maintenant, comme je veux garder la forme, je fais attention. Je joue au badminton et au rugby après les cours. J'espère que je garderai mes **bonnes habitudes**[2] toute ma vie.

Grade 6-7

Tick list:
- ✓ tenses: present, imperfect, future
- ✓ quantifiers ('très', 'plein de')
- ✓ complex structures, e.g. 'pour' + infinitive

Vous écrivez un article sur la vie saine pour le bulletin d'information scolaire. Décrivez:

[1]lots of   [2]good habits

- *comment vous restez en bonne santé*
- *votre avis sur le fast-food*
- *comment vous êtes resté(e) en bonne santé quand vous étiez plus jeune*
- *vos idées pour rester en bonne santé dans l'avenir*

*Écrivez environ **90** mots en **français**. Répondez à chaque aspect de la question.* [16 marks]

To improve:
- + use conjunctions, e.g. 'ainsi que', 'de plus' or 'car'
- + use reflexive verbs

Unhealthy Living

Now onto the topic of drugs, smoking and alcohol. Remember, try to consider different points of view.

La dépendance — Addiction

fumer	to smoke	arrêter	to stop	la cigarette	
s'enivrer	to get drunk	la drogue	drug	électronique	e-cigarette
se droguer	to take drugs	l'alcool (m)	alcohol	le tabagisme	addiction to smoking
être accro (à)	to be addicted (to)	ivre	drunk	nocif / nocive	harmful (for your health)

Les gens boivent pour s'amuser. — *People drink to have fun.*

Le tabagisme cause des maladies graves. — *Smoking addiction causes serious illnesses.*

Il faut sensibiliser le public aux dangers des substances qui créent une dépendance. — *We must increase awareness amongst the public of the dangers of addictive substances.*

Beaucoup de gens veulent arrêter de fumer car c'est mauvais pour la santé. — *Lots of people want to stop smoking because it's bad for your health.*

take drugs — se droguent
lung cancer — le cancer du poumon
heart attacks — les crises (f) cardiaques
warn — avertir
it's expensive — c'est cher
they have difficulty breathing — ils ont du mal à respirer

Ils ne boivent que le weekend — They only drink at the weekend

Question
Est-ce que tu penses que les jeunes boivent trop?
Do you think that young people drink too much?

Simple Answer
Oui, parce qu'ils boivent chaque weekend quand ils sortent en boîte.
Yes, because they drink every weekend when they go clubbing.

Extended Answer
Oui, plein de jeunes ont besoin d'une boisson alcoolisée pour s'amuser, donc ils boivent beaucoup quand ils sortent en boîte. Moi, je trouve ça effrayant car l'alcool a des effets nocifs.
Yes, many young people need an alcoholic drink to have fun, so they drink a lot when they go clubbing. I think it's frightening because alcohol has harmful effects on your health.

SPEAKING Use 'il faut' to say what should be done to solve a problem...

Take a look at this sample answer to get an idea of what you could say in the speaking exam.

Qu'est-ce que tu penses de l'alcool ?

Moi, je n'aime pas du tout l'alcool. Ce n'est pas le **goût**[1] qui me dégoûte, ce sont plutôt les conséquences nocives. Ceux qui boivent beaucoup ne pensent pas à leur santé. De plus, l'alcoolisme me fait peur — j'ai plein d'amis qui ont besoin d'une boisson alcoolisée **afin de**[2] se détendre et s'amuser. Quand j'aurai des enfants, je les avertirai des effets nocifs de la consommation excessive de l'alcool. Je crois qu'il faut faire plus pour **lutter contre**[3] ce problème.

Grade 6-7

Tick list:
✓ tenses: present, future
✓ complex structures ('pour' + inf.)
✓ connectives: 'de plus', 'quand'

To improve:
+ tenses: perfect, imperfect
+ include intensifiers ('très', 'vraiment')

Now try answering these questions out loud. Aim to talk for two minutes.
- *Qu'est-ce que tu penses de l'alcool ?*
- *Pourquoi les jeunes boivent-ils ?*
- *Selon toi, quels sont les dangers de l'alcool et du tabagisme ? [10 marks]*

[1]taste
[2]in order to
[3]to fight against

Remember, in the general conversation part of the exam, you'll need to ask the examiner at least one question too.

Illnesses

The topic of illnesses crops up in French exams time and time again, so you can be sure it's worth learning. You need to know specific vocab for various illnesses, as well as how to talk about wider health issues.

La maladie — Illness

tomber malade	to fall ill
se sentir mal	to feel unwell
vomir	to vomit
tousser	to cough
un rhume	a cold
la grippe	flu
l'obésité (f)	obesity
le médicament	medicine
la crise cardiaque	heart attack
le sida	AIDS
le médecin / le docteur	doctor
l'ordonnance (f)	prescription
guérir	to cure / treat

Remember, 'avoir' (to have) is an irregular verb. Have a look at p.132 to find out more.

Grammar — avoir mal + au / à l' / à la / aux

The preposition '**à**' combines with definite articles (see p.109):

J'ai mal (**à + le**) **au** ventre (m) / **au** dos (m).
I have tummy / back pain.

J'ai mal (**à + l'**) **à l'**estomac (m, starts with vowel).
I've got a stomach ache.

J'ai mal (**à + la**) **à la** tête (f) / **à la** main (f).
I've got a headache. / My hand hurts.

J'ai mal (**à + les**) **aux** oreilles (f) / **aux** pieds (m).
I've got earache. / My feet hurt.

Des problèmes de santé — Health problems

Health isn't just about going to the doctor's — you need to be prepared to discuss wider issues, too.

J'attrape souvent des rhumes. Je tousse, et j'ai mal à la gorge. J'ai aussi le nez qui coule.
I often catch colds. I cough, and I get a sore throat. I also get a runny nose.

Quand je me sentais mal et j'avais envie de vomir, le médecin m'a donné(e) une ordonnance.
When I felt ill and I wanted to vomit, the doctor gave me a prescription.

De temps en temps, je me sens déprimé(e).
From time to time, I feel depressed.

Le sida reste un grand problème dans les pays en développement.
AIDS remains a big problem in developing countries.
→ *in underdeveloped countries — dans les pays en voie de développement*

À cause des médias, les jeunes s'inquiètent souvent de leur poids et de leur apparence.
Because of the media, young people often worry about their weight and their appearance.

Il y a toujours de la pression pour être très mince et se conformer aux stéréotypes.
There's always pressure to be very thin and to conform to stereotypes.
→ *handsome / beautiful — beau / belle*

 We're all allergic to exams — but you still need to revise...

You see this article in a French magazine. Translate it into **English**. [9 marks]

Je vais souvent à l'hôpital pour rendre visite à ma grand-mère, qui est malade depuis l'année dernière. Au début, j'étais triste, mais elle commence à aller mieux. À l'avenir, je voudrais être médecin pour aider les personnes qui souffrent. J'aimerais trouver de nouveaux médicaments pour les guérir et faire des recherches sur des maladies graves.

Listening Questions

Ignoring the next four pages would be an unhealthy revision choice — pick that pen up again.
The best way to see what you've learnt is to test yourself with some realistic exam practice.

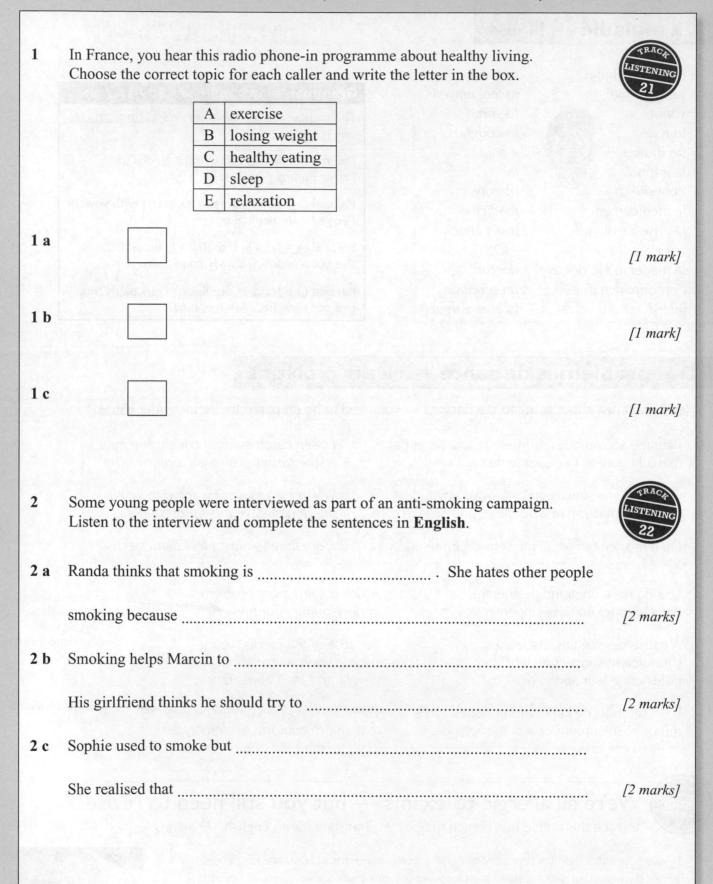

1   In France, you hear this radio phone-in programme about healthy living.
     Choose the correct topic for each caller and write the letter in the box.

A	exercise
B	losing weight
C	healthy eating
D	sleep
E	relaxation

1 a   ☐

[1 mark]

1 b   ☐

[1 mark]

1 c   ☐

[1 mark]

2   Some young people were interviewed as part of an anti-smoking campaign.
     Listen to the interview and complete the sentences in **English**.

2 a   Randa thinks that smoking is .... She hates other people

     smoking because ....   *[2 marks]*

2 b   Smoking helps Marcin to ....

     His girlfriend thinks he should try to ....   *[2 marks]*

2 c   Sophie used to smoke but ....

     She realised that ....   *[2 marks]*

Speaking Question

Candidate's Role

- Your teacher will play the role of the doctor. They will speak first.

- You should use *vous* to address the doctor.

- – ! – means you will have to respond to something you have not prepared.

- – ? – means you will have to ask the doctor a question.

> Vous allez chez le médecin parce que vous vous sentez mal.
>
> - Symptômes (**deux** détails).
>
> - !
>
> - Dernier repas (**deux** détails).
>
> - ? Conseils.
>
> - Autres problèmes de santé.

Teacher's Role

- You begin the role-play using the introductory text below.

- You should address the candidate as *vous*.

- You may alter the wording of the questions in response to the candidate's previous answers.

- Do not supply the candidate with key vocabulary.

> Introductory text: *Vous allez chez le médecin parce que vous vous sentez mal. Moi, je suis le médecin.*
>
> - Quels sont vos symptômes ?
>
> - ! Depuis quand vous sentez-vous mal ?
>
> - Quelle était la dernière chose que vous avez mangée ?
>
> - ?
>
> - Avez-vous d'autres problèmes de santé ?

Reading Questions

1   Translate the following passage into **English**.

> Il y a beaucoup de gens qui voudraient être maigres comme les célébrités qu'on voit à la télévision. C'est souvent un problème parmi les jeunes. L'année dernière, ma meilleure amie voulait être plus mince et elle a fait un régime. Elle était fatiguée tout le temps. C'était vraiment triste.

....

....

....

....

....

....

[9 marks]

2   Translate the following passage into **English**.

> Demain il y aura un match important pour mon équipe de football. Pourtant, je m'inquiète parce que les joueurs ont eu beaucoup de problèmes de santé. Chloé s'est cassé le bras et ne pourra pas jouer demain. Michelle a mal à l'oreille et sa mère ne la laisse pas sortir de la maison. En plus, deux autres filles sont malades.

....

....

....

....

....

....

[9 marks]

Writing Questions

1 Vous écrivez une lettre à votre journal local sur les dangers du tabagisme.

Décrivez:

- les problèmes de santé associés au tabagisme

- les avantages potentiels si les gens arrêtaient de fumer.

Écrivez environ **150** mots en **français**. Répondez à chaque aspect de la question.

[32 marks]

2 Translate the following passage into **French**.

> I would like to be in good shape, so I try to eat well. I think that it is important to be healthy when you are young. I used to eat a lot of ice cream but now I prefer to eat balanced meals. Also, I exercise three times a week. I walk to school instead of taking the bus.

....

....

....

....

....

....

....

....

[12 marks]

Revision Summary for Section Seven

You guessed it — it's time to see how well those last few pages sunk in with a few more questions. Try to answer everything without looking at what you've just learnt. Find out which bits you've got sorted, and which bits need another look.

Healthy Living (p.69) ☑

1) What's the French for...?
   a) in good health   b) to stay in shape   c) healthy living   d) to relax ☑

2) Noémi says: 'C'est très important de se détendre. Je fais de l'exercice au moins deux fois par semaine, et je me détends le soir en lisant des magazines.' What is she saying? ☑

3) Qu'est-ce que tu fais pour rester en bonne forme? ☑

4) 'I used to take the bus to get to school, but now I walk there.' How would you say this in French? ☑

5) Damien wants to eat a more balanced diet. Which of the following options would help him to achieve this?
   a) ne manger que des légumes   c) manger beaucoup de matières grasses
   b) manger des repas équilibrés   d) manger plus de sucre ☑

Unhealthy Living (p.70) ☑

6) Translate these phrases into French.   a) to get drunk   b) to stop smoking   c) to take drugs ☑

7) 'La dépendance est un problème qui touche beaucoup de gens.'
   Translate this sentence into English. ☑

8) Your French penfriend tells you: 'Je déteste le tabagisme. Ce n'est pas cool, c'est dangereux. Le tabac cause des maladies graves comme le cancer du poumon.' How does she feel about smoking? Why? Answer in English. ☑

9) À ton avis, pourquoi les jeunes s'enivrent-ils? ☑

10) In French, write down three ways that smoking can be harmful for your health. ☑

Illnesses (p.71) ☑

11) Translate the French words below into English.
    a) l'ordonnance   b) le poids   c) la pression   d) le médecin   e) la grippe ☑

12) Jérôme says: 'Je suis malade. J'ai mal à la gorge.' What's he saying? ☑

13) You're at the doctor's. In French, say: 'I have a stomach ache and I feel unwell.' ☑

14) Translate this sentence into English. 'Ma sœur est tombée malade avant-hier, et elle a dû aller à l'hôpital.' ☑

15) What does 'être déprimé' mean?
    a) to be deprived   b) to be depressed   c) to be obese   d) to be unhealthy ☑

16) Marcel works for a world health charity. He says: 'Les pays en voie de développement ont besoin de plus de ressources pour lutter contre les maladies graves.' What does this mean in English? ☑

Environmental Problems

That's right — it's time to start thinking about all things green, natural and... polluted. Poor old Mother Nature.

L'environnement (m) — The environment

l'effet (m) de serre	*the greenhouse effect*	jeter	*to throw away*
le réchauffement de la Terre	*global warming*	gaspiller	*to waste*
la couche d'ozone	*ozone layer*	les déchets (m) / les ordures (f)	*rubbish*
augmenter	*to increase*	la pollution	*pollution*
mondial(e)	*worldwide*	pollué(e)	*polluted*
le charbon	*coal*	le déboisement	*deforestation*
le gaz carbonique	*carbon dioxide*	détruire	*to destroy*
le gaz d'échappement	*exhaust fumes*	protéger	*to protect*
le pétrole	*oil*	l'énergie (f) renouvelable	*renewable energy*

Ce n'est pas écologique — It's not environmentally friendly

Les gens jettent souvent des choses recyclables dans la poubelle.

People often throw recyclable things in the bin.

paper — du papier
glass — du verre

Un sac en plastique peut prendre des années à se décomposer.

A plastic bag may take years to decompose.

an aluminium can — une boîte en aluminium

L'emballage est un gaspillage des ressources naturelles de la Terre.

Packaging is a waste of the Earth's natural resources.

of raw materials — des matières (f) premières

La pollution est un risque sanitaire — Pollution is a health hazard

La pollution est causée par les activités humaines.

Pollution is caused by human activity.

Parfois, les usines polluent les lacs et les rivières avec des produits chimiques nocifs.

Sometimes, factories pollute lakes and rivers with harmful chemicals.

Dans les grandes villes, la pollution de l'air peut provoquer des problèmes de santé.

In cities, air pollution may cause health problems.

Le gaspillage de l'eau — Water wastage

Nous gaspillons de l'eau dans la vie quotidienne.

We waste water in everyday life.

Il faut prendre des mesures pour économiser l'eau, comme prendre une douche au lieu d'un bain.

We need to take action to save water, such as having a shower instead of a bath.

Il n'y a qu'un litre d'eau potable pour chaque cent litres d'eau sur la planète.

There is only one litre of drinkable water for every hundred litres of water on the planet.

Environmental Problems

You might prefer hiding away in a darkened room to roaming the hills and basking in the glories of nature, but you still need to have an opinion about environmental problems, so listen up...

La destruction des habitats — The destruction of habitats

Le déboisement contribue à l'effet de serre et mène à la perte des écosystèmes.

Deforestation contributes to the greenhouse effect and leads to the loss of ecosystems.

Certaines espèces sont menacées d'extinction.

Certain species are threatened by extinction.

Il y a des problèmes graves — There are some serious problems

Question

Est-ce que l'environnement est important pour toi?
Is the environment important to you?

À ton avis, quelles sont les plus grandes menaces pour l'environnement?
In your opinion, what are the biggest threats to the environment?

Simple Answer

Oui, je m'intéresse beaucoup à l'environnement.
Yes, I'm very interested in the environment.

Je crois que les plus grandes menaces sont le déboisement, le réchauffement de la Terre et la pollution de l'air.
I believe that the biggest threats are deforestation, global warming and air pollution.

Extended Answer

Oui, pour moi il y a de grands problèmes pour la Terre, et je pense que c'est à nous de la protéger.
Yes, for me there are big problems for the Earth, and I think that it's up to us to protect it.

D'abord, il y a l'utilisation mondiale des énergies fossiles, comme le charbon, qui mène à une augmentation du gaz carbonique. Le déboisement et les gaz d'échappement produisent aussi le gaz carbonique qui est responsable du réchauffement de la Terre.

En plus, je trouve qu'on a trop de déchets — une famille moyenne jette plus d'une tonne de déchets chaque année!

Enfin, il y a le gaspillage de l'eau. Malgré les 780 millions personnes dans le monde qui n'ont pas d'eau potable, ici on gaspille de l'eau chaque jour.

Firstly, there is the global use of fossil fuels, like coal, which leads to an increase in carbon dioxide. Deforestation and exhaust fumes also produce carbon dioxide which is responsible for global warming.

Furthermore, I find that we have too much rubbish — an average family throws away more than a tonne of rubbish each year!

Lastly, there's water wastage. Despite the 780 million people in the world who don't have drinking water, we waste water each day here.

Grammar — adjective position

In French, adjectives usually come after the noun. However, this isn't always the case, e.g.

Il y a un <u>grand problème</u>.   ***There is a <u>big problem</u>.***

Adjectives such as <u>beau</u> — *beautiful*, <u>joli</u> — *pretty*, <u>jeune</u> — *young*, <u>gentil</u> — *kind*, <u>grand</u> — *big*, <u>petit</u> — *small* usually come before the noun. See p.111 for more.

Le déboisement abîme le <u>beau paysage</u>.
Deforestation ruins the <u>beautiful landscape</u>.

Les <u>petites actions</u> peuvent avoir un <u>grand effet</u>.
<u>Small actions</u> can have a <u>big impact</u>.

Learning these pages will help you avoid problems in the exam...

Here's a lovely writing question for you — translate the following passage into **French**. *[12 marks]*

Pollution has caused some serious problems for the environment. It has destroyed many habitats. I think that people do not do enough to protect the planet. Every day, we throw away recyclable materials and waste natural resources. In the future, we will have to use renewable energy instead of coal and oil.

Problems in Society

Social problems, natural disasters, war... this section just keeps getting better and better. It's enough to make you want to pull the duvet over your head and stay there. Here's something to pass the time...

Les problèmes sociaux — Social problems

'SDF' stands for 'sans domicile fixe' (without a permanent home).

le voyou	*yob / hooligan*	les SDF, les sans-abri (m / f)	*homeless people*
la bande	*gang*	le chômage	*unemployment*
l'attaque (f)	*attack*	la pauvreté	*poverty*
agresser	*to attack*	l'immigration (f)	*immigration*
le harcèlement	*harassment*	le tremblement de terre	*earthquake*
harceler	*harass*	l'incendie (m)	*fire*
effrayant(e)	*frightening*	l'inondation (f)	*flood*
voler	*to steal*	la guerre	*war*
l'émeute (f)	*riot*	l'égalité (f)	*equality*

La violence chez les jeunes — Youth violence

En rentrant à la maison, j'ai été agressé(e).   *On the way home, I was attacked.*

threatened — menacé(e)
hit — battu(e)

J'ai peur des bandes dans mon quartier.   *I'm scared of the gangs in my neighbourhood.*

of the hooligans — des voyous (m)

On me harcèle au collège.   *People harass me at school.*

make fun of me — se moque de moi

L'inégalité sociale — Social inequality

Le chômage est un problème grave dans les pays européens.   *Unemployment is a serious problem in European countries.*

L'inégalité sociale entre les riches et les pauvres peut provoquer des émeutes violentes.   *Social inequality between the rich and the poor can provoke violent riots.*

Grammar — 'avoir besoin de...'

'Avoir besoin de' means to <u>need</u> something.

Nous <u>avons besoin d'</u>emplois.   *We <u>need</u> jobs.*

You can also use 'avoir besoin de' with a verb, to say you need to <u>do</u> something.

Le gouvernement <u>a besoin de</u> prendre des mesures pour aider les chômeurs.
The government <u>needs to</u> take action to help the unemployed.

Les effets de la guerre — The effects of war

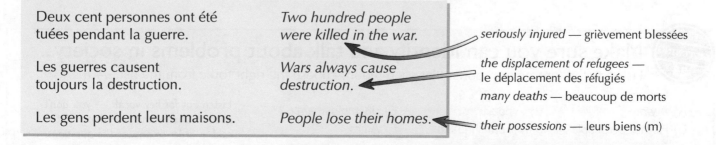

Deux cent personnes ont été tuées pendant la guerre.   *Two hundred people were killed in the war.*

seriously injured — grièvement blessées

Les guerres causent toujours la destruction.   *Wars always cause destruction.*

the displacement of refugees — le déplacement des réfugiés
many deaths — beaucoup de morts

Les gens perdent leurs maisons.   *People lose their homes.*

their possessions — leurs biens (m)

Section Eight — Social and Global Issues

Problems in Society

Yep, another page on big global issues. It's all pretty bleak, this stuff, but it is important, so learn it well.

Les catastrophes naturelles — Natural disasters

Des milliers de personnes ont dû quitter leurs maisons après les inondations l'année dernière.

Thousands of people had to leave their homes after the floods last year.

Un incendie a ravagé le village.

A fire devastated the village.

Le gouvernement prend des mesures pour aider les victimes du tremblement de terre.

The government is taking measures to help the victims of the earthquake.

Le problème principal est... — The main problem is...

You need to prepare this topic <u>thoroughly</u> — it's tricky. Have a think about how to answer this question.

Question

À ton avis, quels sont les problèmes principaux pour les SDF?

In your opinion, what are the main problems facing homeless people?

Simple Answer

Je crois que le plus grand problème est qu'ils ne peuvent pas trouver un emploi pour pouvoir payer un logement.

I think the biggest problem is that they cannot find a job to be able to afford accommodation.

Extended Answer

Je pense que les problèmes des SDF sont complexes. Si on est au chômage, on n'a pas les moyens de payer un logement. Cependant, il n'est pas possible de trouver un emploi sans domicile fixe. Il s'agit d'un cercle vicieux.

En outre, les sans-abris ont parfois des dettes, ce qui rend leur situation encore plus difficile.

En dernier lieu, ils sont vulnérables aux attaques violentes parce qu'ils vivent dans la rue.

I think homeless people's problems are complicated. If people are unemployed, they can't afford to pay for accommodation. However, it is not possible to find a job without a permanent address. It's a vicious circle.

Besides, homeless people sometimes have debts, which makes their situation even more difficult.

Finally, they are vulnerable to violent attacks because they live on the streets.

socialement exclu(e)	*socially excluded*
déprimé(e)	*depressed*
vulnérable	*vulnerable*
supporter	*to tolerate / to put up with*
l'ennui (m)	*problem*
le souci	*worry / concern*

Grammar — On doit... / Il faut...

Use '<u>on doit...</u>' (from 'devoir') or '<u>il faut...</u>' (from 'falloir') to say '<u>we must</u>'. The verb which follows is in the <u>infinitive</u>.

<u>On doit</u> aider les pauvres.
<u>We must</u> help the poor.

<u>Il faut</u> empêcher les guerres.
<u>We must</u> prevent wars.

'Il faut' is an impersonal verb — see p.149.

You can also use the verb 'devoir' to say that <u>someone</u> needs to do something.

Les politiciens <u>doivent</u> donner la priorité à la question de l'inégalité sociale.
Politicians <u>must</u> prioritise the issue of social inequality.

TRACK LISTENING 23

Make sure you can identify and talk about problems in society...

Listen to the four news reports. For each report, choose the right topic from the list. *[4 marks]*

A) A war
B) Homeless people
C) A flood
D) An earthquake
E) Unemployment
F) A fire

Listen out for key vocab — you don't need to understand everything that's said in order to answer the questions.

Contributing to Society

You might be feeling a bit down about the state of the world, but fear not — there's plenty you can do to make things better. Just don't go recycling this book before you've learnt it all...

Comment pouvons-nous aider? — How can we help?

le travail bénévole	voluntary work	éteindre	to switch off
l'association (f) caritative	charity	faire du recyclage / recycler	to recycle
mener une campagne	to lead a campaign	le centre de recyclage	recycling centre
améliorer	to improve	les produits (m) bio	green products
défavorisé(e)	disadvantaged	être vert(e)	to be green
combattre	to combat	sauver	to save

Qu'est-ce que tu peux faire? — What can you do?

Je vais mener une campagne pour aider les réfugiés.

I am going to lead a campaign to help refugees.

Pour conserver l'énergie, il faut se souvenir d'éteindre les lumières quand on quitte la maison.

To save energy, you must remember to switch off the lights when you leave the house.

Grammar — se souvenir de

'Se souvenir de' means 'to remember'. It's a reflexive verb so it needs a reflexive pronoun (p.142 has more about this).

Je me souviens toujours de trier mes déchets quand je fais du recyclage.
I always remember to sort my rubbish when I recycle.

Question	Simple Answer	Extended Answer
Tu aimes aider les autres? Pourquoi / pourquoi pas?	Oui, c'est gratifiant d'aider les autres.	Oui, dans mon temps libre, je fais du travail bénévole pour une association caritative qui aide les chômeurs à se préparer aux entretiens d'embauche. En travaillant ensemble, nous pouvons améliorer la vie des gens défavorisés.
Do you like helping others? Why / why not?	*Yes, it is rewarding to help others.*	*Yes, in my free time I do voluntary work for a charity which helps the unemployed to prepare for job interviews. By working together, we can improve the lives of disadvantaged people.*

un défi intéressant	an interesting challenge
ça vaut la peine	it's worthwhile

This is a great topic for using the conditional and future tenses...

Look at the example below for some suggestions about how to tackle a photo card question.

Est-ce que tu fais du recyclage ?
Pourquoi / pourquoi pas ?

À mon avis, protéger l'environnement c'est très important. Je recycle autant que possible — le verre, le plastique et même mes vieux vêtements. En plus, j'ai mené une campagne à l'école pour encourager les élèves à faire du recyclage. Je pense que si chaque personne prenait une ou deux mesures pour combattre le gaspillage des ressources, nous pourrions sauver la planète.

Grade 6-7

Tick list:
✓ detailed answer
✓ tenses: perfect, imperfect, present, conditional

To improve:
+ more adjectives and adverbs
+ use 'il faut...' or 'on doit...'

Now try answering these questions yourself. [10 marks]

- *Qu'est-ce qu'il y a sur la photo ?*
- *Qu'est-ce que tu as déjà fait pour protéger l'environnement ?*
- *La société fait assez pour la Terre ? Pourquoi / pourquoi pas ?*

© iStock.com/Jani Bryson

Listening Questions

Nearly there... just four pages of exam practice, then this section is almost done and dusted.
Don't forget to keep coming back to any questions you're unsure about — practice makes perfect.

1   Listen to this podcast on recycling. Answer the questions in **English**.

TRACK LISTENING 24

1 a   Why is recycling important?

....
[1 mark]

1 b   What should people do to help? Give **two** details.

    1. ....

    2. ....
[2 marks]

1 c   Name **two** things that can be recycled.

....
[2 marks]

2   Listen to this local radio report about a charity fundraising event.
       Choose the correct answer for each question and write the letter in the box.

TRACK LISTENING 25

2 a   People living in the town have just put on...

A	a week of sporting competitions.
B	a charity sports day.
C	an inter-school rugby tournament.

[1 mark]

2 b   The mayor came up with the idea because...

A	her mother died from cancer.
B	there is a cancer hospital in town.
C	she is interested in medical research.

[1 mark]

2 c   The events included...

A	a race around the town.
B	a boxing tournament.
C	a dressing up competition.

[1 mark]

Speaking Question

- Spend a couple of minutes looking at the photo and the questions below it.

- You can make notes on a separate piece of paper.

© iStock.com/sirichai_raksue

You will be asked the following **three** questions, and **two** questions you haven't prepared:

- Qu'est-ce qu'il y a sur la photo ?

- À ton avis, quelles activités humaines contribuent à la pollution ?

- Quelles sont les solutions aux problèmes de pollution ?

Teacher's Material

- Allow the student to develop his / her answers as much as possible.

- You need to ask the student the following questions **in order**:

  - Qu'est-ce qu'il y a sur la photo ?

  - À ton avis, quelles activités humaines contribuent à la pollution ?

  - Quelles sont les solutions aux problèmes de pollution ?

  - Qu'est-ce que tu penses du déboisement ?

  - Qu'est-ce que tu suggérerais pour protéger les espèces menacées d'extinction ?

Reading Questions

1 Read this website post that Karim wrote about traffic in Nice.

> Je vis au centre de Nice. J'adore la ville, mais ce qui m'énerve c'est qu'il y a beaucoup de pollution à cause de la circulation intense. Il y a toujours des embouteillages, et le gaz d'échappement cause la pollution atmosphérique. Selon moi, le gouvernement a une responsabilité à assumer — il faut créer plus de zones piétonnes et d'espaces verts au centre de la ville, et construire plus de pistes cyclables. On devrait encourager les gens à marcher ou à utiliser les transports en commun, comme le train ou l'autobus, au lieu de conduire. Si vraiment on doit aller au travail en voiture, on pourrait partager le voyage avec des collègues.

According to Karim, which **two** statements are **true**? Write the letters in the boxes.

A	Cars should be completely banned in the centre of Nice.
B	Increasing the number of cycle lanes would help reduce pollution.
C	There is not enough public transport.
D	People should car share instead of driving to work separately.

[2 marks]

2 Translate the following passage into **English**.

> J'habite dans une grande ville où il y a beaucoup de violence, et j'ai vraiment peur des bandes dans mon quartier. Le soir, il y a des endroits que j'évite, surtout parce qu'une fois j'ai été agressé en rentrant à la maison. C'était effrayant. Il faut faire quelque chose mais je ne sais pas quoi.

....

....

....

....

....

....

[9 marks]

Writing Questions

1 Vous écrivez une lettre au chef d'une association caritative française au sujet de votre candidature pour un travail bénévole.

Décrivez:

- votre motivation pour aider les gens

- le travail bénévole que vous avez déjà fait

- les problèmes sociaux que vous avez remarqués dans la société

- comment vous aideriez l'association à faire son travail.

Écrivez environ **90** mots en **français**. Répondez à chaque aspect de la question.

[16 marks]

2 Translate the following passage into **French**.

> I think that it is very important to protect the environment. There is a lot that we could do at home. For example, in the winter I always switch off the central heating during the day. Yesterday, I took a shower instead of a bath because that uses less water.

....

....

....

....

....

....

....

....

[12 marks]

Revision Summary for Section Eight

Just before you tuck into the delights of Section Nine, here's a page of lovely revision questions for you to tackle. Try to answer all of the questions without cheating — make a note of any you find tricky and then go back through the section. Reward yourself with a big old tick when you can answer a question.

Environmental Problems (p.77-78) ☑

1) What do these words mean in English?
   a) le déboisement   b) l'effet de serre   c) le gaz carbonique   d) le gaz d'échappement ☑

2) 'Global warming is a worldwide problem.' Translate this sentence into French. ☑

3) Does caring for the environment matter to you? Answer in French, giving at least three reasons. ☑

4) An environmental leaflet warns: 'La pollution commence à abîmer notre planète. Nos lacs et nos rivières sont devenus pollués, ce qui menace les écosystèmes qui existent depuis des millions d'années.' What is it saying? ☑

5) Est-ce qu'il y a des problèmes d'environnement dans ta région? Répondez en français. Utilisez des phrases complètes. ☑

6) Danielle says: 'On gaspille des ressources tous les jours. On jette les déchets, sans faire du recyclage. Mais ce qui m'énerve le plus, c'est qu'on ne pense pas aux générations futures.' Does she think we do enough for the environment? Why / Why not? Answer in English. ☑

Problems in Society (p.79-80) ☑

7) What's the French for...?
   a) harassment   b) unemployment   c) poverty   d) inequality   e) homeless people ☑

8) 'Pour la plupart, les jeunes ne sont pas violents.' What does this sentence mean in English? ☑

9) Penses-tu que le chômage soit un grand problème? Répondez en français. Utilisez des phrases complètes. ☑

10) Saïd says: 'J'ai peur de ne pas trouver d'emploi.' What is Saïd afraid of? Answer in English. ☑

11) You're listening to the news. You hear that: 'There has been an earthquake and a flood in Japan.' How would you say this in French? ☑

Contributing to Society (p.81) ☑

12) In French, describe one example of what a charity might do to help people in war zones. ☑

13) Your friend wants to do something to help 'les sans-abris'. Who does he want to help? ☑

14) 'J'aimerais être vert, mais les produits bios sont trop chers.' Translate this sentence into English. ☑

15) In French, write down three things you could do to help the environment. ☑

16) Your penfriend has written to you about what she does to help others: 'Je fais du travail bénévole pour une association caritative qui aide les jeunes défavorisés. Parfois c'est dur, mais cela en vaut la peine.' What does this mean in English? ☑

17) How would you say 'I'm leading a campaign against bullying' in French? ☑

18) Que faut-il faire pour améliorer la vie des pauvres? ☑

Where to Go

We're all going on a summer holiday... This page is all about different countries and places you can go to.

Les pays (m) du monde — The countries of the world

l'Angleterre (f)	*England*	l'Inde (f)	*India*
la Grande-Bretagne	*Great Britain*	l'Amérique (f)	*America*
les États-Unis (m)	*United States*	l'Afrique (f)	*Africa*
l'Allemagne (f)	*Germany*	l'Asie (f)	*Asia*
le Brésil	*Brazil*	l'Europe (f)	*Europe*
la Chine	*China*	à l'étranger	*abroad*
l'Espagne (f)	*Spain*	la mer	*sea*
la Russie	*Russia*	la plage	*beach*
la Belgique	*Belgium*	la Méditerranée	
la Suisse	*Switzerland*		*the Mediterranean*

Grammar — to go to...

To say you're going to a <u>country</u>, you need the correct form of '<u>aller</u>' *(to go)* and the correct <u>preposition</u>. Use:

- <u>au</u> for masc. sing. countries starting with a consonant.
- <u>aux</u> for plural countries.
- <u>en</u> for masc. sing. countries starting with a vowel and all <u>fem. sing.</u> countries.

If you're going to a <u>town</u>, you just need '<u>à</u>'.

Les vacances (f) — Holidays

Je vais aller en France, et après ça, j'irai en Écosse pour trois jours.

I'm going to go to France, and after that, I will go to Scotland for three days.

> to Paris — à Paris
> to Wales — au pays de Galles

J'ai passé les vacances au bord de la mer.

I spent the holidays at the seaside.

> in the mountains — à la montagne

Je suis allé(e) en Asie — au Japon.

I went to Asia — to Japan.

Question	**Simple Answer**	**Extended Answer**
Quels sont vos projets pour les vacances?	Je vais passer deux semaines en Algérie.	À la fin d'août, j'irai dans le sud de l'Inde pour trois semaines avec deux amis. Nous visiterons des sites historiques.
What are your plans for the holidays?	*I'm going to spend two weeks in Algeria.*	*At the end of August, I will go to the south of India for three weeks with two friends. We'll visit historical sites.*

READING

Make sure you use the right version of 'au' or 'en' with places...

Lisez l'email de Françoise qui parle de ses vacances. Répondez aux questions en **français**.

Salut Marc,

Les grandes vacances sont arrivées enfin ! Mais je ne suis pas contente : ma famille n'a pas de projets pour les vacances. Nous ne pouvons pas arriver à une décision. Moi, je voudrais aller en Angleterre parce que j'ai envie de voir un match de football anglais. Ma sœur pense que nous devrions passer les vacances au bord de la mer. Elle veut aller chaque jour à la plage. Ma mère préférerait aller à Berlin car elle s'intéresse aux musées. Cependant, mon père dit que nous allons tous rester en France. Il croit que nous devrions faire du camping car il adore la vie en plein air. Et toi, où vas-tu passer les vacances ?

Amitiés,
Françoise

e.g. Françoise n'est pas contente. Pourquoi ?

La famille de Françoise n'a pas de projets pour les vacances.

1. Comment veut-elle passer les vacances ? Donnez **deux** détails. *[2]*

2. Qu'est-ce qu'elle dit au sujet de sa sœur ? Donnez **deux** détails. *[2]*

3. Que veut faire son père ? Donnez **deux** détails. *[2]*

Accommodation

I know it's hard thinking about holidays while you're revising, but here's some stuff on accommodation.

Le logement — Accommodation

loger	to stay	faire du camping	to go camping
l'hôtel (m)	hotel	l'auberge (f) de jeunesse	youth hostel
le camping	campsite	la chambre d'hôte	bed and breakfast
la tente	tent	la colonie de vacances	holiday camp

Je cherche un hôtel qui n'est pas cher.   *I'm looking for a hotel that isn't expensive.* ← *a luxury hotel — un hôtel de luxe*

Il cherche un hôtel au bord de la mer.   *He's looking for a hotel at the seaside.* ← *in Nice — à Nice*

in the town centre — au centre-ville

Est-ce qu'il y a une auberge de jeunesse ici?   *Is there a youth hostel here?*

Où aimez-vous loger? — Where do you like to stay?

Question

Quel est votre type de logement préféré?

What's your favourite type of accommodation?

Simple Answer

J'aime loger dans les hôtels car c'est plus pratique.

I like staying in hotels because it's more practical.

Extended Answer

Je préfère faire du camping parce qu'il y a beaucoup de choses qu'on peut faire à la campagne. En plus, je trouve qu'on peut voir plus de choses de l'endroit qu'on visite.

I prefer to go camping because there are many things you can do in the countryside. Also, I find that you can see more of the place you're visiting.

Je préfère loger dans une auberge de jeunesse parce que c'est moins cher qu'un hôtel.   *I prefer to stay in a youth hostel because it is less expensive than a hotel.* ← *I like getting to know other people — j'aime faire la connaissance de nouvelles personnes*

J'aime faire du camping parce que j'adore la vie en plein air.   *I like camping because I love life in the open air.* ← *nature — la nature*

to explore the countryside — explorer la campagne

Je n'aime pas les colonies de vacances. Je préférerais rester chez moi.   *I don't like holiday camps. I would prefer to stay at home.*

On peut se détendre plus si on loge dans un hôtel parce qu'on ne doit pas cuisiner.   *You can relax more if you stay in a hotel because you don't have to cook.* ← *because the rooms are already prepared — parce que les chambres sont déjà préparées*

TRACK LISTENING 26

Avoid always using 'j'aime' — add in 'je préfère' and 'je trouve'...

You are listening to an audio book of 'Le tour du monde en quatre-vingts jours' by Jules Verne. This extract features Phileas Fogg, Mrs Aouda and Passepartout. Read the sentences below, and decide which three of them are true. The first one has been done for you.

e.g. Passepartout felt as if he was in England.   **true**

A. The bar was on the first floor of the hotel.

B. Soup, biscuits and cheese were provided.

C. They had to pay for their meal.

D. Mrs Aouda thought it was very American.

E. They had plenty to eat.   *[2 marks]*

Getting Ready to Go

And the boring but necessary admin bit... This page is about booking your holiday and getting ready to go.

Les préparatifs (m) — Preparations

réserver	to book / to reserve
la valise	suitcase
les bagages (m)	luggage
la pièce d'identité	ID
le passeport	passport
l'agence (f) de voyages	travel agency
la climatisation	air conditioning
le sac de couchage	sleeping bag
l'emplacement (m)	pitch
la chambre	room
le lit à deux places	double bed
les lits (m) jumeaux	twin beds
donner sur	to overlook

Grammar — from...to...

To say 'from...to...' when booking something, use 'du...au...'.

Je voudrais réserver une chambre du 25 août au 27 août.
I'd like to reserve a room from the 25th August to the 27th August.

J'ai mis mon passeport et mes lunettes de soleil dans ma valise. | *I put my passport and my sunglasses in my suitcase.*

J'ai réservé une chambre du 5 mai au 12 mai. | *I booked a room from the 5th May to the 12th May.*

Faire une réservation — To make a reservation

Je voudrais réserver une chambre avec un lit à deux places. | *I would like to book a room with a double bed.*

Nous voudrions réserver un emplacement pour une tente du 13 juillet au 17 juillet. Nous sommes deux adultes et un enfant. | *We would like to reserve a pitch for one tent from the 13th July to the 17th July. We are two adults and one child.*

Je préfère avoir une chambre simple avec climatisation qui donne sur la mer. | *I prefer to have a single room with air conditioning which overlooks the sea.*

with twin beds — à lits jumeaux

with bunk beds — à lits superposés

a campervan — un camping-car

a caravan — une caravane

SPEAKING

Hope you've got all that vocab packed and ready for the exam...

Emma is having a conversation with a French travel agent about booking a hotel.

Vous parlez avec un agent de voyage (AV).

Grade 8-9

AV :	Bonjour. Je peux vous aider ?
Emma :	Bonjour ! Je voudrais réserver une chambre dans un hôtel à Nice, s'il vous plaît.
AV :	Oui, bien sûr. Pour combien de personnes et pour combien de nuits ?
Emma :	Pour deux adultes. Je voudrais une chambre avec lits jumeaux du 3 juin au 5 juin, s'il vous plaît.
AV :	D'accord. Vous avez des préférences particulières ?
Emma :	Je préférerais un hôtel au bord de la mer, avec une piscine et une chambre **climatisée**[1] parce qu'il fera chaud.
AV :	Ah oui. Vous avez choisi votre destination à cause du temps ?
Emma :	Oui, mais aussi parce que j'aime la culture dans le sud de la France. Je trouve que tout le monde est très **détendu**[2].

[1]air-conditioned
[2]relaxed

Tick list:
✓ tenses: present, perfect, future, conditional
✓ complex and relevant vocab

To improve:
+ more varied conjunctions

*Respond to the travel agent's questions yourself. You should aim to talk for around 2 minutes in **French**. Address the travel agent as 'vous'.*

[15 marks]

How to Get There

A vital thing about going on holiday is getting there. The transport vocab will be useful in other contexts too.

Comment y aller — How to get there

l'arrivée (f)	*arrival*	la voiture	*car*	conduire	*to drive*
le départ	*departure*	l'autobus (m)	*bus*	l'autoroute (f)	*motorway*
manquer	*to miss*	le train	*train*	la route	*way / road*
la carte	*map*	l'avion (m)	*plane*	le vol	*flight*
l'horaire (m)	*timetable*	le bateau	*boat*	louer	*to rent / to hire*

Voyager — To travel

Je suis allé(e) en train. *I went by train.*

Je préfère les voitures aux bus — les bus sont peu fiables. *I prefer cars to buses — buses are not very reliable.*

Nous avons manqué le bateau. *We missed the boat.*

Grammar — monter, descendre

Use 'monter <u>dans</u>' to say 'to get <u>on</u>'.
Je monte <u>dans</u> le train.   I get <u>on</u> the train.
Use 'descendre <u>de</u>' to say 'to get <u>off</u>'.
Il descend <u>du</u> bus.   He gets <u>off</u> the bus.

Nous allons louer une voiture. Puis, selon la carte, nous devons prendre l'autoroute. *We're going to hire a car. Then, according to the map, we need to take the motorway.*

J'ai regardé l'horaire — le TGV devrait arriver à six heures. Mais il est en retard. *I looked at the timetable — the TGV should arrive at six o'clock. But it's late.*

'TGV' stands for 'train à grande vitesse' (high-speed train). The French national rail company is called SNCF.

En avion — By plane

Il faut arriver à l'aéroport deux heures avant l'heure de départ. *You must arrive at the airport two hours before the departure time.*

check in — s'enregistrer

Le vol était retardé à cause d'un problème technique. *The flight was delayed due to a technical problem.*

to bad weather — du mauvais temps

Question	Simple Answer	Extended Answer
Est-ce que tu aimes voler?	Oui, les avions sont le moyen de transport le plus sûr.	J'ai peur de voler parce que mon imagination me fait toujours envisager le pire. Mais les avions sont si pratiques et rapides!
Do you like flying?	*Yes, aeroplanes are the safest mode of transport.*	*I'm scared of flying because I always imagine the worst. But planes are so convenient and fast!*

READING

Remember that 'aller' (to go) takes 'être' in the past tense...

Translate this social media post about holidays into **English**. *[9 marks]*

La semaine prochaine, je vais aller en vacances aux États-Unis. En particulier, je voudrais voir New York. J'y ai réservé un hôtel de luxe avec une grande piscine. Cependant, le voyage m'inquiète beaucoup. J'ai peur de voler, et je serai dans l'avion pendant sept heures.

What to Do

So you've chosen a destination, booked your accommodation and got there... now what do you do?

Le tourisme — Tourism

l'office (m) de tourisme	*tourist office*	la cathédrale	*cathedral*	le tour	*tour*
les renseignements (m)	*information*	le château	*castle*	le plan de ville	*town plan*
le site touristique	*tourist attraction*	le musée	*museum*	la carte postale	*postcard*
le parc d'attractions	*theme park*	la visite guidée	*guided tour*	se faire bronzer	*to sunbathe*

En vacances, j'ai visité... — On holiday, I visited...

Question

Qu'est-ce que tu as fait en vacances?

What did you do on holiday?

Simple Answer

J'ai visité une cathédrale et je suis allé(e) à la plage.

I visited a cathedral and I went to the beach.

Extended Answer

J'ai décidé d'aller au musée pour apprendre autant que possible sur la région. Ça m'intéressait beaucoup.

I decided to go to the museum to learn as much as possible about the region. It was really interesting.

L'un de mes plus grands plaisirs, c'est faire **une visite guidée**.

One of my greatest pleasures is going on a guided tour.

J'adore **me faire bronzer à la plage. Malheureusement, j'ai oublié ma crème solaire.**

I love sunbathing at the beach. Unfortunately, I forgot my suncream.

La cathédrale m'a beaucoup plu(e).

I liked the cathedral a lot.

a boat tour — un tour en bateau

my swimming costume — mon maillot de bain

my sunglasses — mes lunettes (f) de soleil

the zoo — le zoo
the fair — la foire

Grammar — plaire and pleuvoir

'Plaire' means *'to please'* and 'pleuvoir' means *'to rain'*. They both have the same past participle — 'plu'.
Il m'a beaucoup plu(e). *I liked it a lot. (It pleased me a lot.)* **Il a beaucoup plu.** *It rained a lot.*

Make sure you know how to spell the key vocab correctly...

Jack has written a blog about his plans for his holiday in France.

Cet été, je vais passer deux semaines à Cherbourg pour améliorer mon français. J'ai quelques projets pour réaliser ce **but**[1]. Je logerai avec une famille française, donc je parlerai français tous les jours. Je vais faire une visite guidée pour essayer de faire la connaissance de la ville et des gens français.

[1]aim
[2]coast

Je vais visiter les sites historiques car on peut y apprendre beaucoup. L'été dernier, je suis allé à Vienne et j'ai visité un château historique — les histoires des gens qui y ont vécu m'ont beaucoup intéressées.

J'irai sur la **côte**[2] aussi parce que je veux passer des jours relaxants à la plage.

Tick list:
✓ tenses: present, perfect, both futures
✓ correct use of 'y'

To improve:
+ use the conditional
+ give opinions using adjectives

Vous écrivez un blog sur vos projets pour les vacances. Décrivez :
* *ce que vous aimez faire en vacances*
* *les vacances dernières*

*Écrivez environ **150** mots en **français**. Répondez aux deux aspects de la question.*

[32 marks]

Listening Questions

If at first you don't succeed, try and try again. You'll be working against the clock in the exam, so knowing what you're likely to come across is essential — the last thing you want to do is panic.

1   You telephone a hotel in France to book your summer holiday.
     Listen to the answerphone message.

TRACK LISTENING 27

1 a   Which option do you need for a summer holiday?
      Write the correct number in the box.

[1 mark]

1 b   What would you find on the hotel website?

      ....
[1 mark]

1 c   Give **two** details should you provide if you wish to speak to someone.

      1. ....

      2. ....
[2 marks]

2   Écoutez ces interviews. Choisissez **deux** phrases qui
     sont **vraies** et écrivez les bonnes lettres dans les cases.

TRACK LISTENING 28

2 a   Zamzam

A	Elle passe ses vacances avec sa famille.
B	Elle va toujours aux magasins pendant le séjour.
C	Elle achète de la nourriture avant de partir en vacances.
D	Elle part à la campagne.

[2 marks]

2 b   Rayad

A	Il aime faire du camping.
B	Il aime les vacances à la campagne.
C	Il n'est pas obligé de payer ses vacances.
D	Il aime la nourriture.

[2 marks]

2 c   Nathalie

A	L'auberge de jeunesse ne coûtait pas cher.
B	Elle avait sa propre salle de bains dans l'auberge.
C	Les dortoirs n'étaient pas propres.
D	Elle va y retourner l'année prochaine.

[2 marks]

Speaking Question

Candidate's Material

- Spend a couple of minutes looking at the photo and the questions below it.

- You can make notes on a separate piece of paper.

© iStock.com/MauritsVink

You will be asked the following **three** questions, and **two** questions you haven't prepared:

- Qu'est-ce qu'il y a sur la photo ?

- Quel mode de transport préfères-tu ? Pourquoi ?

- Parle-moi de tes dernières vacances.

Teacher's Material

- Allow the student to develop his / her answers as much as possible.

- You need to ask the student the following questions **in order**:

  - Qu'est-ce qu'il y a sur la photo ?

  - Quel mode de transport préfères-tu ? Pourquoi ?

  - Parle-moi de tes dernières vacances.

  - Où aimes-tu loger quand tu vas en vacances ? Pourquoi ?

  - Où seraient tes vacances idéales ? Pourquoi ?

Reading Questions

1 Read this online advert for holiday jobs. Answer the questions below in **English**.

> Vous vous ennuyez pendant les grandes vacances ? Vous ne savez pas quoi faire ?
>
> Plus d'un quart des jeunes en France partent en vacances avec leur famille parce qu'ils pensent que c'est trop cher de partir seul ou avec des copains.
>
> Alors vous êtes parmi ceux qui n'ont pas beaucoup d'argent ? Pourquoi ne pas trouver un job d'été ? Vous pouvez travailler dans une colonie de vacances dans un autre pays européen. Comme ça, vous apprendrez une autre langue tandis que vous gagnerez un peu d'argent.

1 a Why do over a quarter of young French people go on holiday with their parents?

.... *[1 mark]*

1 b Where does the article suggest young people work? Give **one** detail.

.... *[1 mark]*

1 c What are the **two** advantages of working there?

1. ....

2. .... *[2 marks]*

2 Complete this travel blog using words from the list below.
Write the correct letter in each box.

> Je suis ici en Bosnie-Herzégovine depuis seulement trois jours et je suis déjà
>
> tombée amoureuse du pays ! Une fois arrivée à l'auberge de jeunesse, j'ai ⬚C⬚ tout
>
> de suite à m'amuser. Il y a de nombreux jeunes qui voyagent en Europe comme moi et
>
> tout le monde a des histoires intéressantes à ⬚⬚.
>
> Quant au pays, la Bosnie a un ⬚⬚ tragique et on peut le découvrir dans les
>
> nombreux musées. Les gens ici sont très aimables et j'ai déjà ⬚⬚ des spécialités
>
> nationales. Demain je ⬚⬚ le train au petit matin pour aller à Sarajevo.

A	passé	C	commencé	E	partager
B	prendrai	D	manquais	F	goûté

[4 marks]

Writing Questions

1 Vous écrivez un article sur votre blog sur vos vacances récentes.
Vous voulez recommander votre destination.

Décrivez:

• la destination et comment vous y êtes allé(e)

• où vous êtes resté(e) et les lieux que vous avez visités.

Écrivez environ **150** mots en **français**. Répondez à chaque aspect de la question.

[32 marks]

2 Translate the following passage into **French**.

> Last year my family stayed in a small hotel in England. What a disaster! Our room was very small. The bathroom was really dirty, it was disgusting. The food in the restaurant was terrible and the waiter was rude. Next year we will go to China and visit a theme park.

....

....

....

....

....

....

....

[12 marks]

Revision Summary for Section Nine

Here's another delightful revision summary. You know the drill by now — go through the questions and make a note of which ones you struggle with. Keep going over them again and again, until you're a fully-fledged French expert, then tick away, my friend...

Where to Go (p.87) ☑

1) A well-travelled friend says to you: 'I went to Brazil, China, France and Russia.' How would you say this in French?

2) Tell your friend that you're going to go to Nottingham next weekend.

3) Où es-tu allé(e) en vacances l'année dernière?

4) Your best friend asks you 'Quels sont tes projets pour les vacances?' What is he asking?

Accommodation (p.88) ☑

5) In French, write down as many different types of accommodation as you can.

6) Describe a holiday you went on when you were younger. Say who you went with and where you stayed in French.

7) You're going to Paris. Imagine you're on the phone to the tourist information office. In French, say that you would like to stay in a youth hostel that isn't too expensive.

8) Albert says: 'Je déteste faire du camping parce que je suis toujours fatigué. Je préfère loger dans un hôtel.' What is he saying?

9) Aimes-tu aller en vacances avec ta famille? Pourquoi / Pourquoi pas?

Getting Ready to Go (p.89) ☑

10) You're ringing a hotel. Say that you'd like to reserve a room with a double bed from the 12th July to the 26th July.

11) 'C'était un désastre. Les lits superposés se sont cassés, donc j'ai dû dormir par terre. De plus, la climatisation ne marchait pas.' Why was Jean-Luc dissatisfied with his hotel room? Answer in English.

12) Write down the French words for the travel-related vocabulary below:
   a) suitcase   b) luggage   c) sleeping bag   d) travel agency

13) Imagine you're at an airport. In French, say that you've forgotten your passport.

How to Get There (p.90) ☑

14) Tell your French friend that you're going to miss your flight.

15) An advert in the departures lounge says: 'Les transports en commun ne sont pas toujours fiables. Pour profiter de vos vacances, louez une voiture pendant votre séjour.' What is it advertising? Answer in English.

16) Comment est-ce que tu vas en vacances normalement?

17) 'If I had the money, I would go on holiday to Asia. I would travel by train and get to know other people.' How would you say this in French?

What to Do (p.91) ☑

18) You're on holiday in Brittany. Ask a local where the museum is.

19) Victoire is telling you about her holiday. 'Nous sommes allés à la plage tous les jours et à la fin de la semaine nous avons fait un tour en bateau. Mon père a organisé une visite guidée du château, mais je l'ai trouvée ennuyeuse.' Translate her sentences into English.

20) Qu'est-ce que tu aimes faire en vacances?

School Subjects

Talking about subjects is pretty straightforward — plus, you're probably bursting to say that you adore all things French-related. Explaining your opinion will get you more marks, so use this page to prepare properly.

Les matières (f) — Subjects

For more school subjects, see p.201.

For how to pronounce the letters of the French alphabet, look at p.16.

l'allemand (m)	*German*	la religion	*religious studies*
l'espagnol (m)	*Spanish*	la littérature anglaise	*English literature*
le français	*French*	le dessin	*art*
l'instruction (f) civique	*citizenship*	l'EPS (éducation physique	
la chimie	*chemistry*	et sportive) (f)	*PE (physical education)*
la physique	*physics*	l'informatique (f)	*IT (information technology)*

Ma matière préférée c'est... — My favourite subject is...

Moi, j'adore l'EPS. C'est chouette parce que je ne dois pas me concentrer et les cours sont détendus.

I love PE. It's great because I don't have to concentrate and the lessons are relaxed.

À mon avis, la physique est affreuse. C'est trop compliqué et je n'aime pas faire les expériences.

In my opinion, physics is awful. It's too complicated and I don't like doing the experiments.

my teacher is funny — mon / ma professeur est amusant(e)

I love doing exercise — j'adore faire de l'exercice

is boring — est ennuyeuse
is useless — ne sert à rien

Question	**Simple Answer**	**Extended Answer**	
Quelle est ta matière préférée?	J'aime assez les maths. Les réponses sont toujours claires.	J'aime assez les maths car c'est logique, mais je préfère la littérature anglaise. C'est fascinant et je m'intéresse aux histoires des autres.	j'aime bien *I really like*
What's your favourite subject?	*I quite like maths. The answers are always clear.*	*I quite like maths because it's logical, but I prefer English literature. It's fascinating and I'm interested in other people's stories.*	j'adore *I love*

WRITING — Always explain your opinions — it'll gain you marks...

Cho a envoyé un email à sa copine pour lui parler de ses matières préférées.

Au lycée, ma matière préférée c'est le français parce que c'est tellement intéressant. J'aime assez le dessin et la technologie, mais je les trouve difficiles car je n'ai pas de **côté artistique**[1].

L'année dernière, j'ai étudié l'espagnol, et je m'intéressais beaucoup à cette matière. Malheureusement, le professeur d'espagnol a quitté le lycée, et j'ai dû **laisser tomber**[2] cette matière.

Je déteste l'allemand — pour moi c'est vraiment une langue affreuse. C'est dommage car j'aime apprendre les langues. Je voudrais étudier d'autres langues dans l'avenir et, si j'ai de la chance, peut être je pourrais devenir **traductrice**[3].

Grade 8-9

[1] *artistic side*
[2] *to drop*
[3] *translator*

Tick list:
✓ tenses: present, perfect, imperfect, conditional, future
✓ si clause
✓ good use of conjunctions ('parce que', 'car', 'mais', 'si')

To improve:
+ include more varied sentence structures, e.g. 'pour' + infinitive

Vous écrivez un email à un(e) copain / copine pour donner votre avis sur les matières scolaires. Décrivez :

- *les matières que vous aimez / n'aimez pas étudier et pourquoi*
- *les matières que vous avez trouvées difficiles cette année*
- *les matières que vous voulez faire dans l'avenir*
- *pourquoi vous pensez que les matières que vous étudiez sont utiles (ou pas)*

*Écrivez environ **90** mots en **français**. Répondez à chaque aspect de la question.* [16 marks]

School Routine

You probably know your school routine off by heart — now it's time to learn how to speak about it in French...

Aller à l'école — To go to school

For more modes of transport, see p.90.

la salle de classe	*classroom*
le cours	*lesson*
l'emploi (m) du temps	*timetable*
la récré(ation)	*break*
les vacances (f)	*holidays*
le trimestre	*term*
la semaine	*week*
la rentrée	*return to school (after the summer)*
en retard	*late*
de bonne heure	*early*
tous les jours	*every day*
aller à pied	*to go on foot*

Question

Comment vas-tu à l'école?
How do you get to school?

Simple Answer

J'y vais à pied.
I walk there.

Extended Answer

Normalement, j'y vais à pied parce que j'habite près du lycée. Par contre, quand il pleut, ma mère m'emmène en voiture.

Normally, I walk there because I live close to college. However, when it's raining, my mum takes me in the car.

Grammar — 'y' (there)

'Y' is a pronoun — it means 'there'. It can replace nouns that are <u>locations</u>. It normally goes <u>before the verb</u> — see p.122-123.

J'y vais ce week-end.
I'm going there this weekend.

Une journée typique — A typical day

See p.2 for more about stating the time.

You might be asked to describe your <u>school day</u>, so make sure you know how to talk about <u>different times</u>.

La journée scolaire commence à neuf heures, et elle finit à quinze heures trente. Il y a deux récrés de vingt minutes, et on prend le déjeuner à midi.

The school day starts at nine o'clock, and it finishes at three thirty pm. There are two twenty-minute breaks, and we have lunch at midday.

J'ai un cours de maths chaque jour. Par contre, je ne fais qu'une heure d'EPS par semaine.

I have a maths lesson every day. On the other hand, I only do one hour of PE a week.

C'est une journée fatigante. Si j'avais le choix, je commencerais les cours plus tard.

It's a tiring day. If I had the choice, I would start lessons later.

Pendant la récré — During break

Je fais partie de l'équipe scolaire de natation, donc je m'entraîne souvent pendant la récré.

I'm part of the school swimming team, so I often train during break.

the holidays — les vacances
the term — le trimestre

Normalement, je reste dehors avec mes amis et nous jouons au football. Mais parfois nous allons à la cantine.

Normally, I stay outside with my friends and we play football. But sometimes we go to the canteen.

Make sure you go over this again and again and again...

Écoutez Nicolas qui parle de son emploi du temps.
Complétez les phrases suivantes en **français**.

e.g. Nicolas pense que la chimie est très ...*intéressante*...

1. Nicolas dit qu'il arrive à l'école en retard à cause de .... [1]
2. Nicolas se sent très fatigué après les cours le .... [1]
3. Dans l'avenir, Nicolas va jouer au .... [1]

School Life

The French system is a little different to ours, and you need to understand it in case it pops up in your exams.

La vie scolaire — School life

bien équipé(e)	*well equipped*	l'élève (m / f)	*pupil*	apprendre	*to learn*
mal équipé(e)	*badly equipped*	l'internat (m)	*boarding school*	être en seconde	*to be in year 11*

Où vas-tu à l'école? — Where do you go to school?

Grammar — present tense + 'depuis'

To say you've been doing something since a certain age, use the <u>present tense</u> with 'depuis' (*since*). See p.133 for more on this.
J'étudie le français depuis l'âge de six ans.
I've been studying French since the age of six.

(2 - 6 years)	la maternelle	*nursery school*
(6 - 11 years)	l'école (f) primaire	*primary school*
(11 - 15 years)	le collège	*secondary school*
(15 - 18 years)	le lycée	*sixth form college*
(15 - 18 years)	le lycée professionnel	*technical college*

Je vais au collège près de chez moi. Je l'aime bien, et mes professeurs ont un bon sens de l'humour.

I go to the secondary school close to my home. I really like it, and my teachers have a good sense of humour.

are very engaging — sont très passionnants

Mon école est un internat. J'y vais depuis l'âge de onze ans.

My school is a boarding school. I've been going there since the age of eleven.

a state / private / religious school — une école publique / privée / confessionnelle

Décris ton école — Describe your school

Mon collège est très vieux, mais c'est génial à l'intérieur. Les couloirs sont vifs et pleins de couleur.

My school is very old, but it's great inside. The corridors are lively and full of colour.

it's modern — c'est moderne

the atmosphere is very different — l'ambiance (f) est très différente

Au total, il y a environ trois cents élèves. Il y a deux terrains de sport.

In total, there are around three hundred pupils. There are two sports pitches.

sports halls — gymnases (m)

It's useful to know how the French school system works...

Lisez ces commentaires d'un forum sur la vie scolaire.

Karine : Je vais au lycée à Paris et je suis en seconde. Les cours de sciences me fascinent parce que nos laboratoires scolaires sont très bien équipés : on peut faire plein d'expériences. Il y a une grande piscine, donc je peux faire de l'exercice après les cours, ce qui m'aide à me relaxer.

Alain : Je vais au lycée professionnel, et je prends des cours pour devenir mécanicien. Malheureusement, il faut que tout le monde étudie les maths. Je les déteste : le prof est vraiment ennuyeux, donc je n'arrive pas à m'intéresser aux cours.

Identifiez la bonne personne pour chaque phrase. Écrivez 'K' pour Karine, 'A' pour Alain ou 'K+A' pour Karine et Alain.

e.g. Ses cours le préparent pour un emploi particulier. **A**

1. Avoir plus de ressources l'encourage à apprendre. [1]

2. Les qualités du professeur sont très importantes pour l'intéresser aux cours. [1]

3. On se détend en faisant du sport. [1]

School Pressures

School can be pretty stressful — you're trying to study and get the grades you need whilst maintaining a social life and doing your hobbies. Here's how to talk about it in French — let all that stress out...

Le règlement — School rules

la pression	*pressure*	le bulletin scolaire	*school report*
les devoirs (m)	*homework*	la retenue	*detention*
la note	*mark*	permettre	*to allow*
les résultats (m)	*results*	passer un examen	*to sit an exam*
l'examen (m)	*examination*	échouer	*to fail*
l'erreur (f)	*error / mistake*	réussir un examen	*to pass an exam*
les incivilités (f)	*rudeness*	redoubler	*to resit the year*

Watch out — 'passer un examen' doesn't mean 'to pass an exam', it means 'to take an exam'.

L'uniforme scolaire aide à rendre tous les élèves égaux.	*School uniform helps to make all pupils equal.*
Il est interdit de courir dans les couloirs.	*It is forbidden to run in the corridors.*
Si on enfreint le règlement, on sera en retenue.	*If you break the school rules, you'll be in detention.*

prevents students from being individual — empêche les élèves d'être individuels

to wear make-up at school — de se maquiller à l'école

to be rude to the teachers — d'être impoli(e) envers les professeurs

If you forget your homework — Si on oublie ses devoirs

If you're late — Si on est en retard

Être sous pression — To be under pressure

If you're asked for your <u>views on school</u>, this is a great chance to <u>add detail</u> to your answer.

Il y a beaucoup de pression à l'école à obtenir de bonnes notes.	*There's a lot of pressure at school to get good marks.*
J'ai étudié dur cette année donc j'espère réussir mes examens.	*I studied hard this year so I hope to pass my exams.*
Je me sens sous forte pression car j'ai peur de devoir redoubler.	*I feel under lots of pressure because I'm scared of having to repeat the year.*

to be fashionable — d'être à la mode

to get a good school report — obtenir un bon bulletin scolaire

my older brother is very gifted — mon frère aîné est très doué

Keep learning this vocab if you want to get great 'résultats'...

Here's a photo question. Use the example to get an idea of what to say.

Es-tu sous pression dans ta vie scolaire ?

Moi, je me sens sous assez de pression. Il y a des devoirs chaque semaine pour l'anglais, les mathématiques et les sciences ; d'ailleurs, si nous n'obtenons pas de bonnes notes, les profs nous en donnent plus. Je voudrais aller à l'université, donc je dois réussir tous mes examens. Pourtant, il est difficile de trouver assez de temps pour étudier et aussi de passer du temps avec ses amis.

Grade 8-9

Now respond to the following questions. You should talk for about 2 minutes.

- *Qu'est-ce qu'il y a sur la photo ?*
- *Que penses-tu du règlement scolaire ? Pourquoi ?*
- *Comment était ton école primaire ?*
- *Es-tu sous pression dans ta vie scolaire ?*   [10 marks]

Tick list:
✓ tenses: present, conditional
✓ pronouns ('nous', 'en')
✓ reflexive verb

To improve:
+ more tenses: talk about the past
+ include some intensifiers, e.g. 'très'

Education Post-16

It's more than likely you've given this a lot of thought already, so you've already done the hardest part. All that's left is to work out how to say it in French — here's a little something to help you on your way...

L'enseignement postscolaire — Further education

You might have to discuss your plans for <u>future studies</u>, so it's important to know some <u>key vocabulary</u>.

laisser tomber	*to drop*
former	*to train*
en première	*in year 12*
en terminale	*in year 13*
le conseiller d'orientation / la conseillère d'orientation	*careers adviser*
le bac(calauréat)	*A-levels*
l'apprentissage (m)	*apprenticeship*
l'apprenti(e) (m / f)	*apprentice*
la licence	*degree*
l'université (f), la faculté	*university*
l'année (f) sabbatique	*gap year*

'Collège' means 'secondary school' in French. The French equivalent of technical college is a 'lycée professionnel'. For more about the school system, see p.99.

Grammar — 'avoir' constructions + infinitive

'<u>Avoir envie de</u>' means '<u>to want</u>' to do something.
'<u>Avoir l'intention de</u>' means '<u>to intend</u>' to do something.
Both of these constructions are followed by an infinitive (see p.133).

J'ai envie d'<u>aller</u> à l'université.
I want <u>to go</u> to university.

Elle a l'intention de <u>faire</u> un apprentissage.
She intends <u>to do</u> an apprenticeship.

Mes études à l'avenir — My future studies

Question	Simple Answer	Extended Answer
Pourquoi as-tu choisi de passer / ne pas passer le bac? *Why have you chosen to do / not to do A-levels?*	J'ai besoin du bac pour faire mon métier préféré. *I need A-levels to do my preferred job.*	Pour moi, ce n'est pas un choix. Il faut avoir une licence pour faire mon métier préféré, et pour faire ça, j'ai besoin du bac. *For me, it isn't a choice. You have to have a degree to do my preferred job, and to do that, I need A-levels.*
	Je préférerais être apprenti(e). *I'd prefer to be an apprentice.*	Pour moi, il s'agit de l'argent. Je voudrais trouver un emploi et gagner de l'argent dès que possible. J'ai parlé au conseiller d'orientation et il m'a conseillé de faire un apprentissage. *For me, it's about money. I would like to find a job and earn money as soon as possible. I've spoken to the careers adviser and he advised me to do an apprenticeship.*

J'ai l'intention d'aller au lycée l'année prochaine pour passer le bac.	*I plan to go to sixth form next year to do A-levels.*	*to study history, maths and French* — pour étudier l'histoire, les maths et le français
Avant d'aller à l'université, j'aimerais prendre une année sabbatique pour découvrir le monde.	*Before going to university, I would like to take a gap year to discover the world.*	*do some voluntary work* — faire du travail bénévole

WRITING ## 'Future plans' is a common topic, so prepare your answers now...

Translate the following passage into **French**. *[12 marks]*

To celebrate the end of the exams, I watched films with my friends. We are very happy because it is the holidays. Next September, I will go to the sixth form college to do A-levels and I would like to get good results. However, my best friend wants to do an apprenticeship.

Career Choices and Ambitions

Deciding what to do with your life isn't exactly plain sailing, but don't worry about having to reveal your grand plans to the world in French. If you're uncertain, don't let it stop you — just make something up.

Le monde du travail — The world of work

le petit job	part-time job
le boulot	job (informal)
l'emploi (m)	job (formal)
l'entretien (m)	interview
l'employé(e) (m / f)	employee
l'employeur (m) / l'employeuse (f)	employer
le débouché	job opportunity / prospect
le / la patron(ne)	boss
enrichissant(e)	enriching / rewarding
le salaire	salary
l'ingénieur (m / f)	engineer
l'avocat(e) (m / f)	lawyer
l'infirmier (m) / l'infirmière (f)	nurse

See the vocab list on p.202 for more jobs.

Grammar — articles with jobs / professions

In French, you <u>don't need</u> an indefinite article ('<u>un</u>' / '<u>une</u>') when you describe someone's job.

Ma mère <u>est avocate</u>.   *My mother's <u>a lawyer</u>.*

Je veux <u>être infirmier</u>.   *I want <u>to be a nurse</u>.*

Grammar — venir + de + infinitive

'<u>Venir + de + infinitive</u>' means '<u>to have just done something</u>'. Don't forget that 'venir' (*to come*) is an <u>irregular</u> verb.

Je <u>viens d'aller</u> à un entretien.
I <u>have just been</u> to an interview.

Mon père <u>vient de prendre</u> sa retraite.
My dad <u>has just taken</u> his retirement.

Ton métier idéal — Your ideal job

Question

Quel est ton métier idéal? Pourquoi?

What is your ideal job? Why?

Simple Answer

Je rêve d'être médecin afin de soigner les malades.

I dream of being a doctor so that I can care for sick people.

Extended Answer

Je crois qu'être vétérinaire serait idéal pour moi car c'est un métier enrichissant — dans notre société les animaux domestiques font partie de nos familles. Pour moi, c'est important de trouver de la satisfaction dans mon travail.

I believe that to be a vet would be ideal for me because it's an enriching job — in our society, pets are part of our families. For me, it's important to find job satisfaction.

As-tu un petit-job? — Do you have a part-time job?

Je suis vendeur / vendeuse. Je travaille le week-end pour gagner de l'argent. Ça me permet de sortir avec mes amis.

I'm a shop assistant. I work at the weekend to earn money. It allows me to go out with my friends.

Je travaille dans un café. Mon salaire n'est pas très bon, mais je travaille dur.

I work in a café. My salary isn't very good, but I work hard.

I babysit — Je fais du babysitting

I work at a hairdresser's — Je travaille dans un salon de coiffure

I like working there — j'aime y travailler

Remember you don't need 'un(e)' to talk about someone's job...

Your French pen pal sends you this message. Translate it into **English**. *[9 marks]*

Quand j'étais plus jeune, j'avais envie d'être boulanger parce que j'adorais faire des gâteaux. Aujourd'hui, je m'intéresse toujours à la cuisine, et j'aimerais être chef quand je quitterai l'école. J'ai un petit job dans la cuisine d'un restaurant. Je ne gagne pas beaucoup d'argent, mais j'espère que l'expérience sera utile dans l'avenir.

Listening Questions

Here come your final four pages of exam practice — give them your best shot. Don't forget that there's also a full practice exam at the end of this book — it's fantastic preparation for the real thing.

1   Pendant un échange scolaire, vous entendez ces jeunes qui parlent de leurs études. Écrivez la bonne lettre dans la case pour compléter les phrases.

TRACK LISTENING 30

1 a   Pour Karine...

A	les langues ne sont pas faciles.
B	la chimie est difficile.
C	c'est très utile de savoir parler une autre langue.

[1 mark]

1 b   Nadia pense que c'est essentiel de...

A	parler avec les autres.
B	ne pas perdre son temps devant un écran.
C	savoir bien utiliser un ordinateur.

[1 mark]

1 c   Salim pense que...

A	les jeunes utilisent trop les ordinateurs.
B	c'est toujours nécessaire d'utiliser un ordinateur.
C	les ordinateurs aident à étudier les maths.

[1 mark]

2   Écoutez ces publicités et choisissez les **deux** phrases qui sont **vraies**. Écrivez les bonnes lettres dans les cases.

TRACK LISTENING 31

2 a

A	Pour ce travail, il faut aimer être seul.
B	Les diplômes sont importants.
C	C'est un travail de vacances.
D	Un sens de l'humour est essentiel.
E	On travaille dans un hôpital.

[2 marks]

2 b

A	Pour ce travail, il faut avoir passé des examens.
B	Il faut payer les repas.
C	On travaille tous les jours de la semaine.
D	C'est un travail qui en vaut la peine.
E	Le travail est très facile.

[2 marks]

Speaking Question

Candidate's Role

- Your teacher will play the role of your French friend. They will speak first.

- You should use *tu* to address your friend.

- – ! – means you will have to respond to something you have not prepared.

- – ? – means you will have to ask your friend a question.

> Tu parles de ta routine scolaire avec ton ami(e) français(e).
>
> - Transport au collège.
>
> - !
>
> - Les devoirs — votre opinion et une raison.
>
> - ? Matières étudiées.
>
> - Activités extrascolaires.

Teacher's Role

- You begin the role-play using the introductory text below.

- You should address the candidate as *tu*.

- You may alter the wording of the questions in response to the candidate's previous answers.

- Do not supply the candidate with key vocabulary.

> Introductory text: *Tu parles de ta routine scolaire avec ton ami(e) français(e).*
> *Moi, je suis ton ami(e).*
>
> - Comment vas-tu au collège ?
>
> - ! Qu'est-ce que tu as fait pendant la récré hier ?
>
> - Que penses-tu des devoirs ?
>
> - ? Allow the candidate to ask you a question.
>
> - Quelles activités extrascolaires est-ce que tu fais ?

Section Ten — Current and Future Study and Employment

Reading Questions

1   Translate the following passage into **English**.

> Je vais aller au lycée près de chez moi. Le bâtiment est très moderne et les salles de classe sont grandes. En plus, je pourrai chanter dans la chorale et jouer dans l'orchestre. Malheureusement, ma meilleure amie n'ira pas au lycée avec moi, car elle veut aller au lycée professionnel.

....

....

....

....

....

....

[9 marks]

2   Read these Internet posts about further education.
     Identify the people by writing either **Y** (Yuki), **A** (Ankit), **M** (Marc) or **L** (Lucie).

Yuki	Si on veut faire un travail manuel, c'est mieux de faire un apprentissage. En travaillant comme apprenti, on apprend un métier et on ne perd pas de temps.
Ankit	Je trouve que si on veut une carrière intéressante, il est essentiel de continuer ses études. Moi, je veux réussir mon bac et après ça, on verra.
Marc	C'est très important de réussir aux examens. Je vais continuer mes études parce que je sais ce que je veux faire plus tard et j'ai besoin de qualifications.
Lucie	Je pense qu'on peut étudier et travailler en même temps. On peut trouver un travail à temps partiel donc gagner de l'argent et avoir un diplôme.

Example: Who wants to learn on the job?   ☐ Y

2 a   Who has already decided on a career path?   ☐

[1 mark]

2 b   Who thinks it's a good idea to have a part-time job while studying?   ☐

[1 mark]

2 c   Who will make plans after doing A-levels?   ☐

[1 mark]

Writing Questions

1   Vous écrivez un email à votre correspondant(e) luxembourgeois(e) sur vos
    ambitions pour l'avenir.

    Décrivez:

    • votre carrière de rêve

    • les matières que vous avez étudiées l'année dernière

    • l'expérience de travail dont vous avez besoin

    • vos projets pour une année sabbatique.

    Écrivez environ **90** mots en **français**. Répondez à chaque aspect de la question.

    [16 marks]

2   Translate the following passage into **French**.

I am fed up with school because there is a lot of pressure. The lessons are boring and I don't like them. Yesterday, my teacher got angry and I had detention during the lunch break. Also, we have to wear a school uniform but I would prefer to choose my clothes myself.

    ....

    ....

    ....

    ....

    ....

    ....

    ....

    [12 marks]

Revision Summary for Section Ten

What better way to round off a section on study and employment than with another revision summary? Use these questions to help you discover the gaps in your knowledge — then go back afterwards and plug those holes.

School Subjects (p.97) ☑

1) Say what your GCSE subjects are in French. ☑
2) What's your favourite subject? Which subject(s) don't you like? Answer in French. ☑

School Routine (p.98) ☑

3) What's the French for...? a) lesson b) timetable c) holidays d) term ☑
4) In French, describe a normal day at school. Say what time you start, when you eat lunch and when you finish. ☑
5) How would you say, in French, that you have five lessons every day and that each lesson lasts 50 minutes? ☑
6) Qu'est-ce que tu fais normalement pendant la récré? ☑

School Life (p.99) ☑

7) Your French penfriend writes you an email describing his school life. 'Je suis en seconde et je vais à un lycée en banlieue parisienne. C'est un internat de garçons et j'y vais depuis l'âge de quinze ans.' Translate this into English. ☑
8) In French, say: 'My school has 800 pupils, a football pitch and a swimming pool.' ☑
9) Imagine the council has given you money to improve your school. What would you do with it? Answer in French, giving three suggestions. ☑

School Pressures (p.100) ☑

10) Translate these words and phrases into English:
    a) le règlement b) échouer c) la note d) les devoirs e) le bulletin scolaire ☑
11) 'La semaine dernière j'ai eu une retenue car je me suis maquillée à l'école.' Why did Alina get into trouble last week? How was she punished? ☑
12) In French, write down one advantage and one disadvantage of having a school uniform. ☑
13) Do you feel pressured at school? Why / Why not? Answer in French. ☑

Education Post-16 (p.101) ☑

14) What's the French for 'further education'? ☑
15) Your French friend says: 'Je suis en terminale. J'étudie pour le bac car je veux aller à l'université pour faire une licence d'informatique.' What's she saying? ☑
16) Est-ce que tu vas continuer tes études après les examens? Pourquoi / Pourquoi pas? ☑
17) In French, say: 'I want to take a gap year and do some voluntary work.' ☑

Career Choices and Ambitions (p.102) ☑

18) What's the French for...? a) job b) job opportunity c) salary d) interview ☑
19) Quel serait ton métier idéal? Pourquoi? ☑
20) In French, tell your friend: 'I've just started a new part-time job. I work in a supermarket at the weekend. I like working there, but it's tiring.' ☑

| Nouns | # Words for People and Objects |

Nouns are words for people and objects. This is important in French because all nouns have a gender.

Every noun in French is masculine or feminine

1) Whether a noun is <u>masculine</u> or <u>feminine</u> affects loads of things. The words for '<u>the</u>' and '<u>a</u>' are <u>different</u> and, if that wasn't enough, <u>adjectives</u> change to match the gender too.

2) '<u>Le</u>' in front of a noun means it's <u>masculine</u>. '<u>La</u>' in front means it's <u>feminine</u>.

> le livre (m) intéressant   *the interesting book*

> la matière (f) intéressante   *the interesting subject*

For more on how adjectives change to fit the gender, see p.110.

3) When you <u>learn</u> a <u>noun</u>, learn the <u>article</u> too — don't think 'chien = dog', think '<u>le</u> chien = the dog'.

Sometimes you can guess which gender a word is

If you have to <u>guess</u> whether a noun is <u>masculine</u> or <u>feminine</u>, use these <u>rules of thumb</u>:

It's probably <u>masculine</u> if...   ...it <u>ends in</u>:   -age, -al, -er, -eau, -ing, -in, -ment, -ou, -ail, -ier, -et, -isme, -oir, -eil   ...<u>or</u> it's a   male person, language, day, month or season.

It's probably <u>feminine</u> if...   ...it <u>ends in</u>:   -aine, -ée, -ense, -ie, -ise, -tion, -ance, -elle, -esse, -ière, -sion, -tude, -anse, -ence, -ette, -ine, -té, -ure   ...<u>or</u> it's a   female person.

These rules don't work every time — there are some exceptions.

Nouns can also be made plural

1) Nouns in French are <u>usually</u> made <u>plural</u> by adding an '<u>s</u>' — the <u>same</u> as in English.

> le chat *the cat* ⟹ les chats *the cats*

2) When you make a noun <u>plural</u>, instead of '<u>le</u>' or '<u>la</u>' to say '<u>the</u>', you have to use '<u>les</u>' — see p.109.

3) Some nouns can't be made plural by sticking an '<u>s</u>' on the end — they have <u>irregular plural forms</u>:

Noun ending	Example	Meaning	Irregular plural ending	Example
-ail	le travail	work	-aux	les travaux
-al	le journal	newspaper	-aux	les journaux
-eau	le bureau	office	-eaux	les bureaux
-eu	le jeu	game	-eux	les jeux
-ou	le chou	cabbage	-oux	les choux ⟹

Only a handful of nouns follow this rule — e.g. 'genou' (*knee*), 'bijou' (*jewel*) — most nouns ending in 'ou' are <u>regular</u>.

4) Some nouns <u>don't change</u> in the plural form. These are usually nouns that end in <u>-s</u>, <u>-x</u> or <u>-z</u>.

> la croix *the cross* ⟹ les croix *the crosses*

> la souris *the mouse* ⟹ les souris *the mice*

Using the correct gender will help boost your marks...

Add 'le' or 'la' to these words and then put the whole thing into its plural form.

1. cadeau (*present*)   **3.** citron (*lemon*)   **5.** voiture (*car*)

2. piscine (*swimming pool*)   **4.** cheval (*horse*)   **6.** pâtisserie (*cake shop*)

'The', 'A' and 'Some'

'The' and 'a' are some of the most common words in a language, so it's a good idea to revise them well...

Un, une — A

The word for 'a' depends on the gender of the noun (see p.108).

'Un' and 'une' are indefinite articles.

'Un' is used with masculine words... | un café (m)   *a coffee*

...and 'une' is used with feminine ones. | une tasse (f)   *a cup*

Le, la, l', les — The

1) The word for 'the' is different depending on the gender and number of the noun:

These are definite articles.

Masculine singular	Feminine singular	Before vowels / 'h' (sometimes)	Masc. or fem. plural
le	la	l'	les

2) For words starting with a vowel, 'le' or 'la' is shortened to 'l''. This makes them easier to say.

l'avion (m)   *the aeroplane*   l'émission (f)   *the programme*

3) Some words starting with an 'h' also take 'l'' instead of 'le' or 'la'. Sadly there's no rule for when this happens — you just have to learn it.

l'homme (m)   *the man*

'De' and 'à' change before 'le' and 'les'

1) 'De' (of / from) and 'à' (to / at) are prepositions (see p.128).

2) Be careful when you use them before a definite article (le/la/l'/les). They combine with 'le' and 'les' to make new words.

	le	la	l'	les
à +	au	à la	à l'	aux
de +	du	de la	de l'	des

Je reste à + le collège. ⟹ Je reste au collège.   *I'm staying at school.*
Je viens de + le Canada. ⟹ Je viens du Canada.   *I come from Canada.*
Je vais à + les États-Unis. ⟹ Je vais aux États-Unis.   *I'm going to the United States.*

Du, de la, de l', des — 'Some' or 'any'

1) If you want to say 'some' or 'any', use 'de' with the correct definite article (see the table above). These are called partitive articles.

2) In negative sentences (see p.143), you only use 'de', regardless of the gender or whether it's singular or plural.

Je n'ai pas de pain.   *I haven't got any bread.*   Je n'ai pas de pantalon.   *I haven't got any trousers.*

3) You also just use 'de' after most quantities — such as 'beaucoup de' (lots of) or 'un peu de' (a bit of).

J'ai un peu de fromage.   *I have a bit of cheese.*

Knowing how to use French articles is crucial...

Fill in the gaps with the correct article.
1. L'homme a un peu ...... pain.
2. Les étudiants viennent ...... Maroc.
3. Je vais ...... pays de Galles.
4. Nous avons ...... bananes.
5. Ils n'ont pas ...... raisins.
6. Il va ...... bibliothèque.

Adjectives | **Words to Describe Things**

Adjectives are very useful, but they're a little bit tricky in French...

Adjectives describe things — here are some common ones

beau / belle	*beautiful*	affreux / affreuse	*awful*	nouveau / nouvelle	*new*	
triste	*sad*	long(ue)	*long*	lent(e)	*slow*	
normal(e)	*normal*	facile	*easy*	pratique	*practical*	
intéressant(e)	*interesting*	difficile	*difficult*	amusant(e)	*funny*	

French adjectives 'agree' with the thing they're describing

1) In English, adjectives don't <u>change form</u> — even when the word being described is plural, e.g. <u>big</u> boots.

2) In French, most adjectives <u>change</u> to match the <u>gender</u> and <u>number</u> of the word they're <u>describing</u>.

3) You often add an '-e' to the adjective if the word being described is <u>feminine</u> (see p.108).
   But <u>don't</u> do this if the word <u>already ends</u> in 'e'.

> le livre intéressant   *the interesting book*

> la vie intéressante   *the interesting life*

4) Add an '-s' to the adjective if the word being described is <u>plural</u> (see p.108).
   This means that with <u>feminine plurals</u>, you're adding '-es'.

> les livres intéressants   *the interesting books*

> les vies intéressantes   *the interesting lives*

Some adjectives don't follow these rules

Adjectives with <u>certain endings</u> follow <u>different</u> rules:

Ending	Important examples	Masculine singular	Feminine singular	Masculine plural	Feminine plural
-x	heureux *(happy)*, sérieux *(serious)*, ennuyeux *(boring)*, dangereux *(dangerous)*	heureux	heureuse	heureux	heureuses
-on, -en, -el, -il	bon *(good)*, mignon *(sweet)*, cruel *(cruel)*, gentil *(kind)*	bon	bonne	bons	bonnes
-er	premier *(first)*, dernier *(last)*, fier *(proud)*, cher *(expensive)*, étranger *(foreign)*	premier	première	premiers	premières
-f	sportif *(sporty)*, actif *(active)*, vif *(lively)*, négatif *(negative)*	sportif	sportive	sportifs	sportives
-c	blanc *(white)*, sec *(dry)*	blanc	blanche	blancs	blanches

These double the last letter + add 'e' in the feminine.

'Sèche' (f. sing.) and 'sèches' (f. pl.) have an accent added to them.

Adjectives — très sérieux, et un peu ennuyeux, mais utiles...

Translate these phrases into **French**, making sure the adjectives agree.

1. The proud mother.   **3.** The slow cat.   **5.** The lively dogs.   **7.** A kind woman.

2. A sad girl.   **4.** A blue house.   **6.** The white cars.   **8.** An expensive jacket.

Words to Describe Things
Adjectives

Adjectives add details to what you've written, which will get you those extra marks. So they're pretty useful...

Some adjectives don't follow the rules

1) These adjectives are <u>irregular</u>.

2) Some <u>change</u> before <u>masculine singular</u> nouns starting with a <u>vowel</u> because it's <u>easier</u> to say.

3) Some adjectives <u>never change</u>, e.g. '<u>marron</u>' (brown) and '<u>orange</u>' (orange).

Masculine singular	Before a masc. sing. noun starting with a vowel	Fem. sing.	Masc. plural	Fem. plural
vieux (old)	vieil	vieille	vieux	vieilles
beau (beautiful)	bel	belle	beaux	belles
nouveau (new)	nouvel	nouvelle	nouveaux	nouvelles
fou (mad)	fol	folle	fous	folles
long (long)	long	longue	longs	longues
tout (all)	tout	toute	tous	toutes
rigolo (funny)	rigolo	rigolote	rigolos	rigolotes

Most adjectives go after the word they're describing...

1) In French, <u>most</u> adjectives follow the <u>noun</u> (the word they're describing).

> J'ai une voiture rapide. *I have a fast car.*

2) You can also <u>use adjectives</u> in sentences with <u>verbs</u> such as '<u>être</u>' (to be) and '<u>devenir</u>' (to become). The adjective still needs to <u>agree</u> with the noun though.

> Ils sont prêts maintenant. *They are ready now.*
> Elle devient grande. *She is becoming tall.*

Adjectives are always masculine singular after 'ce', e.g. 'c'est nouveau' (it's new).

...but there are some odd ones which go before

'Grand(e)' goes after the noun when it's describing a person.

1) These adjectives almost always go <u>before</u> the noun:

bon(ne)	good	nouveau / nouvel(le)	new	grand(e)	big / tall
mauvais(e)	bad	beau / bel(le)	beautiful	haut(e)	high
jeune	young	premier / première	first	joli(e)	nice / pretty
vieux / vieil(le)	old	petit(e)	small / short	faux / fausse	false

Adjectives have to agree regardless of whether they come before or after the noun.

> J'ai une petite maison, avec un joli jardin et une belle vue.
> *I have a small house, with a pretty garden and a beautiful view.*

2) Some adjectives <u>change meaning</u> depending on whether they go <u>before</u> or <u>after</u> a word. For example, '<u>propre</u>' means '<u>own</u>' before a noun but '<u>clean</u>' after it. '<u>Ancien</u>' is another example:

> l'ancien château ⟹ *the former castle*
> le château ancien ⟹ *the old castle*

Learn which adjectives go where...

Without looking at the page above, pick the sentences that have the adjective(s) in the right place.

1. C'est un chien jeune.
2. Le long train est bleu.
3. Elle est une fille sportive.
4. Tu as lu un ennuyeux livre.
5. J'ai une voiture rouge nouvelle.
6. Vous avez la meilleure maison.

Adjectives
Words to Describe Things

They're no ordinary adjectives on this page — they're possessives, indefinites and demonstratives. Fancy.

Words like 'my' and 'your' show who an object belongs to

1) <u>Possessive adjectives</u> show that something <u>belongs</u> to someone. They go <u>before the noun</u>.

notre cousin	*our cousin*

2) They <u>match</u> the <u>thing being described</u> — <u>NOT</u> the <u>person</u> it belongs to. The <u>different</u> forms are in this table.

	My	Your (inf. sing.)	His / her / its	Our	Your (formal, pl.)	Their
Masculine singular	mon	ton	son	notre	votre	leur
Feminine singular	ma	ta	sa	notre	votre	leur
Plural	mes	tes	ses	nos	vos	leurs

3) So, for example, it's <u>always</u> 'mon père' *(my father)* even if a <u>girl</u> is talking.

Voici mon père et ma mère.
Here is my dad and my mum.

This means that 'son', 'sa' or 'ses' could all mean either 'his' or 'her'. You can usually tell which one it's meant to be by using the context.

4) <u>Before vowels</u>, or words starting with '<u>h</u>' that take '<u>l''</u>, you use the <u>masculine</u> possessive adjective — even if the noun is <u>feminine</u>. It's <u>easier to say</u>.

Mon amie s'appelle Ana.	*My friend's called Ana.*

Quelque, chaque — Some, each

1) '<u>Quelque</u>' *(some)* and '<u>chaque</u>' *(each)* are <u>indefinite adjectives</u>. They <u>don't</u> have a set of <u>different</u> forms for masculine, feminine or plural.

'Quelque chose' is a fixed phrase that uses 'quelque'. It means 'something'.

2) '<u>Quelque</u>' <u>doesn't</u> have a <u>feminine</u> form, but it <u>does</u> add an '-s' when it changes from <u>singular</u> to <u>plural</u>.

J'ai acheté quelques bonbons au magasin qui est à quelque distance de chez moi.
I bought some sweets at the shop which is some distance from my house.

3) '<u>Chaque</u>' <u>never</u> changes whether it's describing something <u>masculine</u> or <u>feminine</u>.

Je lis chaque nuit.	*I read every night.*

Ce, cet, cette, ces — This, these

1) To say '<u>this</u>' or '<u>these</u>', you need the right form of '<u>ce</u>':

Masculine singular	Feminine singular	Masc. words that take 'l''	Masculine or feminine plural
ce	cette	cet	ces

Choose the one that matches the noun you're describing.

2) These are <u>demonstrative adjectives</u> — they're used when you use '<u>this</u>' as a <u>describing word</u>.

Ce film est terrible.	*This film is terrible.*

Cet homme est grand.	*This man is tall.*

You need to be able to use all of these adjectives correctly...

Complete these sentences using the correct translation of the words in brackets.

1. ...... père n'aime pas ...... nouvelle voiture. (my, his)
2. ...... amis ne vont pas à ...... lycée. (your (sing. inf.), our)
3. ...... hôtel est grand. (this)
4. ...... cuisinière a ...... légumes. (this, some)

Words to Compare Things

When you're describing something, it's often useful to be able to compare it to something else. Doing this will also make your language more complex and gain you marks — hurrah! Here's how to do it...

Plus..., le plus... — More..., the most

You can do this with most adjectives.

1) In French you <u>couldn't</u> say, for example, 'weird<u>er</u>' or 'weird<u>est</u>' — you have to say '<u>more weird</u>' or 'the <u>most weird</u>', using '<u>plus</u>' and '<u>le plus</u>'. Use '<u>que</u>' to say '<u>than</u>'.

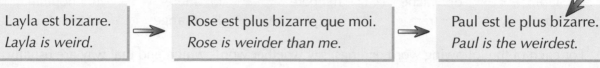

Layla est bizarre. *Layla is weird.*	Rose est plus bizarre que moi. *Rose is weirder than me.*	Paul est le plus bizarre. *Paul is the weirdest.*

2) To say '<u>less</u>' or '<u>the least</u>', you use the word '<u>moins</u>' in the <u>same</u> way as '<u>plus</u>'.

fort *strong*	moins fort *less strong*	le moins fort *the least strong*

3) If you want to say something is the <u>same</u>, use '<u>aussi...que</u>' *(as...as)*.

Cette émission est aussi passionnante que l'autre.   *This programme is as exciting as the other one.*

4) '<u>Plus</u>', '<u>moins</u>' and '<u>aussi</u>' form <u>comparative adjectives</u>. '<u>Le plus</u>' and '<u>le moins</u>' form <u>superlative adjectives</u> — they're saying something is '<u>the most</u>', rather than directly <u>comparing</u> it to something else.

The adjectives still need to agree

1) If you're using <u>comparatives</u> or <u>superlatives</u>, the adjectives still need to <u>agree</u> with the <u>word</u> they're <u>describing</u>.

Elle est plus sportive.   *She is more sporty.*

2) If you're saying '<u>the most</u>' or '<u>the least</u>', you have to make '<u>the</u>' agree as well.

Jean et Françoise sont les plus jeunes. *Jean and Françoise are the youngest.*

There are some exceptions

1) There are some <u>odd ones out</u> when it comes to making <u>comparisons</u> — just like in English. Unfortunately, these tend to be words that come up a lot.

2) With these words, you <u>don't</u> use '<u>plus</u>' or '<u>moins</u>':

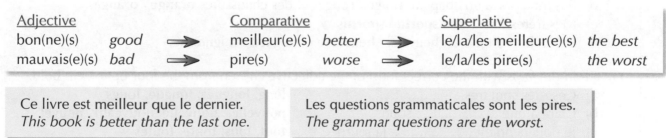

<u>Adjective</u>		<u>Comparative</u>		<u>Superlative</u>	
bon(ne)(s)	*good*	meilleur(e)(s)	*better*	le/la/les meilleur(e)(s)	*the best*
mauvais(e)(s)	*bad*	pire(s)	*worse*	le/la/les pire(s)	*the worst*

Ce livre est meilleur que le dernier. *This book is better than the last one.*	Les questions grammaticales sont les pires. *The grammar questions are the worst.*

Make sure you can use comparatives and superlatives accurately...

Translate these phrases into **French**. Remember those pesky adjective agreements...

1. Navid and Pauline are the strongest.
2. Your grandma is older than my grandad.
3. This shop is the least expensive.
4. Julie is as active as Thérèse.
5. His ideas are the worst.
6. French is the best.

Quick Questions

Knowing all this grammar is vital, so you need to make sure it sticks in your mind. Test what you've read with these quick questions — don't move on until you can answer them all correctly.

1) Write down whether each of these words is masculine or feminine.
   a) chien
   b) lapin
   c) sœur
   d) souris
   e) vache
   f) frère
   g) chat
   h) père
   i) pomme
   j) oiseau
   k) mère
   l) orange
   m) maison
   n) hôpital
   o) école

2) For each of the following word endings, say whether words which end that way are usually masculine or feminine.
   a) -tion
   b) -ou
   c) -er
   d) -ière
   e) -ée
   f) -elle
   g) -ment
   h) -sion
   i) -isme
   j) -esse
   k) -ail
   l) -ise
   m) -té
   n) -ure
   o) -et

3) For each of these words, swap the indefinite article ('un' or 'une') for the definite article ('le', 'la' or 'l'').
   a) une maison
   b) un jardin
   c) un professeur
   d) une orange
   e) une robe
   f) un hôpital
   g) un abricot
   h) un hiver

4) Fill in the gaps in these sentences using the correct partitive article ('de', 'du', 'de la', 'de l'' or 'des').
   a) Sophia a .... oranges.
   b) Je n'ai pas .... poires.
   c) Ils ont gagné .... argent.
   d) Elle prend .... soupe.
   e) Il mange beaucoup .... chips.
   f) Richard n'a pas .... chaussettes.
   g) Il me donne .... chocolat.
   h) Je veux .... frites.

5) Underline all of the adjectives in the following sentences.
   a) L'examen était facile.
   b) Tes amis sont amusants et gentils.
   c) Thomas a un vieux chien.
   d) C'est une belle femme.
   e) Le film est triste.
   f) Alice habite dans une grande maison.
   g) J'ai une bonne idée.
   h) Le voyage sera long et ennuyeux.

6) Cross out the incorrect form of the adjectives in bold to complete the sentences.
   a) Alexandre a les yeux **bleu / bleus**.
   b) J'habite dans une maison **moderne / modernes**.
   c) La **premier / première** question est très **difficile / difficiles**.
   d) Susanna porte un chapeau **rouge / rouges** et des chaussures **orange / oranges**.
   e) Mes frères sont assez **sportif / sportifs**.
   f) Le cochon d'Inde est **heureux / heureuse** et **mignon / mignonne**.

7) Fill in the gaps with the correct form of the adjective chosen from the four options in **bold**.
   a) Ces rues sont très ....   **long, longues, longue, longs**
   b) Clara a une .... souris.   **nouvelles, nouvelle, nouveaux, nouvel**
   c) Je dors pendant .... la journée.   **tout, tous, toute, toutes**
   d) Ton professeur est ....   **rigolote, rigolotes, rigolos, rigolo**

Quick Questions

Quick Questions

8) Fill in the gaps in these sentences using the correct form of the adjectives in brackets.
   a) Elle porte une robe .... (blanc)
   b) En France, il y a beaucoup de gens .... (étranger)
   c) Florence et Charlotte sont les .... (dernier)
   d) Cette chemise est trop .... (cher)
   e) Mes chaussettes sont .... (sec)

9) Add the adjective in brackets to the correct gap in the sentences.
   a) J'ai une .... chemise .... (bleue)
   b) Nous sommes au .... étage .... (premier)
   c) Loïc habite dans un .... appartment .... (petit)
   d) Il chante des .... chansons .... (étrangères)
   e) C'est une .... peinture .... (bonne)

10) What's the French for...?
   a) my dog
   b) their car
   c) your house
   d) my friend
   e) his shoes
   f) her brother
   g) our parents
   h) your horse

11) Translate the following sentences into French.
   a) My bicycle is red.
   b) Is your (sing.) coat blue?
   c) His mother lives in Ireland.
   d) Did you (formal) speak to your grandmother?
   e) They haven't done their homework.
   f) Have you (informal) seen her money?

12) Rewrite each of these sentences, replacing the English word in brackets with the correct form of 'chaque' or 'quelque.'
   a) Je joue au rubgy (each) week-end.
   b) Eric a acheté (some) légumes.
   c) (Each) élève doit faire ses devoirs.
   d) Il a trouvé (some) livres intéressants.

13) Fill in the gaps in these sentences using the correct demonstrative adjective ('ce', 'cette' or 'ces').
   a) Je pense que .... travail est un peu ennuyeux.
   b) .... hôpital est merveilleux.
   c) Je ne me souviens pas de .... film.
   d) .... animaux sont malheureux.
   e) Les hommes vont aux États-Unis .... année.

14) Translate these sentences into French using 'le plus', 'la plus' or 'les plus'.
   a) This festival is the most exciting.
   b) I am strange, but he is the strangest.
   c) These trees are the greenest.

Words to Describe Actions

Words that describe actions are called adverbs. Like adjectives, they're useful for adding more detail to your French and gaining you marks. Nifty...

Adverbs describe how something's being done

1) In English, you don't say 'I run <u>slow</u>' — you add '<u>-ly</u>' on the end to say 'I run <u>slowly</u>'. 'Slowly' is an <u>adverb</u>.

2) In French, you add '<u>-ment</u>' on the <u>end</u> of an <u>adjective</u> to make an <u>adverb</u>. But <u>first</u> you have to make sure it's in the <u>feminine form</u> (see p.110-111).

> adroit *(skilful)* ⟹ adroite (feminine form) **+** -ment ⟹ adroitement *(skilfully)*

3) Unlike adjectives, <u>adverbs</u> don't have to <u>agree</u> — they're <u>describing</u> an <u>action</u>, not the <u>person</u> doing it.

Elle court adroitement. *She runs skilfully.*	Nous courons adroitement. *We run skilfully.*

There are some small exceptions

'Présentement' and 'lentement' follow the normal rule and use their feminine adjective forms + '-ment'.

1) Some adjectives <u>don't</u> follow the rules above.

2) If an adjective ends in '<u>-ant</u>' or '<u>-ent</u>', the '<u>nt</u>' is replaced with '<u>-mment</u>'.

> fréquent *(frequent)* ⟹ fréque- + -mment ⟹ fréquemment *(frequently)*
> récent *(recent)* ⟹ réce- + -mment ⟹ récemment *(recently)*

3) With <u>some</u> adjectives ending in '<u>-e</u>', the '<u>e</u>' changes to '<u>é</u>' when they become <u>adverbs</u>.

> énorme *(enormous)*   énormément *(enormously)*

> précise *(precise)*   précisément *(precisely)*

4) If an adjective's <u>masculine</u> form ends in a <u>vowel</u>, you can just add '<u>-ment</u>' to it to make an <u>adverb</u> — you <u>don't</u> need to use the <u>feminine</u> form.

> poli *(polite)*   poliment

5) '<u>Gentiment</u>' *(gently, kindly)* is <u>completely irregular</u>. It comes from '<u>gentil</u>' *(gentle, kind)*.

Some adverbs don't use '-ment'

Some <u>adverbs</u> are quite <u>different</u> from their <u>adjectives</u>.

bon(ne)	*good* ⟹	bien	*well*
mauvais(e)	*bad* ⟹	mal	*badly*
rapide	*fast* ⟹	vite	*fast*

Nous jouons bien au tennis.	*We play tennis well.*
Elle écrit mal.	*She writes badly.*
Tu parles vite.	*You talk fast.*

Remember, adverbs don't have to agree...

Turn these adjectives into adverbs.

1. triste *(sad)*

2. négatif *(negative)*

3. sérieux *(serious)*

4. fier *(proud)*

5. absolu *(absolute)*

6. lent *(slow)*

7. mauvais *(bad)*

8. constant *(constant)*

Words to Describe Actions

Adverbs don't just describe how something's being done — you can use them to specify the time and place it's happening as well. Read on for more...

Adverbs can describe when something's being done

1) <u>Adverbs of time</u> describe <u>when</u>, or <u>how frequently</u>, something happens.

tous les jours	*every day*	il y a...	*...ago*	immédiatement	*immediately*
normalement	*normally*	récemment	*recently*	en même temps	*at the same time*
souvent	*often*	avant	*before*	tôt	*early*
quelquefois	*sometimes*	déjà	*already*	tard	*late*
jamais	*never*	maintenant	*now*	bientôt	*soon*

2) You can also form <u>phrases</u> to describe the <u>day</u>, <u>month</u>, <u>season</u> or <u>year</u> something happens using the adjectives '<u>dernier</u>' *(last)* and '<u>prochain</u>' *(next)*. They can go at the <u>start</u> or <u>end</u> of a <u>sentence</u>.

> Je vais partir lundi prochain.
> *I'm going to leave next Monday.*

> L'année dernière, je suis allé(e) en Italie.
> *Last year, I went to Italy.*

See p.135 for more on the future tense and p.136-139 for more on the past tenses.

3) Words to describe <u>different days</u> can be used as adverbs.

hier	*yesterday*	avant-hier	*the day before yesterday*
aujourd'hui	*today*	après-demain	*the day after tomorrow*
demain	*tomorrow*		

Some adverbs describe location

<u>Adverbs of place</u> usually come <u>after</u> the <u>verb</u> in a phrase or sentence.

ici	*here*
là	*there*
là-bas	*over there*
partout	*everywhere*
quelque part	*somewhere*
loin	*far*
près	*near*

Elle court partout.	*She runs everywhere.*
Il marche loin chaque jour.	*He walks far every day.*
Je fais mes devoirs ici.	*I do my homework here.*
Il gare sa voiture là-bas.	*He parks his car over there.*

If there's a direct object, e.g. 'les devoirs', the adverb always goes after it.

Phrases can be used as adverbs

You can use <u>adverbial phrases</u> in the <u>same</u> way as <u>adverbs</u>. They often come at the <u>beginning</u> of a <u>sentence</u>.

Adverbial phrases are often really handy when you're giving your opinion on something.

> En général, les lapins sont mignons.
> *In general, rabbits are cute.*

par conséquent	*consequently*
en tout cas	*anyway*

tout à fait	*absolutely*
de toute façon	*anyway*

Adverbs — learn them <u>well</u>, revise them <u>often</u> and you'll go <u>far</u>...

Translate these sentences into **French**. Make sure you use the right adverbs.

1. I play tennis over there.

2. You (sing.) sing every day.

3. I normally go to town by bus.

4. They're (fem.) going over there.

5. Consequently, I like my subjects.

6. I like this new teacher now.

Words to Compare Actions

You can also use adverbs to compare how people do things, or to say they're the best or worst at something.

Comparative adverbs compare actions

1) '<u>Plus</u>' is used to say someone is doing something '<u>more...</u>' than someone else. Use '<u>que</u>' to say '<u>than</u>'.

'Plus' comes
before the adverb.

> Jean lit plus vite que Souad.   *Jean reads more quickly than Souad.*

2) You can use '<u>moins</u>' to say '<u>less...</u>' — use it in the <u>same</u> way as '<u>plus</u>'.

> Souad lit moins souvent que Danielle.   *Souad reads less often than Danielle.*

3) There are <u>two</u> expressions for when something is done <u>equally</u>.
   Use '<u>aussi...que</u>' to say '<u>as...as</u>' and '<u>autant que</u>' to say '<u>as much as</u>'.

> Danielle lit aussi vite que Jacques.   *Danielle reads as fast as Jacques.*

> Danielle lit autant que Jacques.   *Danielle reads as much as Jacques.*

Le plus — The most

1) '<u>Le plus...</u>' is a <u>superlative adverb</u> — you use it to
   say someone does something '<u>the most...</u>'.

> Vivienne chante le plus musicalement.
> *Vivienne sings the most musically.*

2) You always use '<u>le</u>' because adverbs <u>don't</u> have to <u>agree</u>
   with the <u>person</u> doing the action — they're describing the
   <u>action</u> itself. This is <u>different</u> from <u>adjectives</u>.

> Ils conduisent le plus dangereusement.
> *They drive the most dangerously.*

'Bien' and 'mal' are the odd ones out

1) '<u>Bien</u>' *(well)* and '<u>mal</u>' *(badly)* <u>don't</u> follow the rules. You just need to learn their
   <u>comparative</u> and <u>superlative</u> forms.

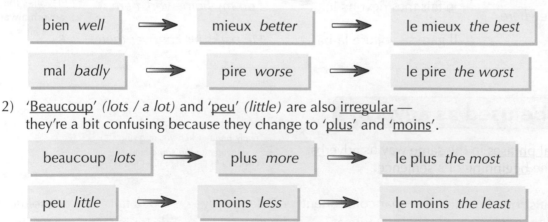

| bien *well* | ⟹ | mieux *better* | ⟹ | le mieux *the best* |
| mal *badly* | ⟹ | pire *worse* | ⟹ | le pire *the worst* |

2) '<u>Beaucoup</u>' *(lots / a lot)* and '<u>peu</u>' *(little)* are also <u>irregular</u> —
   they're a bit confusing because they change to '<u>plus</u>' and '<u>moins</u>'.

| beaucoup *lots* | ⟹ | plus *more* | ⟹ | le plus *the most* |
| peu *little* | ⟹ | moins *less* | ⟹ | le moins *the least* |

Use comparatives to make sure you write as well as possible...

Translate the words in brackets to fill in the gaps in these sentences.

1. Thomas joue du piano .... *(the best)*
2. François va à l'étranger .... *(the most frequently)*
3. Lucie court ...... Emmanuel. *(more than)*
4. Je regarde la télévision .... *(the least often)*
5. Tu ris ...... moi. *(as much as)*
6. Je chante ...... toi. *(worse than)*

Words to Say How Much

Intensifiers and quantifiers change the meaning of adjectives and adverbs slightly, so you can give more precise descriptions and impress the examiners.

Intensifiers strengthen what you're saying

1) Words such as 'trop' *(too)* and 'assez' *(quite)* can add <u>detail</u> to your sentences. They're called <u>intensifiers</u>.

trop	*too*	assez	*quite*
très	*very*	peu	*not very*

2) You can use them to <u>emphasise</u> an <u>adjective</u>, or to say <u>what</u> something's like or what you <u>think</u> of it.

3) <u>Intensifiers</u> can be used with <u>adjectives</u> — they always go <u>before</u> them.

Camille est trop sérieuse.
Camille is too serious.

La géographie est peu intéressante.
Geography is not very interesting.

4) You can use intensifiers with <u>adverbs</u>. They go <u>before</u> the adverb.

J'écris très vite. *I write very fast.*

Ils courent assez lentement. *They run quite slowly.*

Quantifiers help you say how many or how much

1) <u>Quantifiers</u> let you say roughly how much of something you have, without being specific, e.g. '<u>lots</u>' or '<u>not many</u>'.

trop de	*too many, too much*
beaucoup de	*lots of, many*
assez de	*enough*
peu de	*little, not much, not many*
un peu de	*a little, a little bit of*

2) Many are the <u>same</u> words as above, followed by '<u>de</u>'.

J'ai assez de chaussures. *I have enough shoes.*

3) With <u>quantifiers</u>, 'de' doesn't change to agree with the noun, but it changes to '<u>d</u>' before a <u>vowel</u>.

Nous avons peu d'argent. *We have little money.*

Il a trop d'examens. *He has too many exams.*

Adverbs can be intensifiers

1) Some <u>adverbs</u> can act as <u>intensifiers</u> as well. Here's a <u>list</u> to give you an idea:

particulièrement	*particularly*
vraiment	*really*
incroyablement	*incredibly*
énormément	*enormously*
exceptionnellement	*unusually*

Ce film est vraiment passionnant. *This film is really exciting.*

2) The <u>adjectives</u> still have to <u>agree</u> but the <u>adverbs</u> don't.

La montagne est incroyablement haute.
The mountain is incredibly high.

Intensifiers will make your French incredibly good...

Correct these sentences — find incorrectly written quantifiers / intensifiers and wrong genders / agreements.

1. Elle est trèse vive.

2. Ils ont une peu d'eau.

3. Le musicien est vraiment doué.

4. C'est assez d'intéressant.

5. Tu as beaucoup des chaussettes.

6. L'homme a trop chocolat.

Quick Questions

From time to time, I like to do some practice questions. Each question is based on the pages you've just read, so if there's something you're stuck on, go back and refresh your memory.

Quick Questions

1) Turn each of these adjectives into adverbs.
   a) facile
   b) précis
   c) heureux
   d) évident
   e) gentil
   f) complet
   g) clair
   h) stupide
   i) deuxième
   j) calme
   k) incroyable
   l) honnête

2) Translate these sentences into French.
   a) Zanna writes as much as Étienne.
   b) The black dog is the oldest.
   c) Chocolate cakes are the best.
   d) I play tennis better than my sister.

3) Use the correct form of 'bien', 'mal', 'peu' and 'beaucoup' to fill the gaps in these sentences.
   a) Julian joue du banjo .... que Claude.   (bien)
   b) Ayesha nage le .... dans la mer.   (mal)
   c) Lucie écrit le .... au collège.   (peu)
   d) Matthieu cuisine .... à la maison que Charles.   (beaucoup)

4) Fill in the gaps in these sentences with the correct adverb from the list.
   a) ...., nous sommes montées dans la tour.   demain
   b) Je vais .... au cinéma.   déjà
   c) ...., il se douche à six heures.   souvent
   d) Ils vont voyager ....   normalement
   e) Ton cadeau est .... arrivé.   hier

5) Use a French adverb to fill the gap in each of these sentences and match the English translation.
   a) Je l'ai vu ....   *I saw it over there.*
   b) Elle a perdu son portable ....   *She has lost her mobile phone somewhere.*
   c) Mon père a ses papiers ....   *My dad has his papers everywhere.*
   d) L'aéroport est assez .... de la ville.   *The airport is quite far from the town.*
   e) Venez ...., s'il vous plaît.   *Come here, please.*

6) Translate each of these adverbial phrases into English.
   a) en général
   b) tout à fait
   c) de temps en temps
   d) l'année prochaine
   e) en retard
   f) en tout cas
   g) la semaine dernière
   h) en même temps

7) Translate these quantifiers into English.
   a) un peu de
   b) assez de
   c) trop de
   d) peu de
   e) beaucoup de

8) Now use the quantifiers to fill in these gaps, using the clues in brackets to help you.
   a) Elles ont .... poissons.   (they don't need any more)
   b) Elle a .... argent.   (more than she needs)
   c) Mon ami a .... serpents.   (more than a few)
   d) Le magicien a eu .... succès.   (not much)

I, Me, You, We, Them

I'm sure you're thrilled by the idea of learning lots of pronouns. They're useful words though — they'll help your French sound less repetitive. You use them all the time in English — probably without realising...

Subject pronouns replace the subject of the sentence

1) <u>Subject pronouns</u> are words like '<u>I</u>' and '<u>you</u>':

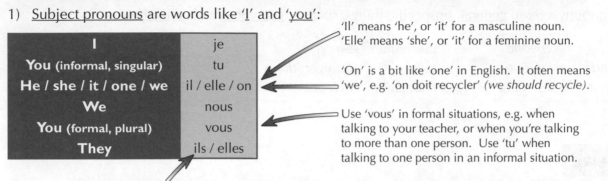

I	je
You (informal, singular)	tu
He / she / it / one / we	il / elle / on
We	nous
You (formal, plural)	vous
They	ils / elles

'Il' means 'he', or 'it' for a masculine noun. 'Elle' means 'she', or 'it' for a feminine noun.

'On' is a bit like 'one' in English. It often means 'we', e.g. 'on doit recycler' *(we should recycle)*.

Use 'vous' in formal situations, e.g. when talking to your teacher, or when you're talking to more than one person. Use 'tu' when talking to one person in an informal situation.

'Ils' is for a group of masculine nouns, or a mixture of masculine and feminine. 'Elles' is for a group of feminine nouns.

2) Subject pronouns can <u>replace</u> the <u>subject</u> (the person or thing <u>doing</u> the action in a sentence). Using them means you <u>don't</u> have to <u>keep saying</u> the same noun over and over again.

> Mon frère est musicien. Il est fana de musique rock.

> *My brother is a musician. He is a fan of rock music.*

'My brother' can be replaced with 'he' to sound less repetitive.

There are different pronouns for the direct object...

The <u>direct object</u> is the <u>person</u> or <u>thing</u> that the action is <u>being done to</u> — direct object pronouns <u>replace</u> the <u>noun</u> used as the direct object:

Remember, when 'le' or 'la' is followed by a word beginning with a vowel, it becomes 'l''.

Me	**You** (inf sing.)	**Him / her / it**	**Us**	**You** (formal, pl.)	**Them**
me	te	le / la	nous	vous	les

> Il voit son amie. ⟹ Il la voit.
> *He sees his friend.* ⟹ *He sees her.*

...and for the indirect object

<u>Indirect objects</u> are things that are <u>affected</u> by the <u>action</u> being done, but not <u>directly</u>. They often have '<u>to</u>' or '<u>for</u>' before them in English:

Me	**You** (informal singular)	**Him / her / it**	**Us**	**You** (formal, plural)	**Them**
me	te	lui	nous	vous	leur

> Il donne le cadeau à son amie.
> *He gives the present to his friend.*

> Il lui donne le cadeau.
> *He gives her the present.*

Pronouns are tricky, so make sure you learn this page...

Replace the words in bold with the correct pronoun from the brackets.

1. Hélène (lui / la / les) donne le livre **à son ami**.
2. **Emilie** (Elle / Tu / La) aime les chiens.
3. Tu peux (leur / elles / les) voir **les tortues**?
4. Avez-vous le livre? Non, elle (il / l' / le) a **le livre**.
5. **Moi et mon amie** (Nous / Elles / La) allons au cinéma.
6. Non, **les tortues** (les / elles / ils) ne sont pas ici.

Something, There, Any

There are even pronouns for unspecified things, e.g. 'everyone'. There are a couple of tricky little ones on this page too, so have a good read and then try the questions at the bottom of the page to test yourself.

Use indefinite pronouns for unspecified things

Indefinite pronouns refer to general, unspecific things, such as 'everyone' and 'something'.

quelqu'un	*someone*	plusieurs	*several*
tout le monde	*everyone*	tout	*all / everything*
quelque chose	*something*	chacun(e)	*each one*

Tout le monde aime le chocolat.
Everyone likes chocolate.

Y — There

1) 'Y' can mean 'there'. It replaces the noun for a location which has already been mentioned.

Elle va à la banque.   *She's going to the bank.* ➞ Elle y va.   *She's going there.*

This is often used to talk about weather. See p.63.

2) It's also used in some common expressions.

Allons-y!   *Let's do it! / Let's go!*   Vas-y!   *Do it! / Go on!*   Il y a...   *There is / There are...*

3) It means 'it' or 'them' after verbs followed by 'à'.

Je pense à l'idée.   *I'm thinking about the idea.* ➞ J'y pense.   *I'm thinking about it.*

En — Of it, of them, some, any

1) 'En' has a few meanings — depending on the context, it can mean 'of it', 'of them', 'some' or 'any'.

As-tu peur des guêpes? Oui, j'en ai peur.   *Are you scared of wasps? Yes, I'm scared of them.*

As-tu des oranges? Oui, j'en ai.   *Have you got any oranges? Yes, I have some.*

As-tu des poires? Non, je n'en ai pas.   *Have you got any pears? No, I don't have any.*

2) It means 'it' or 'them' after verbs followed by 'de'.

Tu as besoin d'aide.   *You need help.* ➞ Tu en as besoin.   *You need it.*

Indefinite pronouns? J'en ai besoin.

Choose the correct sentences and have a go at rewriting the ones that are wrong.
1. Il y a une cuisine si vous en avez besoin.
2. Toutes le monde sait que c'est vrai.
3. A-t-elle des livres? Oui, elle y a.
4. J'y réfléchis.
5. Tu connais le château? J'en suis allé(e).
6. Il y en a plusieurs.

Position and Order of Object Pronouns | Pronouns

To give you a break from learning pronouns, some of this page is about the order they go in instead...

Object pronouns always go before the verb

1) If there's <u>more than one pronoun</u>, they go in a <u>certain</u> order:

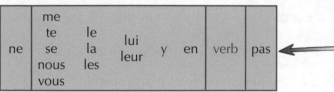

| ne | me
te
se
nous
vous | le
la
les | lui
leur | y | en | verb | pas |

In negative sentences, 'ne' goes before the object pronouns and 'pas' goes after the verb. See p.143 for more about negatives.

> Elle me le donne.
> *She gives it to me.*

2) With <u>compound</u> tenses, which use 'avoir' or 'être' before the main verb, the pronouns go <u>before both verbs</u>.

> Elle me l'a donné.   *She gave it to me.*

The perfect (p.136-137) and pluperfect (p.147) are compound tenses.

3) Certain verbs (vouloir, pouvoir, devoir) are often used with the <u>infinitive</u> of another verb. The <u>object pronouns</u> go <u>between</u> them.

> Je peux le lui donner.   *I can give it to him / to her.*

Use pronouns to emphasise who you're talking about

1) <u>Emphatic pronouns</u> make it really <u>clear</u> who you're talking about.

2) You need them...

Me	moi
You (informal singular)	toi
Him / her / one	lui / elle / soi
Us	nous
You (formal, plural)	vous
Them (m / f)	eux / elles

- if the words are <u>on their own</u>, or after '<u>c'est</u>'.

> Qui parle? Moi! C'est moi!   *Who's speaking? Me! It's me!*

- to <u>compare</u> people or things — the emphatic pronoun goes after 'que' *(than)*.

> Il est plus petit que toi.   *He's smaller than you.*

- for <u>giving instructions</u>. (See p.145 for more on how to do this.)

> Écoutez-moi!   *Listen to me!*

> Donne-lui ton portable!   *Give him your mobile!*

- <u>after prepositions</u> such as '<u>for</u>' or '<u>with</u>'.

> Tu le fais pour elle.   *You do it for her.*

> Je suis allé avec eux.   *I went with them.*

3) You can add '<u>-même</u>' on the end of an <u>emphatic pronoun</u> to say '<u>-self</u>'. Add an '<u>s</u>' if it's <u>plural</u> ('<u>-mêmes</u>').

> On le fait soi-même.   *One does it oneself.*

Don't forget that by itself, 'même' means 'even', e.g. 'même si' (even if).

> Elles l'ont écrit elles-mêmes.   *They wrote it themselves.*

Getting your pronouns in the right order will impress the examiner...

Unscramble the words in these sentences and then translate them into English.

1. donne. lui Il le
2. ai l' qui C'est écouté. moi
3. l' toi- Tu as écrit même.
4. nous. êtes allés Vous y avec
5. t' Elle dit. a
6. vais en parler. Je lui

Pronouns — Relative and Interrogative Pronouns

These help link bits of a sentence together so you're not stuck with lots of short phrases. Read on for more...

'Qui' and 'que' are relative pronouns

1) Relative pronouns introduce extra information about something you've mentioned in your sentence.

2) 'Qui' is used if you're referring to the subject of the sentence — the person or thing doing the action.

> La femme qui a volé le portefeuille.   *The woman who stole the wallet.*

3) 'Que' is used to refer to the object of the sentence — the person or thing that something's being done to.

> Le portefeuille que la femme a volé.   *The wallet that the woman stole.*

You can use 'qui' and 'que' to ask questions

See p.4-5 on questions.

1) In questions, 'qui' and 'que' are interrogative pronouns. 'Qui' means 'who', and 'que' means 'what'.

2) They can be the subject of a question. 'Que' changes to 'qu'est-ce qui' when it's the subject.

> Qui parle?   *Who is speaking?*   Qu'est-ce qui se passe?   *What is happening?*

3) You can also use 'qui' and 'que' as the object of the question.

> Qui connaissez-vous?   *Who do you know?*   Que savez-vous?   *What do you know?*

4) 'Qui' and 'que' can be used after prepositions (words such as 'with' or 'for' — see p.128-129). 'Que' changes to 'quoi' after a preposition but 'qui' stays the same.

> Tu parles avec qui?   *Who are you talking to?*   De quoi parles-tu?   *What are you talking about?*

Dont — Of which, whose, about which...

You only need to recognise 'dont' — you don't have to use it.

'Dont' has several meanings and can be used in different ways:

• To replace 'de' when 'de' is used with a verb. For example, 'parler de' (to talk about).

> L'araignée dont on a parlé.   *The spider we talked about. (The spider about which we talked.)*

• To say 'whose'. 'Dont' replaces the 'de' used to show possession.

> La chef dont les repas sont délicieux.
> *The chef whose meals are delicious.*

Literally 'The chef of whom the meals are delicious'.

• To talk about something that's part of a group.

> J'ai trois films dont un est une comédie.   *I've got three films, of which one is a comedy.*

Make sure you learn the difference between 'qui' and 'que'...

Translate these sentences, making sure you're using the correct pronoun.

1. The man who is sporty.   **3.** I've got five pencils which are red.   **5.** The car that she drives is slow.

2. The pizza that I like eating.   **4.** Who do you run with?   **6.** What are you thinking about?

Possessive and Demonstrative Pronouns | Pronouns

There are pronouns for showing who owns something, as well as for saying 'this one' and 'that one'.

Possessive pronouns show something belongs to someone

1) Possessive pronouns replace a noun that belongs to someone — they're words like 'mine' and 'yours'. You need to be able to recognise them for the exam — but you don't have to use them.

> Le ballon rouge est ici. C'est le mien. *The red ball is here. It's mine.*

2) They agree with the gender and number of the noun being replaced — have a look at the table:

	Mine	Yours (informal singular)	His / her / its	Our	Yours (formal, plural)	Their
Masculine singular	le mien	le tien	le sien	le nôtre	le vôtre	le leur
Feminine singular	la mienne	la tienne	la sienne	la nôtre	la vôtre	la leur
Plural (m / f)	les miens / miennes	les tiens / tiennes	les siens / siennes	les nôtres	les vôtres	les leurs

> Il y a trois bananes — ce sont les miennes. *There are three bananas — they're mine.*

Celui, celle, ceux, celles — This, these, those

> Don't worry — you don't have to use these, just know what they mean.

Masculine singular	celui
Feminine singular	celle
Masculine plural	ceux
Feminine plural	celles

1) 'Celui', 'celle', 'ceux' and 'celles' are demonstrative pronouns. They mean 'this', 'this one' 'those' or 'the one(s)'.

> J'aime ce gâteau, mais celui qu'on a mangé hier était meilleur. *I like this cake, but the one we ate yesterday was better.*

2) They're used with '-ci' on the end to mean 'this one' or 'this one here'. Adding '-là' on the end changes the meaning to 'that one' or 'that one there'.

> Il y a deux gâteaux. J'aime celui-ci, mais celui-là est meilleur. *There are two cakes. I like this one, but that one there is better.*

'Celui-ci' and 'celui-là' are used to point things out.

Ceci, cela, ça — This, that, that

1) 'Ceci', 'cela' and 'ça' are also demonstrative pronouns. They're used for more general things, not when you're pointing something out.

2) You need to be able to use these ones, so take a look at these examples:

> Ceci est intéressant. *This is interesting.*

> Cela n'est pas vrai! *That isn't true!*

> Je n'aime pas faire ça. *I don't like doing that.*

'Ça' is a more informal way to say 'that'.

Demonstrate your knowledge of pronouns in the task below...

Translate the words in brackets to fill in the gaps.

1. Le stylo là est .... *(yours, informal)*
2. Celle-là est .... *(hers)*
3. ...... n'est pas drôle! *(that)*
4. Ces chiens sont .... *(ours)*
5. Où as-tu vu ...... ? *(that)*
6. C'est .... *(yours, formal)*

Quick Questions

Pronouns may seem tricky at first, but with practice, they'll be a doddle. Speaking of practice, here are some more quick questions to be getting on with. See if you can do them without cheating.

1) For each of these sentences replace the underlined subject with the correct subject pronoun.
   a) <u>Amy</u> aime le chocolat.
   b) <u>Le chien</u> a mangé mes chaussures.
   c) <u>Les garçons</u> détestent les filles.
   d) <u>Mark</u> joue au football.
   e) <u>La souris</u> est sous la table.
   f) <u>Emma et Sarah</u> sont allées au cinéma.

2) For each of these sentences, fill in the correct French direct object pronoun.
   a) Je regarde la télévision. — Je .... regarde.
   b) Paul lit le journal. — Paul .... lit.
   c) Je déteste les chats et les chiens. — Je .... déteste.

3) Translate these indefinite pronouns into French.
   a) something   b) someone   c) everyone   d) each one   e) several

4) Use 'y' or 'en' to fill in the gaps in these sentences.
   a) On .... va s'il fait beau.
   b) Est-ce que tu peux m' .... acheter?
   c) Je n' .... vais pas à cause des monstres.
   d) Les vacances, parlons-............ .
   e) Tu .... es déjà allée?
   f) On ne s' .... sortira jamais!

5) Rearrange the French words to make a complete sentence, making sure the pronouns are in the correct order.
   a) le Nous pouvons leur donner.
   b) attend. t' Mon y père
   c) en Vous achetez. lui
   d) Elle y rencontre. les
   e) la offerte. lui avais Je
   f) téléphoné leur a hier. Il

6) Fill in the gaps in these sentences with 'qui', 'que' or 'qu'.'
   a) Le lapin .... tu as tué était délicieux.
   b) C'est un homme .... aime le poulet.
   c) Les sandales .... il porte avec des chaussettes sont laides.
   d) Le gendarme .... a volé ma voiture était vieux.

7) Translate each of these sentences into English.
   a) Le fermier a une poule dont les œufs sont parfaits.
   b) Il avait trois gâteaux dont deux étaient pleins de fruits.
   c) La maladie dont elle souffre lui donne un nez bleu.

8) Write the correct possessive pronouns in the gaps to complete the following sentences.
   a) Donnez-nous le mouton d'or — c'est ....
   b) Cette carotte longue est à Anaïs — c'est ....
   c) Passe-moi les saucisses — ce sont ....
   d) La veste rouge est à Larry — c'est ....

9) Translate these sentences into English.
   a) Je n'aime pas cette robe. Je préfère celle-là.
   b) As-tu lu ces livres? Celui-ci est très bon, mais celui-là est ennuyeux.
   c) J'aime les chiens, mais ceux-là sont vraiment méchants.

Joining Words

Conjunctions link words together. They help make your French sound more natural and more sophisticated, too — because nothing says sophistication like accurate French conjunctions...

Use conjunctions to make longer sentences

1) Here are some __common__ conjunctions:

mais	*but*	ou bien	*or else*	ainsi	*therefore / so*
et	*and*	puis	*then*	ensuite	*then / next*
ou	*or*	donc	*therefore / so*	ni...ni	*neither...nor*

A clause is a group of words that has a subject and a verb. For more on verbs, see p.131

2) Some conjunctions __link__ two __clauses__ or __sentences__ together. They make the sentences sound more __natural__.

J'ai un petit job.	**donc**	Je mets de l'argent de côté chaque mois.	J'ai un petit job, donc je mets de l'argent de côté chaque mois.
I have a part-time job.	**therefore**	*I save some money every month.*	*I have a part-time job, therefore I save some money every month.*

Les fleurs sont bleues claires et l'herbe est verte. *The flowers are light blue and the grass is green.*

3) 'Ou' (*or*) is used to give __more than one__ option.

Amélie veut être infirmière.	**ou**	Amélie veut être ingénieur.	Amélie veut être infirmière ou ingénieur.
Amélie wants to be a nurse.	**or**	*Amélie wants to be an engineer.*	*Amélie wants to be a nurse or an engineer.*

Make sure you don't get mixed up between 'ou' (or) and 'où' (where).

Some conjunctions add extra information to a sentence

1) Some conjunctions can also add __extra detail__ to a __sentence__.

2) Often these conjunctions introduce a __reason__ for something happening, a __contradiction__ or a __condition__.

parce que	*because*	pendant que	*while*	comme	*like*
puisque	*since*	par contre	*on the other hand*	y compris	*including*
quand	*when*	lorsque	*when / as soon as*	si	*if*
cependant	*however*	par exemple	*for example*	même si	*even if*

Je déteste le tabac parce que c'est mauvais pour la santé.
I hate smoking because it's bad for your health.

Conjunctions can go at the beginning of sentences, too.

Même s'ils sont délicieux, je ne les veux pas. *Even if they're delicious, I don't want them.*

Using conjunctions will make your sentences sound more natural...

Match the French conjunctions below with their English definitions.

1. therefore **3.** however **5.** including   **a)** pendant que **c)** y compris **e)** cependant
2. or else   **4.** while   **6.** since   **b)** ou bien   **d)** ainsi   **f)** puisque

Prepositions

Prepositions may not be much to look at, but size is no guarantee of power. These fellas are some of the most useful words in the French language — and, luckily, they're also some of the easiest to pronounce.

À — 'to', 'in' or 'at'

1) Prepositions are short words like 'to' and 'from'. They let you add extra information to sentences.

2) 'À' can mean 'to', 'in' or 'at'. It changes to 'au' and 'aux' when it's followed by 'le' and 'les' (see p.109).

Je vais au magasin.	Je suis à la maison.	J'habite aux États-Unis.
I'm going to the shop.	*I'm at home.*	*I live in the United States.*

You can't use 'à' for feminine countries, or countries beginning with a vowel. Look at the paragraph on 'en' below to find out more.

3) Some verbs are followed by 'à' when they go before a noun. Here are some examples:

(s')intéresser à	*to be interested in*	rendre visite à	*to visit (someone)*
jouer à	*to play (a game)*	penser à	*to think about*

'En' doesn't mean 'on'

See p.129 for the difference between 'en' and 'dans'.

1) 'En' can mean 'in' or 'to'. It's used instead of 'à' for feminine countries and countries starting with a vowel.

Clare habite en France.	*Clare lives in France.*	Je vais en Iran en mai.	*I'm going to Iran in May.*

2) You should use 'en' to say how long an action takes:

Elle a lu l'article en cinq minutes.	*She read the article in five minutes.*

For something happening in a specific season, month or year, you usually use 'en'.

3) 'En' is also used to describe what something is made of.

une veste en cuir	*a leather jacket*

De — 'of' or 'from'

French doesn't have apostrophes to show belonging — it uses 'de' instead.

1) 'De' often means 'of'.

une tasse de thé	*a cup of tea*	Je porte la robe de ma mère.	*I'm wearing my mother's dress.*

2) 'De' can also mean 'from'. It changes to 'du', 'de la' or 'des' when it's next to a definite article (see p.109).

Jean revient de la plage (f).	*Jean is coming back from the beach.*

3) Some verbs are followed by 'de' when they go before a noun. Learn these important examples:

Il s'agit de	*it's about*	avoir besoin de	*to need*	jouer de	*to play (an instrument)*
changer de	*to change*	avoir envie de	*to want*	partir de	*to leave*

Revise these prepositions carefully...

Translate these phrases into **French** using the correct prepositions.

1. I play football. **3.** It's about a young boy. **5.** I play the clarinet. **7.** He's going to the bank.

2. She visits Manu. **4.** a woollen jumper **6.** They live in France. **8.** You (sing, inf.) come from Wales.

Prepositions

Just for your enjoyment, here are some more handy prepositions...

Chez Natalie — At Natalie's

These prepositions are <u>really important</u> for your exams — try to learn them all.

avec	*with*	à cause de	*because of*	chez	*at the house of*
sans	*without*	au lieu de	*instead of*	grâce à	*thanks to*

Lots of prepositions relate to time

For more on telling the time, see p.2.

1) Prepositions of <u>time</u> tell you <u>when</u> something happened <u>in relation to</u> something else.

avant	*before*	depuis	*since / for*
après	*after*	jusqu'à	*until*
pour	*for*	pendant	*during / for*

> Florence a fini avant les autres.
> *Florence finished before the others.*

2) '<u>Pendant</u>', '<u>depuis</u>' and '<u>pour</u>' are a little bit tricky because they can all be translated as '<u>for</u>'.

3) Use '<u>pendant</u>' for actions that have <u>already happened</u>, or <u>will happen</u> in the future, but <u>aren't happening</u> now.

> J'ai travaillé dans un hôtel pendant deux ans.   *I worked in a hotel for two years.*

See p133 and p.139 for more about 'depuis'.

4) Use '<u>depuis</u>' for actions that <u>began in the past</u>, but are <u>still continuing</u> today.

> J'habite dans le Cumbria depuis trois mois.   *I've lived in Cumbria for three months.*

5) '<u>Pour</u>' (*for*) is used very similarly to in English, but with time, it's <u>only used</u> in the <u>future tense</u>.

> Martine va aller en Suisse pour une semaine.   *Martine is going to go to Switzerland for a week.*

Use prepositions to describe position

1) Some prepositions describe the <u>location</u> of <u>something</u> or <u>someone</u>.

sur	*on*	dans	*in*	devant	*in front of*
sous	*under*	derrière	*behind*	à côté de	*next to*

2) '<u>Dans</u>' (*in*) is normally used to describe when something is <u>actually inside</u> something else.

'En' also means 'in', but it can't mean 'inside' — see p.128.

> Mon passeport est dans ma valise.   *My passport is in my suitcase.*

3) '<u>Dans</u>' is also used to say how much time will pass before an event. E.g. 'dans cinq minutes' (*in five minutes*).

Show off your knowledge of prepositions in the exams...

Choose the correct preposition to complete each of the sentences below.

1. Je suis (à / chez) Paul avec Dima.

3. Je vais aller en vacances (*pendant / pour*) deux semaines.

2. Le magasin est (*sous / dans*) le pont.

4. Je travaille à la pharmacie (*depuis / pendant*) six mois.

Quick Questions

Since we've got through another set of pages, it's time to test what you've learnt. If you can nail your prepositions, your examiner will be very impressed — and you'll be well on your way to good marks.

Quick Questions

1) Translate these conjunctions into English.
   a) mais
   b) ni...ni...
   c) lorsque
   d) comme
   e) ou
   f) quand
   g) depuis que
   h) pendant que
   i) parce que
   j) ou bien
   k) après que
   l) puis

2) These sentences contain the wrong conjunctions. Rewrite them using 'comme', 'puis', 'si', 'et' or 'mais.' You can only use each conjunction once.
   a) Je voudrais une pomme <u>car</u> une poire.
   b) C'est mon anniversaire <u>lorsque</u> je ne sors pas.
   c) <u>Ou</u> tu manges le champignon, je te tuerai.
   d) Je me douche, <u>quand</u> je m'habille.
   e) <u>Ou bien</u> j'étais en retard, j'ai manqué le bus.

3) Fill in the gaps in these sentences using 'à', 'aux', 'dans' or 'en'.
   a) J'habite .... Marseille.
   b) Je vais .... Pays-Bas.
   c) La voiture est .... le garage.
   d) Il va .... Paris ce week-end.
   e) Je voudrais aller .... Afrique.
   f) Mon gilet est .... cuir.
   g) Les chaussures sont .... la boîte.
   h) Il est .... États-Unis en ce moment.

4) Translate the underlined prepositions in the following sentences into French.
   a) The dog is <u>under</u> the table.
   b) Your bag is <u>on</u> the chair.
   c) I left the house <u>without</u> my coat.
   d) I'm going swimming <u>after</u> school.
   e) I had lunch <u>at</u> Juliette's.
   f) We will leave at <u>around</u> midday.
   g) I went to the cinema <u>with</u> my friends.
   h) I arrived <u>before</u> you.

5) Translate the following sentences into English.
   a) Mon père est très fatigué car il travaille tout le temps.
   b) Prends un chocolat si tu veux.
   c) Je suis fatiguée donc je vais me coucher.
   d) Qu'est-ce que tu vas faire pendant les vacances?
   e) Je joue au football avec mon frère.

6) Complete the following sentences using the correct form of 'à' or 'de.'
   a) Je viens .... France.
   b) Je vais donner des bonbons .... enfants.
   c) On peut changer de l'argent .... banque.
   d) Je m'intéresse .... tennis de table.
   e) Le train part .... quai numéro trois.
   f) C'est la voiture .... ma mère.
   g) Je l'ai vu .... télévision.
   h) Luc joue .... guitare.
   i) Pierre joue .... piano.
   j) Ce livre est .... Michel.

7) Translate these sentences into French using the prepositions in brackets.
   a) The school is opposite the swimming pool.   (en face de)
   b) I stayed at home because of the rain.   (à cause de)
   c) There is a supermarket next to the park.   (à côté de)
   d) Aix-en-Provence is near Marseilles.   (près de)

Verbs in the Present Tense

You need to know the present tense inside out and back to front — it crops up all over the place. It also provides the foundations for some trickier tenses later on, so learning it properly now is well worth it.

Verbs are action words

1) A <u>verb</u> is a word that describes an <u>action</u>. 'Eat', 'sing' and 'jump' are all <u>examples</u> of English <u>verbs</u>.

2) <u>Actions</u> can take place in different <u>times</u> — or <u>tenses</u> — the past, present or future.

3) To put a verb in a <u>tense</u>, you need to know its <u>infinitive</u>, e.g. 'être' (*to be*). They're in this <u>form</u> in the <u>dictionary</u>.

The present describes something happening now

1) Use the <u>present tense</u> to describe something <u>that's occurring now</u>.

> *You can use the French present tense to say that something 'is happening' or that something 'happens'.*

| Je mange une pomme. | *I am eating an apple. / I eat an apple.* |

2) You should also use the <u>present tense</u> to describe something that <u>happens regularly</u>.

| Le lundi, je fais du jogging. | *I go jogging on Mondays.* |

3) <u>Verbs</u> in the present tense have <u>different endings</u>, but you always start by finding the verb's <u>stem</u>.

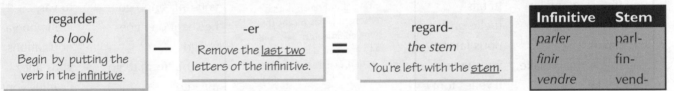

regarder		-er		regard-
to look		Remove the <u>last two</u> letters of the infinitive.		*the stem*
Begin by putting the verb in the <u>infinitive</u>.	**—**		**=**	You're left with the <u>stem</u>.

Infinitive	Stem
parler	*parl-*
finir	*fin-*
vendre	*vend-*

4) Then you add the correct <u>endings</u> to the <u>stem</u> (see below).

Add the right endings to the verb's stem

> The 'il'/'elle'/'on' form of the present tense for '-re' verbs doesn't have an ending.

In French, there are <u>three groups</u> of verbs — verbs ending in '<u>-er</u>', '<u>-ir</u>' and '<u>-re</u>':

'-er' endings

I	je	-e
you (inf. sing)	tu	-es
he/she/it/one	il/elle/on	-e
we	nous	-ons
you (pl., formal)	vous	-ez
they (m/f)	ils/elles	-ent

'-ir' endings

I	je	-is
you (inf. sing)	tu	-is
he/she/it/one	il/elle/on	-it
we	nous	-issons
you (pl., formal)	vous	-issez
they (m/f)	ils/elles	-issent

'-re' endings

I	je	-s
you (inf. sing)	tu	-s
he/she/it/one	il/elle/on	—
we	nous	-ons
you (pl., formal)	vous	-ez
they (m/f)	ils/elles	-ent

E.g. 'regarder'   (*to watch*)
'regard-'   (the stem)
+ '-ons'   ('nous' ending)
nous regardons   (we watch)

E.g. 'finir'   (*to finish*)
'fin-'   (the stem)
+ '-issent'   ('elles' ending)
elles finissent   (they finish)

E.g. 'vendre'   (*to sell*)
'vend-'   (the stem)
+ nothing   ('elle' ending)
elle vend   (she sells)

You can't avoid the present tense, so make sure you learn it...

Have a go putting the verbs below into the present tense. The subject is given in brackets.

1. parler (je)
2. établir (il)
3. remplir (nous)
4. répondre (tu)
5. entendre (elles)
6. commencer (vous)
7. perdre (vous)
8. grossir (ils)
9. allumer (je)
10. vendre (on)

Irregular Verbs in the Present Tense

Irregular verbs don't follow a set pattern. This means that there aren't any concrete rules you can apply to them. The only way to revise them properly is to learn them off by heart.

Some of the most useful verbs are irregular

Lots of <u>important verbs</u> are <u>irregular</u> — this means that they <u>don't follow</u> the usual rules. Here are some of the <u>most common</u> ones that you <u>need to know</u> for your exams:

avoir — to have

I have	j'ai
you (inf. sing.) have	tu as
he/she/it/one has	il/elle/on a
we have	nous avons
you (pl., formal) have	vous avez
they have	ils/elles ont

Make sure you know the difference between 'a' from 'avoir' and the preposition 'à' (see p.128).

être — to be

I am	je suis
you (inf. sing.) are	tu es
he/she/it/one is	il/elle/on est
we are	nous sommes
you (pl., formal) are	vous êtes
they are	ils/elles sont

faire — to make / do

I make	je fais
you (inf. sing.) make	tu fais
he/she/it/one makes	il/elle/on fait
we make	nous faisons
you (pl., formal) make	vous faites
they make	ils/elles font

Remember, you don't usually pronounce the last letter of a word in French if it's a consonant. This means that some endings (e.g. 'fais' and 'fait') are spelt differently but sound exactly the same.

aller — to go

I go	je vais
you (inf. sing.) go	tu vas
he/she/it/one goes	il/elle/on va
we go	nous allons
you (pl., formal) go	vous allez
they go	ils/elles vont

devoir — must / to have to

I must	je dois
you (inf. sing.) must	tu dois
he/she/it/one must	il/elle/on doit
we must	nous devons
you (pl., formal) must	vous devez
they must	ils/elles doivent

'Devoir' is a verb, but 'les devoirs' is a noun meaning 'homework'.

vouloir — to want

I want	je veux
you (inf. sing.) want	tu veux
he/she/it/one wants	il/elle/on veut
we want	nous voulons
you (pl., formal) want	vous voulez
they want	ils/elles veulent

pouvoir — to be able to / can

I can	je peux
you (inf. sing.) can	tu peux
he/she/it/one can	il/elle/on peut
we can	nous pouvons
you (pl., formal) can	vous pouvez
they can	ils/elles peuvent

Don't mix up 'savoir' and 'connaître' — 'savoir' means to know something. To say that you know somebody, use 'connaître'.

savoir — to know

I know	je sais
you (inf. sing.) know	tu sais
he/she/it/one knows	il/elle/on sait
we know	nous savons
you (pl., formal) know	vous savez
they know	ils/elles savent

These verbs crop up everywhere, so you need to learn them...

Each verb below is spelt incorrectly — using the verb tables above, rewrite each of the phrases correctly.

1. nous doivons
2. je veut
3. vous êtez
4. tu doix
5. elle vat
6. ils faient
7. elles pouvent
8. on saix
9. ils avont
10. nous faions

More About the Present Tense

There's still more to learn about the present tense — round off your knowledge with these last few points.

Verbs sometimes stay in their infinitive

1) When one verb <u>follows</u> another in a sentence or phrase, the <u>first verb</u> needs to be in the right form, but the <u>second verb</u> is <u>always</u> in the <u>infinitive</u>.

> Je veux aider les autres.   *I want to help other people.*
>
> 'Je veux' is the <u>first verb</u> in the sentence — it's in the <u>first person singular</u> form of the present tense. Because '<u>aider</u>' comes <u>directly after</u> 'je veux', it's in the <u>infinitive</u> form.

2) Some <u>verbs</u> can be followed <u>directly</u> by an <u>infinitive</u>, but a few verbs need a <u>preposition</u> in between.

commencer à	*to begin*	essayer de	*to try*
réussir à	*to succeed*	décider de	*to decide*
apprendre à	*to learn*	(s')arrêter de	*to stop (oneself)*
arriver à	*to succeed in / to manage*	menacer de	*to threaten*

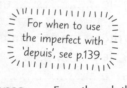

When 'venir de' is followed by an infinitive, its definition changes — it means 'to have just done something'.

'Arriver <u>à</u>' + an <u>infinitive</u> means 'to succeed' in doing something.

> J'essaie de faire plus de sport.   *I'm trying to do more sport.*

> J'apprends à conduire la voiture de mon père.   *I'm learning to drive my dad's car.*

'Depuis' can be used with the present tense

For when to use the imperfect with 'depuis', see p.139.

1) 'Depuis' means '<u>since</u>' or '<u>for</u>' (see p.129).

2) If the <u>action</u> you're talking about is <u>still going on</u> today, use the <u>present tense</u>.

> Il habite à Belfast depuis 1997.   *He's lived in Belfast since 1997.*

Even though the action began in the past, the person is still living in Belfast — so you need the present tense.

> Je travaille comme serveur depuis six mois.   *I've worked as a waiter for six months.*

Swap your subject and verb to form a question

Look at p.4-5 for more on how to ask questions.

1) To form a <u>question</u>, invert (or swap over) the <u>subject pronoun</u> and the <u>verb</u>.

2) When you do this, you <u>always</u> need to add a <u>hyphen</u> (-) between the <u>verb</u> and <u>subject pronoun</u>.

If the last letter of the verb and the first letter of the subject pronoun are both vowels, separate them by adding a 't'. This just makes it easier to pronounce — the 't' doesn't mean anything.

> Elle a mal au ventre. ⟹ A-t-elle mal au ventre?
>
> *She has a stomach ache.* ⟹ *Has she got a stomach ache?*

Remember that questions are important for your speaking exam...

Translate these sentences into **French**. Make sure you invert the subject and the verb for the questions.

1. I'm starting to understand.
2. I want to eat some pizza.
3. I've been studying French for 2 years.
4. I've played football since 1999.
5. Do you like plums?
6. Do you play the piano?

Quick Questions

It's essential you know how to use the present tense, so grab some paper and work through the questions below. Watch out for any irregular verbs — don't let them trip you up.

Quick Questions

1) How would you say the following in French?
   a) I speak   b) you listen   c) we play   d) they hate   e) he listens

2) Write out the correct form of each verb in the present tense. Make sure it matches the subject.
   a) agir — tu ....
   b) acheter — vous ....
   c) finir — je ....
   d) choisir — ils ....
   e) partager — vous ....
   f) punir — elles ....
   g) battre — on ....
   h) attendre — vous ....
   i) mordre — elle ....
   j) vendre — je ....

3) Complete the following sentences by adding the correct verb endings in the present tense.
   a) Il rest...... à la maison. Il regard...... le match de rugby à la télé.
   b) Nous habit...... au troisième étage. Tu mont...... par l'escalier ou par l'ascenseur.
   c) Je mang...... des sandwichs tous les jours à midi. Mes amis mang...... à la cantine.
   d) Vous parl...... à votre amie au téléphone. Elle te donn...... de ses nouvelles.

4) Fill in the gaps in the following sentences with the correct form of the verb in brackets.
   a) Il .... du thé.   (boire)
   b) Ils .... toujours ça.   (dire)
   c) Je .... un journal.   (lire)
   d) Vous .... la porte.   (ouvrir)
   e) Elle .... la fenêtre.   (fermer)
   f) Nous .... sauter haut.   (pouvoir)

5) Write in the present tense forms of the verbs below. Some are irregular.
   a) je .... **faire**
   b) tu .... **aller**
   c) il / elle / on .... **vouloir**
   d) nous .... **devoir**
   e) vous .... **faire**
   f) il / elle / on .... **faire**
   g) nous .... **aller**
   h) vous .... **vouloir**
   i) ils / elles .... **devoir**
   j) je .... **aller**

6) Fill in the gaps in the following sentences with the correct present tense form of être.
   a) Nous .... heureux.
   b) Mon père .... ingénieur.
   c) Les devoirs .... ennuyeux.
   d) Vous .... anglais.
   e) Je .... fatigué.
   f) Elle .... belle.

7) Translate these sentences into French using 'arriver à', 'commencer à' or 'apprendre à.'
   a) I'm learning to play the guitar.
   b) I never manage to eat my breakfast.
   c) It is starting to rain.
   d) I always manage to do my homework.

8) Write the correct form of the present tense of 'avoir' in the gaps.
   a) je ....
   b) tu ....
   c) il / elle ....
   d) nous ....
   e) vous ....
   f) ils / elles ....

9) Rearrange these statements to form questions.
   a) Elle mange de la viande.
   b) Tu vas en ville ce matin.
   c) Il aime le chocolat.
   d) Elle a un petit ami.
   e) Vous savez parler chinois.
   f) Nous devons partir bientôt.

Talking About the Future

You need to be able to talk about things that'll happen in the future, too. Don't worry — there are no crystal balls involved, just some good old-fashioned verb conjugations. Everything you need to know is on this page.

Use 'I'm going' + infinitive

The <u>immediate future</u> is the <u>easiest</u> future tense — it uses the <u>present tense</u> form of '<u>aller</u>' and <u>an infinitive</u>.

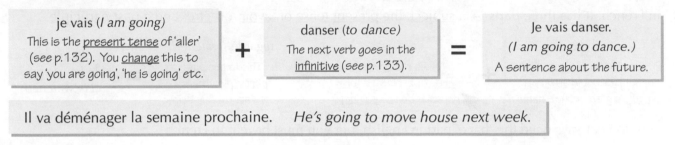

je vais (*I am going*)
This is the <u>present tense</u> of 'aller' (see p.132). You <u>change</u> this to say 'you are going', 'he is going' etc.

+

danser (*to dance*)
The next verb goes in the <u>infinitive</u> (see p.133).

=

Je vais danser.
(*I am going to dance.*)
A sentence about the future.

Il va déménager la semaine prochaine.   *He's going to move house next week.*

La forêt et ses animaux vont disparaître.   *The forest and its wildlife are going to disappear.*

'I will' — the proper future tense

1) Using the proper <u>future tense</u> in French is the same as saying '<u>will</u>' in English, e.g. 'I will bake'.

2) To form the <u>future tense</u>, you need find the verb's <u>infinitive</u> (see p.133) and add on the correct <u>endings</u>. The endings are <u>the same</u> for <u>all verbs</u>:

Future tense endings

I	je	-ai	we	nous	-ons
you (inf. sing.)	tu	-as	you (pl., formal)	vous	-ez
he/she/it/one	il/elle/on	-a	they (m/f)	ils/elles	-ont

These endings might look familiar because they're similar to the present tense of 'avoir'.

3) Verbs <u>ending</u> in '<u>-re</u>' are a bit different — you drop the <u>final '-e'</u> from the <u>infinitive</u> to get the stem.

Verb	Stem
regarder (*to look*)	regarder-
finir (*to finish*)	finir-
vendre (*to sell*)	vendr-

je regarderai   *I will look*

il finira   *he will finish*

Ils vendront les fruits.   *They will sell the fruit.*

Some important verbs have irregular stems

Some <u>important verbs</u> are <u>irregular</u> in the future tense — their <u>stems</u> aren't in the infinitive form:

Verb	Stem	Verb	Stem	Verb	Stem	Verb	Stem	Verb	Stem
aller	ir-	avoir	aur-	venir	viendr-	voir	verr-	pouvoir	pourr-
être	ser-	faire	fer-	vouloir	voudr-	devoir	devr-	recevoir	recev-

The stems are the only irregular part of these verbs — they all use the normal endings listed above.

You will need to use the future tense to access the highest marks...

Put each of these present tense phrases into the immediate and proper future tenses.

1. il va
2. j'ai
3. nous finissons
4. tu regardes
5. elles disent
6. vous faites
7. tu peux
8. elle vient
9. ils sont
10. on vend

Perfect Tense

Talking About the Past

Now you've got the hang of the present and future, it's time to look at the past — that's if you can remember what life was like before revision, of course. The perfect tense can be tricky, so read carefully.

Use the perfect tense for completed actions

1) Use the <u>perfect tense</u> to describe an action that <u>happened</u> and <u>finished</u> in the <u>past</u>.

2) In French, it has <u>three</u> parts — a <u>subject</u>, the <u>present tense</u> of 'avoir' or 'être' and a <u>past participle</u>.

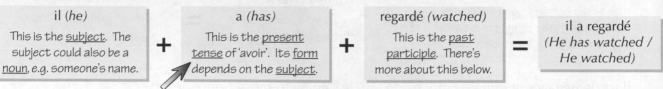

il *(he)*		a *(has)*		regardé *(watched)*		il a regardé
This is the <u>subject</u>. The subject could also be a <u>noun</u>, e.g. someone's name.	**+**	This is the <u>present tense</u> of 'avoir'. Its <u>form</u> depends on the <u>subject</u>.	**+**	This is the <u>past participle</u>. There's more about this below.	**=**	*(He has watched / He watched)*

3) You don't always need the 'have' part in English, but you <u>must</u> have it in French.

Most verbs use 'avoir' in the perfect tense

1) Use the <u>present tense</u> of 'avoir' to make the '<u>have</u>' part of the perfect tense:

avoir — to have

I have	j'ai
you (inf. sing.) have	tu as
he/she/it/one has	il/elle/on a
we have	nous avons
you (pl., formal) have	vous avez
they have	ils/elles ont

Elle a joué au rugby. *She has played rugby. / She played rugby.*

Nous avons acheté un chat. *We've bought a cat. / We bought a cat.*

Remember that the present tense of 'avoir' is irregular. See p.132 for other irregular verbs.

2) Get the <u>past participle</u> of a verb by finding the verb's <u>stem</u> (see p.131) and adding on the <u>correct ending</u>.

3) Verbs ending in '<u>-er</u>', '<u>-ir</u>' and '<u>-re</u>' each have a <u>different</u> ending:

Past participles

'-er' verbs	stem	+	é	e.g. regarder:	regard + é = regardé
'-ir' verbs	stem	+	i	e.g. finir:	fin + i = fini
'-re' verbs	stem	+	u	e.g. vendre:	vend + u = vendu

j'ai mangé *I have eaten / I ate*

il a perdu *he has lost / he lost*

Past participles agree with some direct objects

1) Past participles taking '<u>avoir</u>' only <u>change form</u> if there's a <u>direct object</u> or <u>direct object pronoun</u> (see p.121) <u>before</u> the verb.

2) When this happens, the <u>past participle</u> acts a bit like an adjective and <u>agrees</u> in <u>gender</u> and <u>number</u>.

Les voix (f) que j'ai entendues. *The voices that I heard.*

The object comes before the verb, so the verb needs to agree with it. 'Voix' is feminine and plural, so 'entendues' has an 'e' and an 's' on the end.

Don't move on until you're confident forming the perfect tense...

Change these phrases from the present to the perfect tense.

1. je parle
2. il élargit
3. nous finissons
4. tu vends
5. on grandit
6. elles mangent
7. je réponds
8. vous cherchez

Talking About the Past

That's the easiest bit done and dusted. Now it's time to sit up straight, roll up your sleeves and discover why the perfect tense isn't so perfect after all. It's nothing you can't handle — just take it one step at a time.

'Vivre' becomes 'vécu'

1) Some really important verbs have <u>irregular past participles</u>. This means that they <u>don't use</u> the same endings as regular verbs (see p.136).

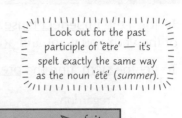
Look out for the past participle of 'être' — it's spelt exactly the same way as the noun 'été' (*summer*).

2) These are the most important ones:

Irregular past participles

avoir (*to have*)	⟹ eu	faire (*to do / make*)	⟹	fait
boire (*to drink*)	⟹ bu	lire (*to read*)	⟹	lu
connaître (*to know someone*)	⟹ connu	mettre (*to put*)	⟹	mis
devoir (*to have to / must*)	⟹ dû	prendre (*to take*)	⟹	pris
dire (*to say / tell*)	⟹ dit	savoir (*to know something*)	⟹	su
écrire (*to write*)	⟹ écrit	venir (*to come*)	⟹	venu
être (*to be*)	⟹ été	vivre (*to live*)	⟹	vécu

Some verbs take 'être' instead of 'avoir'

To see how the present tense of 'être' is formed, see p.132.

1) A few verbs use '<u>être</u>' instead of '<u>avoir</u>' to form the <u>perfect tense</u>.

aller	*to go*	partir	*to leave*	naître	*to be born*	tomber	*to fall*
venir	*to come*	sortir	*to go out*	mourir	*to die*	retourner	*to return*
revenir	*to come back*	descendre	*to go down*	devenir	*to become*	entrer	*to go in*
arriver	*to arrive*	monter	*to go up*	rester	*to stay*	rentrer	*to go back*

2) Just like '<u>avoir</u>' verbs, the correct <u>present tense form</u> of '<u>être</u>' is needed.

> Luc est allé à l'épicerie.   *Luc went to the grocer's.*

> Il s'est habillé.   *He got dressed.*

All reflexive verbs (see p.142) take 'être' in the perfect tense.

Verbs that take 'être' have to agree

1) <u>All verbs</u> that take 'être' in the perfect tense <u>have to agree</u> with their <u>subject</u>.

2) The <u>past participle</u> gains an '<u>s</u>' if the subject is <u>plural</u>, an '<u>e</u>' if it's <u>feminine</u> and '<u>es</u>' if it's <u>feminine and plural</u>.

When a reflexive verb is in the perfect tense, the present tense of 'être' always goes between the reflexive pronoun and the past participle.

> Les filles sont parties il y a une heure.   *The girls left an hour ago.*

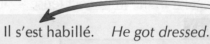

> Ils se sont lavés dans la rivière.   *They washed themselves in the river.*

It's vital you know which verbs take 'être' and which take 'avoir'...

Translate these phrases into **French**. Remember to check if they take 'être' or 'avoir'.

1. they (fem.) put
2. we've read
3. you (sing.) said
4. I went
5. she arrived
6. we had to
7. they (masc.) returned
8. I washed myself

Imperfect Tense | Talking About the Past

Like English, French has more than one past tense — time is a complicated notion, after all. The imperfect tense is really useful though, and dead easy to form. Once you've got the hang of it, you won't look back.

Get the stem from the present tense 'nous' form

1) To form the <u>imperfect tense</u>, you have to find <u>the stem</u> of the verb you want and <u>add on</u> the correct <u>ending</u>.

> The only verb that's irregular in the imperfect tense is 'être' (see below).

2) To get the <u>stem</u>, find the <u>present tense 'nous' form</u> of the verb and <u>take off</u> the '<u>-ons</u>'.

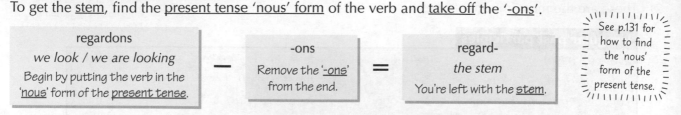

regardons		-ons		regard-
we look / we are looking				*the stem*
Begin by putting the verb in the 'nous' form of the <u>present tense</u>.	**−**	Remove the '<u>-ons</u>' from the end.	**=**	You're left with the <u>stem</u>.

> See p.131 for how to find the 'nous' form of the present tense.

3) When you've got the stem, <u>add on</u> the <u>ending</u> you need. The endings are <u>the same</u> for <u>all</u> verbs:

Imperfect tense endings		
I	je	-ais
you (inf. sing.)	tu	-ais
he/she/it/one	il/elle/on	-ait
we	nous	-ions
you (pl., formal)	vous	-iez
they (m/f)	ils/elles	-aient

Verb	Stem	Imperfect form	
aller	all-	j'	allais
attendre	attend-	tu	attendais
venir	ven-	il/elle/on	venait
faire	fais-	nous	faisions
parler	parl-	vous	parliez
avoir	av-	ils/elles	avaient

'Être', 'avoir' and 'faire' crop up a lot

1) Some verbs crop up more than others, so it's a good idea to become <u>really familiar</u> with them.

2) '<u>Être</u>' is <u>irregular</u> in the <u>imperfect tense</u> — its stem is '<u>ét-</u>'. It uses the regular endings, though:

être (to be)		
I	j'	étais
you (inf. sing.)	tu	étais
he/she/it/one	il/elle/on	était
we	nous	étions
you (pl., formal)	vous	étiez
they (m/f)	ils/elles	étaient

C'était formidable.	*It was great.*

'C'était' (*it was*) is the past tense of 'c'est' (*it is*). C'était + an adjective is useful for descriptions.

Nous étions épuisés.	*We were exhausted.*

La pièce était bondée.	*The room was overcrowded.*

3) All the other verbs are <u>regular</u> — they form the imperfect tense following the <u>normal rules</u>.

4) Make sure you learn '<u>avoir</u>' and '<u>faire</u>' inside out. They're used in lots of handy phrases.

Il y avait...	*There was... / There were...*

Il faisait froid.	*It was cold.*

You need to be able to form the imperfect tense...

These phrases are a mixture of the imperfect and present tense. List all of the phrases that are in the imperfect.

1. nous venions
2. j'attends
3. elle faisait
4. vous veniez
5. j'ai
6. nous remplissons
7. elles vendent
8. tu étais

Talking About the Past

Now you know how to form the imperfect tense, it's a good idea to learn when to use it.

Use the imperfect for descriptions in the past

1) Use the imperfect tense to describe something or someone in the past.

Il était une heure.   *It was one o'clock.*

Il faisait chaud.   *It was hot.*

Yann était heureux de la voir.   *Yann was happy to see her.*

2) The imperfect tense also describes an action that 'was happening' in the past. It's different to the perfect tense (see p.136) because the action isn't complete.

J'attendais le train.   *I was waiting for the train.*

The person hadn't finished waiting for the train, so the action is incomplete.

Il parlait à l'avocat.   *He was talking to the lawyer.*

Imperfect	Perfect
I was going	I went
she was running	she ran
we were waiting	we waited

3) When one action interrupts another action in a past tense sentence, the first action is left unfinished. This means that it needs to be in the imperfect tense.

Je lisais quand le téléphone a sonné.   *I was reading when the telephone rang.*

The second action is in the perfect tense.

Use the imperfect for what used to happen

You can use the imperfect for something you used to do regularly, or something you used to do in general.

You also use the underlined imperfect tense to talk about what you used to do.

J'allais au cinéma tous les jeudis.   *I used to go to the cinema every Thursday.*

This verb is describing someone.

Quand j'avais dix ans, je jouais de la guitare.   *When I was ten, I used to play the guitar.*

Imperfect + 'depuis' — had been

See p.133 for when to use 'depuis' with the present tense.

'Depuis' means 'for' or 'since' (see p.129). In French, when you want to say that something 'had been' happening 'for' or 'since' a certain time, use the imperfect tense with 'depuis'.

This could also mean 'It had been raining since two o'clock.'

Il pleuvait depuis deux heures.   *It had been raining for two hours.*

Il attendait depuis six heures du matin.   *He had been waiting since six o'clock in the morning.*

Learn the difference between the perfect and imperfect tenses...

Decide whether the verbs below should be in the perfect or the imperfect tense, then translate each sentence.

1. I ran.

2. They have eaten.

3. You (sing.) were laughing.

4. He was annoying .

5. It was terrifying.

6. She cried.

7. I used to play basketball.

8. I was tidying up when she arrived.

Quick Questions

Here's a double helping of questions about tenses. Remember — talking about what happened yesterday and what will happen tomorrow is just as important as talking about what's happening right now...

1) Give the immediate future tense of these verbs, matching the person given.
   a) choisir — je   ....
   b) manger — tu   ....
   c) finir — ils   ....
   d) prendre — vous   ....

2) Give the future tense forms of these verbs.
   a) arriver — elles   ....
   b) danser — on   ....
   c) jouer — il   ....
   d) vendre — nous   ....

3) Fill the gaps with the future tense forms of the verbs in brackets.
   a) Vous .... s'il est permis d'amener les chiens.   (ask)
   b) Je te .... toutes les informations.   (give)
   c) Ils .... un article pour le magazine.   (write)
   d) Je .... par raconter une histoire amusante.   (finish)
   e) On .... un bruit très fort.   (hear)

4) What do these mean in English...?
   a) j'irai
   b) nous serons
   c) vous pourrez
   d) ils diront
   e) il devra
   f) elle voudra
   g) tu auras
   h) je ferai

5) Put these verbs into the perfect tense using the correct form of 'avoir' and the past participle.
   a) je (jouer)
   b) tu (vendre)
   c) vous (regarder)
   d) elles (dormir)
   e) il (écouter)
   f) je (manger)
   g) nous (finir)
   h) on (choisir)

6) Write down the past participle of each of these verbs.
   a) lire   ....
   b) avoir   ....
   c) être   ....
   d) mourir   ....
   e) craindre   ....
   f) devoir   ....
   g) conduire   ....
   h) mettre   ....
   i) prendre   ....
   j) vouloir   ....
   k) savoir   ....
   l) naître   ....

7) Put the verbs in brackets in these sentences into the past tense. Make sure you use the correct verb ('avoir' or 'être'), and make any necessary agreements.
   a) Hier soir mon frère (sortir) avec ses amis et il (rentrer) très tard.
   b) Je (vouloir) te téléphoner mais je (devoir) faire mes devoirs.
   c) Le film (finir) à huit heures, donc nous (pouvoir) en voir un autre.
   d) Quand vous (aller) à la discothèque, est-ce que vous (mettre) votre robe rouge?

8) Add the agreements to the past participles of the 'être' verbs below.
   a) Vous (masc. plural) êtes né...... pendant que votre père regardait le football.
   b) Elle est parti...... quand elle a entendu la voix de son copain.
   c) Elles sont entré...... dans une pièce qui était pleine de poissons morts.
   d) Il est venu...... me voir samedi après-midi.

Quick Questions

Quick Questions

9) Fill in the gaps in these sentences with the perfect tense of the irregular verb in brackets.
   a) Il .... le nouveau roman de son écrivain préféré.   (lire)
   b) Tu .... la tasse sur la table.   (mettre)
   c) Les parents .... une carte postale à leurs enfants.   (écrire)
   d) Vous .... en France.   (vivre)

10) Put these verbs into the perfect tense using the correct form of 'être' and the past participle.
   a) je (aller)   c) elle (sortir)   e) nous (monter)   g) tu (tomber)
   b) vous (devenir)   d) il (arriver)   f) ils (partir)   h) elle (entrer)

11) Turn these present tense sentences into the imperfect tense.
   a) Il y a un concert au théâtre.
   b) C'est trop facile.
   c) Dans ma chambre, il y a un lit et une armoire.

12) Write the correct form of 'faire', 'être' or 'avoir' in the imperfect tense.
   a) Les moutons .... du bruit au centre-ville.
   b) Nous .... bronzées après nos vacances.
   c) Tu .... la grippe.
   d) Tu .... très content de recevoir le paquet.
   e) Je .... la vaisselle avec mes doigts de pied.
   f) J' .... un melon et une courgette.

13) Put the verbs in brackets into the imperfect tense.
   a) je (dormir)   c) il (sembler)   e) vous (écouter)
   b) ils (finir)   d) tu (devoir)   f) nous (rester)

14) In each of these sentences there are two verbs. Put the one describing the key event into
    the perfect tense and the one describing the ongoing situation into the imperfect tense.
   a) Susie (téléphoner) pendant que tu (faire) tes devoirs.
   b) Je (manger) tout le gâteau pendant que ma mère (regarder) la télévision.
   c) Il (se casser) la jambe pendant que nous (jouer) au rugby.
   d) Pendant que vous (ranger) votre chambre, je (prendre) une douche.

15) Translate these sentences into English. Write them all as 'was / were ...ing'.
   a) Je regardais la télévision.   c) Nous attendions le facteur.
   b) Elle dansait dans la salle à manger.   d) Ils faisaient beaucoup de bruit.

16) Translate these sentences into English. Write them all as 'used to ...'.
   a) Je jouais du piano.   d) Tu croyais au père Noël.
   b) On allait au parc tous les jours.   e) Vous achetiez le journal.
   c) Nous regardions les actualités.   f) Il mangeait des haricots verts.

Reflexive Verbs and Pronouns

It's time to say goodbye to tenses and hello to reflexive verbs and pronouns. Lots of people get put off by the sight of these, but they're actually really simple — you just need to know a few rules.

Reflexive verbs have an extra part

Reflexive pronouns	
myself	me
yourself (inf. sing.)	te
himself/herself/itself/oneself	se
ourselves	nous
yourselves (pl., formal)	vous
themselves, each other (m/f)	se

1) **Reflexive verbs** describe **actions** that you do **to yourself**, like washing yourself or getting yourself up.

2) These verbs look different because they've got an **extra part** — a **pronoun** that means '**self**', e.g. 'se laver' (*to wash oneself*). The pronoun **changes form** depending on **who's doing** the action.

You can tell which verbs are reflexive by checking in the dictionary. If you look up 'to get up', it'll say 'se lever'.

Je me lave — I wash myself / have a wash

1) Reflexive verbs can end in '**-er**', '**-ir**' or '**-re**'. They form **tenses** in exactly the **same way** as other verbs:

For the present, imperfect and proper future tenses, the reflexive pronoun always goes between the subject and the verb.

se laver — to wash oneself			
I wash myself	je me lave	*one washes oneself*	on se lave
you (inf. sing.) wash yourself	tu te laves	*we wash ourselves*	nous nous lavons
he washes himself	il se lave	*you (pl., formal) wash yourselves*	vous vous lavez
she washes herself	elle se lave	*they wash themselves*	ils/elles se lavent

2) Reflexive verbs are really important — you'll need to use them to talk about your **hobbies** and your **daily routine**. Make sure you learn these useful examples:

se lever	*to get up*	se détendre	*to relax*	s'appeler	*to be called*
se coucher	*to go to bed*	se sentir	*to feel*	se plaindre	*to complain*
s'intéresser à	*to be interested in*	se disputer	*to argue*	s'amuser	*to enjoy oneself*

Reflexives keep their pronouns in all tenses

1) All reflexive verbs take '**être**' in the **perfect tense** — this means they **agree** with their **subject** (see p.137).

2) The **reflexive pronoun** (me, te, se, etc.) always goes between the **subject** and the **present tense** of '**être**'.

Je me suis levé(e) à sept heures ce matin.
I got up at seven o'clock this morning.

Elle s'est lavée.
She washed herself.

'Lavée' has an 'e' on the end here because its subject (elle) is feminine.

3) In the **immediate future tense** (see p.135), the reflexive **infinitive** needs the **pronoun** that **matches its subject**.

Je vais me coucher. *I'm going to go to bed.*

Ils vont se plaindre. *They're going to complain.*

Learn to express yourself with reflexive verbs...

Translate these phrases into **French**. Make sure you put the reflexive pronouns in the right places.

1. we're going to bed
2. you (pl.) argue
3. they (fem.) get up
4. he's interested in
5. you (sing.) enjoyed yourself
6. I'm going to relax
7. she felt
8. we're going to complain

Negative Forms

You've reached the page where you can grumble and moan. Take all your stress out on two of the most important French words ever — 'ne' and 'pas'. (Don't worry — they're only little but they can take it.)

'ne...pas' — not

1) In English, you change a sentence to mean <u>the opposite</u> by adding '<u>not</u>'. In French, you add <u>two words</u> — '<u>ne</u>' and '<u>pas</u>'. They go <u>either side</u> of the <u>verb</u>.

> je suis d'accord ➡ je ne suis pas d'accord
> *I agree* ➡ *I do not agree*

'Suis' is the verb. The 'ne' goes before it, and the 'pas' goes after it.

2) For verbs in the <u>perfect tense</u> (see p.136-137), put the '<u>ne</u>' and '<u>pas</u>' <u>around</u> the bit of '<u>avoir</u>' or '<u>être</u>'.

> Je n'ai pas aimé l'école primaire.
> *I did not like the primary school.*

> Elle n'est pas encore arrivée.
> *She hasn't arrived yet.*

To say 'not yet', add the word 'encore' directly after the 'pas' in a normal negative sentence.

3) To make an <u>infinitive negative</u>, put the '<u>ne</u>' and the '<u>pas</u>' in <u>front</u> of it.

> Elle préfère ne pas parler de son talent.   *She prefers not to talk about her talent.*

'ne...jamais' — never

There are <u>other negatives</u> that work in the <u>same way</u> as 'ne...pas'. Here are some of the most common ones:

ne...jamais	*never*	ne...personne	*nobody / anyone*
ne...rien	*nothing*	ne...ni...ni	*neither...nor*
ne...plus	*no more / no longer*	ne...que	*only / nothing but*

These negatives position themselves around the verb in the same way as 'ne...pas'.

> Je ne vais plus à York.
> *I don't go to York any more.*

> Je ne vais jamais à York.
> *I never go to York.*

> Je ne vais ni à York ni à Belfast.
> *I neither go to York nor Belfast.*

> Il n'y a rien ici.
> *There's nothing here.*

> Je n'en ai plus.
> *I don't have any more of them.*

'Y' and 'en' always go between the 'ne' and the verb.

Articles change to 'de' after a negative

After a <u>negative</u>, indefinite articles ('<u>un</u> / <u>une</u>') and partitives ('<u>du</u>', '<u>de la</u>', '<u>des</u>' — see p.109) usually become '<u>de</u>'.

> Elle n'a plus de pain.   *She doesn't have any more bread.*

'Ne...que' doesn't follow this rule — it keeps its articles. E.g. 'Je n'ai que du café.' (*I only have coffee.*)

The 'de' is only shortened if the next word begins with a vowel or an 'h' which takes 'l'. E.g. 'd'animaux', 'd'hôpital'.

> Je ne veux pas d'argent.   *I don't want any money.*

This page should help you feel more positive about being negative...

Translate these sentences into **French** using the negative phrases you've learnt on this page.

1. I never eat meat.
2. He doesn't have a dog.
3. You (sing.) only drink water.
4. They (masc.) don't like anyone.
5. We don't live together any more.
6. You (pl.) never go there.

Conditional # Would, Could and Should

The conditional is a bit of a mish-mash of different tenses. On the plus side, you already know half of it...

The conditional = future stem + imperfect endings

1) The <u>conditional</u> is where you'd say '<u>would</u>', '<u>could</u>' or '<u>should</u>' in English.

2) Forming the conditional is pretty straightforward — you take the verb's <u>stem</u> from the <u>future tense</u> and add on the <u>endings</u> you learnt for the <u>imperfect tense</u>.

> Be careful — the imperfect 'je' ending ('-ais') sounds just like the future 'je' ending ('-ai'). This can make the future and conditional tenses tricky to tell apart.

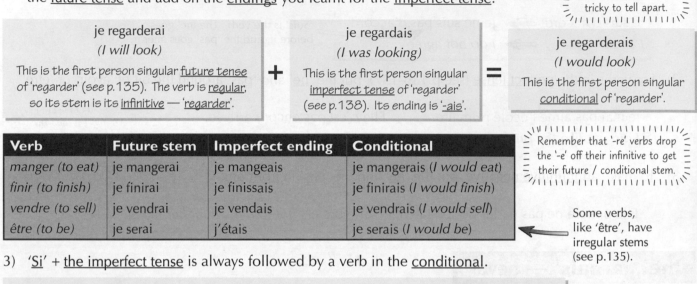

je regarderai
(I will look)

This is the first person singular <u>future tense</u> of 'regarder' (see p.135). The verb is <u>regular</u>, so its stem is its <u>infinitive</u> — 'regarder'.

+

je regardais
(I was looking)

This is the first person singular <u>imperfect tense</u> of 'regarder' (see p.138). Its ending is '<u>-ais</u>'.

=

je regarderais
(I would look)

This is the first person singular <u>conditional</u> of 'regarder'.

> Remember that '-re' verbs drop the '-e' off their infinitive to get their future / conditional stem.

Verb	Future stem	Imperfect ending	Conditional
manger (to eat)	je mangerai	je mangeais	je mangerais (*I would eat*)
finir (to finish)	je finirai	je finissais	je finirais (*I would finish*)
vendre (to sell)	je vendrai	je vendais	je vendrais (*I would sell*)
être (to be)	je serai	j'étais	je serais (*I would be*)

Some verbs, like 'être', have irregular stems (see p.135).

3) '<u>Si</u>' + <u>the imperfect tense</u> is always followed by a verb in the <u>conditional</u>.

> Si j'étais riche, je voyagerais autour du monde. *If I was rich, I'd travel around the world.*

4) To say '<u>could</u>' in French, use the conditional form of '<u>pouvoir</u>' (*to be able to*) followed by <u>an infinitive</u>. To say '<u>should</u>', use the conditional form of '<u>devoir</u>' (*to have to*) followed by <u>an infinitive</u>.

> Elle pourrait aller en France. *She could go to France.*

> Tu devrais te plaindre. *You should complain.*

'Je voudrais' and 'j'aimerais' — I would like

These two verbs are really useful in the <u>conditional</u> — you can use them lots in your <u>speaking assessment</u>:

vouloir (to want)	
I would like	je voudrais
you (inf. sing.) would like	tu voudrais
he/she/it/one would like	il/elle/on voudrait
we would like	nous voudrions
you (pl., formal) would like	vous voudriez
they (m/f) would like	ils/elles voudraient

> Both of these verbs are often followed by an infinitive. Look at p.133 for more on infinitives.

aimer (to like)	
I would like	j'aimerais
you (inf. sing.) would like	tu aimerais
he/she/it/one would like	il/elle/on aimerait
we would like	nous aimerions
you (pl., formal) would like	vous aimeriez
they (m/f) would like	ils/elles aimeraient

> Je voudrais aller à l'hôpital. *I'd like to go to the hospital.*

> J'aimerais du lait. *I would like some milk.*

The examiner would like to see that you can use the conditional...

Put these verbs into the conditional. The subject has been given to you in brackets.

1. améliorer (tu)   3. rendre (nous)   5. aller (elles)   7. être (on)   9. se laver (ils)

2. élargir (il)   4. faire (je)   6. venir (vous)   8. avoir (elle)   10. chercher (vous)

Giving Orders

Learning to order other people about is a pretty important life skill, whatever language you're speaking in. Putting verbs in their imperative lets you do just that — it's really useful and very easy to form.

Imperatives use the present tense

1) <u>Imperatives</u> are words that give an <u>order</u>. They tell someone <u>to do something</u>, or <u>suggest</u> doing something together, e.g. 'sit down' or 'let's eat'.

For when to choose 'tu' or 'vous', see p.121.

2) In French, imperatives are formed using the <u>present tense</u> of the '<u>tu</u>', '<u>nous</u>' and '<u>vous</u>' parts of a verb:

sortir — to go out

'tu' form (inf. sing.)	Sors!	*Get out!*
'nous' form	Sortons!	*Let's go out!*
'vous' form (form., pl.)	Sortez!	*Get out!*

'Tu', 'nous' and 'vous' never appear with an imperative verb — otherwise they would be in the present tense.

Vendons la voiture! *Let's sell the car!*

The 'nous' form always means 'let's'. The action has to involve you and someone else.

Écoutez ceci! *Listen to this!*

Take off the '-s' from the 'tu' form of '-er' verbs

Regular '-er' verbs in the 'tu' form of the present tense normally end in '-es', e.g. 'tu parles'.

1) Watch out for '<u>tu</u>' forms that <u>end</u> in '<u>-es</u>' — you have to <u>lose</u> the <u>final</u> '<u>-s</u>' from the <u>present tense</u>. This means you have to be careful with <u>regular</u> '<u>-er</u>' verbs.

Arrête de me parler! *Stop talking to me!*

Regarde Jean-Paul! *Look at Jean-Paul!*

2) Some verbs have <u>irregular</u> imperatives. They're nothing like the present tense, so you have to <u>learn</u> them.

Imperative form	être — to be	avoir — to have	savoir — to know	aller — to go
tu (*you inf. sing.*)	sois	aie	sache	va
nous (*we*)	soyons	ayons	sachons	allons
vous (*form., pl.*)	soyez	ayez	sachez	allez

Only the 'tu' form of 'aller' has an irregular imperative.

Negative imperatives use 'ne...pas' normally

1) To make an imperative verb <u>negative</u>, put '<u>ne</u>' <u>before</u> the verb and '<u>pas</u>' <u>after</u> it (see p.143).

Ne vendez pas la voiture! *Don't sell the car!*

N'écoute pas! *Don't listen!*

2) Imperative <u>reflexive verbs</u> (see p.142) have an <u>emphatic pronoun</u> (see p.123) that goes <u>after</u> the verb.

Tu te lèves. ⟹ Lève-toi!
You get up. ⟹ *Get up!*

The emphatic pronoun is always joined to the verb by a dash (-).

Tu ne te lèves pas. ⟹ Ne te lève pas!
You don't get up. ⟹ *Don't get up!*

3) When <u>reflexive verbs</u> are <u>imperative</u> and <u>negative</u>, they use their <u>normal pronouns</u> (me, te, etc.). The '<u>ne</u>' goes <u>before</u> the pronoun, and the '<u>pas</u>' goes <u>after</u> the verb.

It's imperative that you learn this page...

Translate these phrases into **French**.

1. Finish your homework! (pl.)
2. Let's organise a party!
3. Listen! (sing.)
4. Let's eat!
5. Don't go! (sing.)
6. Don't run! (pl.)
7. Go to bed! (sing.)
8. Don't argue! (pl.)

Quick Questions

This page covers lots of important grammar points, so don't move on until you can answer each question. After all, knowing how to use negatives and give commands could come in handy...

Quick Questions

1) Fill in the gaps using the correct form of the verb in brackets.
   a) Je .... — j'ai cassé votre vase.   (s'excuser)
   b) Nous .... toujours avec du savon particulier.   (se laver)
   c) Vous .... quand vous jouez au football?   (s'amuser)
   d) Les appartements .... de l'autre côté du supermarché.   (se trouver)
   e) J'ai laissé ma sœur à la maison, parce qu'elle .... mal. (se sentir)
   f) Mes deux petits frères ne .... jamais de bonne heure.   (se coucher)

2) Add any missing agreements to these reflexive verbs in the perfect tense.
   a) Ce matin, elle s'est levé...... à huit heures.
   b) Les élèves (masc.) se sont excusé...... après le cours.
   c) Il s'est lavé...... trois fois avant son rendez-vous avec la princesse.
   d) Elles se sont amusé...... au marché de Noël.

3) Rewrite these sentences to make them negative.
   a) Je mange de la viande.   c) Tu as beaucoup d'argent.
   b) Elle aime faire les courses.   d) Nous allons au cinéma ce soir.

4) Translate these sentences into French.
   a) I eat neither peas nor carrots.   c) We've never been to Russia.
   b) She only wears blue socks.   d) They (fem.) don't speak to anyone.

5) Put the verbs in brackets into the correct conditional form.
   a) Je .... rester à la maison.   (préférer)
   b) Nous .... voir un match de football.   (détester)
   c) Je .... au hockey, si je n'avais pas mal à la jambe. (jouer)
   d) Ils ont dit qu'ils .... le train cet après-midi. (prendre)

6) Translate these sentences into French.
   a) I'd go to the cinema, but I don't have enough money.
   b) We would like to help.
   c) You (informal singular) should arrive at 11 o'clock.

7) Put the missing verb into the French sentences. They all need to be in the imperative form.
   a) .... tes légumes ! (manger)   c) .... à la patinoire ! (aller — nous)
   b) .... gentils ! (être — vous)   d) .... tes devoirs !   (finir)

8) Change these French sentences into commands.
   a) Tu me prêtes ton stylo.   c) Vous vous taisez.   e) Vous vous asseyez.
   b) Tu te couches.   d) Tu t'assieds.   f) Nous nous levons.

9) Make these commands negative.
   a) Sors !   b) Allons à la piscine !   c) Couche-toi !   d) Lève-toi !

'Had done' and '-ing'

It may sound like a made-up tense, but the pluperfect tense is real and you need to know how to use it. It's fairly straightforward, though — plus, you can learn about the present participle once you're done...

J'avais fait — I had done

1) The pluperfect tense is for saying what you had done. It's like the perfect tense — which describes what you have done — but it deals with actions further in the past.

For more about the perfect tense, see p.136-137. For the imperfect tense, look at p.138-139.

2) The pluperfect is made up of the imperfect version of 'avoir' or 'être' + a past participle.

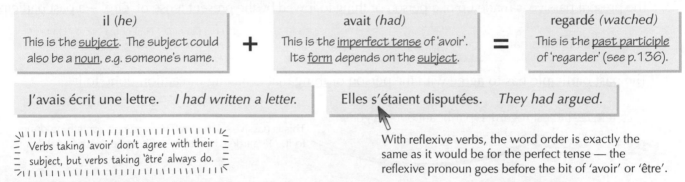

il (he)		avait (had)		regardé (watched)
This is the subject. The subject could also be a noun, e.g. someone's name.	**+**	This is the imperfect tense of 'avoir'. Its form depends on the subject.	**=**	This is the past participle of 'regarder' (see p.136).

J'avais écrit une lettre.   *I had written a letter.*

Elles s'étaient disputées.   *They had argued.*

Verbs taking 'avoir' don't agree with their subject, but verbs taking 'être' always do.

With reflexive verbs, the word order is exactly the same as it would be for the perfect tense — the reflexive pronoun goes before the bit of 'avoir' or 'être'.

'Doing', 'saying' and 'thinking' are present participles

1) To form the present participle, get the imperfect stem of the verb (see p.138) and add '-ant':

Verb	Imperfect stem	Present participle
regarder	regard-	regardant (*watching*)
finir	finiss-	finissant (*finishing*)
vendre	vend-	vendant (*selling*)
faire	fais-	faisant (*doing / making*)

Careful — to say you're 'doing something', e.g. 'I am laughing', you should use the present tense (see p.131-133). If you use two verbs together, e.g. 'I like writing', you use the present tense with an infinitive (see p.133).

Renonçant à l'idée, Clare est retournée chez elle.   *Giving up on the idea, Clare returned home.*

2) 'En' + the present participle usually means 'while doing something' or 'by doing something'.

Il lit le journal en déjeunant.   *He reads the paper whilst having lunch.*

3) Some verbs have irregular stems in the present participle.

Il a réussi en sachant les faits.   *He succeeded by knowing the facts.*

Verb	Irregular stem
avoir (*to have*)	ay-
être (*to be*)	ét-
savoir (*to know*)	sach-

Après avoir mangé — After having eaten

'Avoir' / 'être' + 'past participle' means 'having done something'. This is called the perfect infinitive.

Il regrette d'avoir joué au foot.
He regretted having played football.

Après être arrivées, elles...
After having arrived, they...

Because 'arriver' takes 'être', it needs to agree with its subject.

After having learnt the page, the student attempted the questions...

Translate the following phrases into **French**.

1. I had played
2. we had argued
3. you (pl.) had arrived
4. they (fem.) had been
5. whilst helping
6. by staying
7. after having left
8. after having destroyed

The Passive

Passive sentences in French are structured just like passive sentences in English, so they're dead easy to recognise. But for that theory to work, you need to know what all this passive stuff is in the first place...

La tasse est cassée — The cup is broken

1) In most sentences, there's a person or thing <u>doing</u> the verb, e.g. '<u>The fly bit</u> the man'. These are <u>active sentences</u>. In a <u>passive</u> sentence, the person or thing has <u>something done to it</u>, e.g. '<u>The man was bitten</u> by the fly'.

2) The <u>present passive</u> is made up of a <u>person</u> or <u>thing</u> followed by the <u>present tense</u> of '<u>être</u>' + a <u>past participle</u>.

> Il est aidé par ses parents.   *He is helped by his parents.*

See p.136-137 for more on past participles.

3) The <u>past participle</u> has to <u>agree</u> with the <u>person</u> or <u>thing</u> that is having the <u>action done to it</u>.

> La télé réalité est regardée par beaucoup de gens.
> *Reality TV is watched by lots of people.*

This is passive — 'reality TV' is having something done to it. 'Regardée' has an 'e' so it agrees with 'la télé'.

In the past and the future, only the 'être' bit changes

1) The passive voice can also be <u>in the past</u> or <u>future</u> tenses. It's formed in <u>the same way</u> as it is in <u>the present</u> — the only thing that changes is <u>the tense</u> of '<u>être</u>'.

2) The <u>perfect passive</u> tells you about a passive event that happened in the <u>past</u>. It's formed using the <u>perfect tense</u> of '<u>être</u>' (see p.137) and a <u>past participle</u>.

> La photo a été prise.   *The photo was taken.*

You don't need to be able to form the passive — you just have to know how to recognise it.

3) The <u>imperfect passive</u> describes a passive action that '<u>was happening</u>'. It's formed using the <u>imperfect tense</u> of '<u>être</u>' (see p.138) and a <u>past participle</u>.

> Le livre était écrit pendant la guerre.   *The book was being written during the war.*

4) The <u>future passive</u> is made up of the <u>future tense</u> of '<u>être</u>' and a <u>past participle</u>.

> Tu seras puni(e).   *You will be punished.*

> Les déchets seront jetés.   *The rubbish will be thrown away.*

French often uses 'on' instead of the passive

The passive isn't used very much in French. French speakers often use '<u>on</u>' (*one*) with an <u>active sentence</u> instead.

'One didn't see' sounds quite formal in English, so you'd normally use the passive voice instead.

> On n'a pas vu l'homme.   *One didn't see the man. / The man wasn't seen.*

Don't forget — you only need to be able to recognise the passive...

Identify all of the passive sentences in the list below.

1. L'homme est heurté par la voiture.
2. La fille perd le ballon.
3. Le match est intéressant.
4. La pomme sera mangée par mon oncle.
5. On regarde la télé.
6. La tasse a été cassée.

Impersonal Verbs and the Subjunctive

Right, you're almost there now — just one last page until you're granted grammar freedom. The subjunctive is the crème de la crème of French grammar, but luckily you only have to recognise it in the exam.

Impersonal verbs only work with 'il'

1) <u>Impersonal verbs</u> always have '<u>il</u>' as their subject. Here are some common examples:

il faut	*you must / it is necessary to*	il est nécessaire de	*it's necessary to*
il s'agit de	*it's about*	il pleut / neige	*it's raining / snowing*
il semble	*it seems*	il fait chaud / froid	*it's hot / cold*

Il s'agit d'une mère et ses enfants.   *It's about a mother and her children.*

Il semble injuste d'ignorer la décision.   *It seems unfair to ignore the decision.*

You often use impersonal verbs to talk about the weather. For more about the weather, see p.63.

2) '<u>Il faut</u>' and '<u>il est nécessaire de</u>' are always followed by an <u>infinitive</u>:

See p.133 to learn more about infinitives.

Il faut aller au lycée tous les jours.
You must go to school every day.

Il est nécessaire de lutter contre le réchauffement de la Terre.
It's necessary to fight against global warming.

You may see the subjunctive instead of the infinitive

1) The subjunctive <u>doesn't have</u> an <u>equivalent</u> in English. You don't have to use it in your exams, but you do have to be able to <u>recognise common verbs</u> in the subjunctive:

avoir	être	faire	aller	pouvoir
j'aie	je sois	je fasse	j'aille	je puisse
tu aies	tu sois	tu fasses	tu ailles	tu puisses
il/elle/on ait	il/elle/on soit	il/elle/on fasse	il/elle/on aille	il/elle/on puisse
nous ayons	nous soyons	nous fassions	nous allions	nous puissions
vous ayez	vous soyez	vous fassiez	vous alliez	vous puissiez
ils/elles aient	ils/elles soient	ils/elles fassent	ils/elles aillent	ils/elles puissent

The 'tu' and 'vous' forms of 'avoir' in the subjunctive are the same as its imperatives (see p.145). This is true for 'être', as well.

2) Certain expressions need to be followed by the <u>subjunctive</u> rather than the <u>infinitive</u>, e.g. 'il faut que'.

Il faut que tu fasses la vaisselle.
You must do the washing up.

Il est nécessaire que vous soyez sages.
It is necessary that you're well behaved.

The subjunctive is often used after 'que'.

3) The subjunctive is also used with certain <u>constructions</u>. '<u>Bien que</u>' (*although*), '<u>avant que</u>' (*before*) and '<u>pour que</u>' (*so that*) are all followed by the subjunctive too.

Bien qu'elle ait deux enfants...
Although she has two children...

Avant que vous partiez...
Before you leave...

Pour qu'il fasse ses devoirs...
So that he does his homework...

If I were you, I'd learn this page...

List all phrases below that contain a verb in the subjunctive.

1. Il faut commencer.	**3.** avant que vous alliez	**5.** Il me semble ridicule.	**7.** le stylo que j'ai
2. Le livre que tu veux.	**4.** bien qu'elles soient	**6.** pour que nous puissions	**8.** bien qu'il puisse

Quick Questions

Congrats on reaching the last page of quick questions. Don't speed through it just because it's at the end — give it the time and attention it deserves. You'll kick yourself if you don't revise properly...

Quick Questions

1) Write out the pluperfect forms of the infinitives below, matching the person given.
   a) décrire — il c) partir — elles e) dire — ils g) aller — nous
   b) faire — vous d) vivre — il f) manquer — tu h) manger — je

2) Translate these sentences into English.
   a) J'avais fini.
   b) Mark avait oublié de fermer la fenêtre.
   c) Michelle et Sharon étaient arrivées.
   d) Elle s'était levée à trois heures.
   e) Nous avions perdu la vache.
   f) J'étais parti en voiture.

3) Turn the infinitives below into present participles.
   a) vouloir d) finir g) perdre j) aller
   b) donner e) rendre h) faire k) savoir
   c) acheter f) choisir i) dire l) boire

4) Translate these sentences into English.
   a) Nous nous amusons en lisant des bandes dessinées.
   b) Il reste en forme en jouant au tennis.
   c) Je fais mes devoirs en regardant la télévision.

5) Translate these sentences into French, using the perfect infinitive.
   a) After having made the cake, I ate it. b) After having left, he came back.

6) The following sentences are in the passive. Translate them into English.
   a) Elle est renversée par l'escargot.
   b) Je suis regardé par tout le monde au théâtre.
   c) Louis et Carlo étaient punis par leur prof.
   d) Vous avez été trouvés par les pompiers.

7) What do the following phrases mean...?
   a) il faut c) il semble e) il neige
   b) il est nécessaire de d) il s'agit de f) il fait chaud

8) Match up the French sentences with the English translations.
   a) Il est étrange de voir ces choses. i) It's snowing today.
   b) Il neige aujourd'hui. ii) It is important to wear clothes.
   c) Il est important de porter de vêtements. iii) It's about a man and a cat.
   d) Il s'agit d'un homme et d'un chat. iv) It is strange to see these things.

9) For each of the sentences below, underline the verb in the subjunctive and translate the whole sentence into English.
   a) Il faut que tu viennes — tout le monde sera là !
   b) Il semble qu'ils aient une maladie grave.
   c) Je veux qu'il me dise toute l'histoire.
   d) Il est possible que nous y allions ce soir.

Revision Summary for Section Eleven

This section has a lot of information to take in, so practice is the only way to see if you know your stuff. After doing all those quick questions, there shouldn't be anything on this page that can trip you up.

Nouns and Articles (p.108-109) ☑

1) Underline all of the nouns in the following sentences.
   a) Elle aime manger des carottes.
   b) On parle français au Canada.
   c) J'ai reçu un cadeau de Marcel.
   d) Les cochons nagent.
   e) La poste est fermée.
   f) Samantha habite près de mon frère.

2) Write down the definite ('the'), indefinite ('a') and partitive ('some') articles for the following words.
   a) maison
   b) jeux
   c) chien
   d) journal
   e) chaussure
   f) soleil
   g) travail
   h) jeu

Adjectives and Adverbs (p.110-117) ☑

3) Using the word 'vert' with the correct endings, translate these phrases into French.
   a) the green mountain
   b) the green coat
   c) the green eyes
   d) the green apples
   e) the green man
   f) the green grass

4) Translate these sentences into French, using the adverb formed from the adjective in brackets:
   a) He swims well.   (bon)
   b) Eleanor sings badly.   (mauvais)

Pronouns (p.121-125) ☑

5) Write the correct subject pronouns in the gaps:
   a) Ma souris est malade. .... ne mange rien.
   b) Leur père est infirmier. .... travaille dans un hôpital.
   c) Ses parents sont en vacances. .... rentrent à la maison la semaine prochaine.

Joining Words (p.127) ☑

6) Fill in the gaps with the correct conjunction from the options in brackets:
   a) Je veux me promener, ... il pleut.   (ou, puis, mais)
   b) Il est resté à la maison .... il faisait mauvais.   (ou bien, et, pendant que)
   c) Je bois du chocolat chaud .... il fait froid.   (quand, puis, ou)
   d) J'aime mon cousin .... il est très sympa.   (mais, parce que, ou bien)
   e) Nous allons à l'école .... nous nous amusons.   (puis, si, lorsque)

Different Tenses and the Imperative (p.131-145) ☑

7) What do each of these sentences mean in English? Name the tense used in each one:
   a) Je mange un gâteau.
   b) J'ai mangé un gâteau.
   c) Je mangeais un gâteau.
   d) Je mangerai un gâteau.
   e) J'avais mangé un gâteau.
   f) Je mangerais un gâteau.

8) Change these sentences from the present tense into the imperative.
   a) Tu arrêtes de faire ça.
   b) Nous ne regardons pas le film.
   c) Vous êtes tranquille.
   d) Tu te lèves.
   e) Nous allons au Portugal.

The Passive and the Subjunctive (p.148-149) ☑

9) You hear this headline on the radio: "Un homme a été écrasé par deux chiens géants."
   Rewrite it so it's an active sentence, making sure you don't change the meaning.

10) Final question. What does the following sentence mean?
   "Il faut que tu apprennes toutes les choses dans ce livre avant de le jeter."

The Listening Exam

These pages are crammed full of advice to help you tackle your exams head on, so listen up.

There are four exams for GCSE French

1) Your AQA French GCSE is assessed by four separate exams — Listening, Speaking, Reading and Writing.

2) Each exam is worth 25% of your final mark. You'll get a grade between 1 and 9 (with 9 being the highest).

3) You won't sit all of the papers at the same time — you'll probably have your speaking exam a couple of weeks before the rest of your exams.

The Listening Exam has two sections

If you're sitting foundation tier papers, the format of your exams will be slightly different, but this advice will still be useful.

1) For the listening paper, you'll listen to various recordings of people speaking in French and answer questions on what you've heard.

2) The paper is 45 minutes long (including 5 minutes reading time) and is split into Section A and Section B.

3) Section A is the longer section — the questions are in English, and you'll write your answers in English. Section B is shorter, but the questions are in French and your answers need to be, too.

Read through the paper carefully at the start of the test

1) Before the recordings begin, you'll be given five minutes to read through the paper.

2) Use this time to read each question carefully. Some are multiple choice, and others require you to write some short answers — make sure you know what each one is asking you to do.

3) In particular, look at the questions in Section B, which are written in French. Try to work out what the questions mean. There's a list of exam-style French question words and phrases on the inside front cover of this book to help you prepare for this.

4) Reading the question titles, and the questions themselves, will give you a good idea of the topics you'll be asked about. This should help you predict what to listen out for.

5) You can write on the exam paper, so scribble down anything that might be useful.

Make notes while listening to the recordings

1) You'll hear each audio track twice, and then there'll be a pause for you to write down your answer.

2) While you're listening, it's a good idea to jot down a few details — e.g. dates, times, names or key words. But make sure you keep listening while you're writing down any notes.

3) Listen right to the end, even if you think you've got the answer — sometimes the person will change their mind or add an important detail at the end.

Listen to the speaker's tone, too — this will hint at their mood, e.g. angry or excited.

4) Don't worry if you can't understand every word that's being said — just listen carefully both times and try to pick out the vocabulary you need to answer the question.

Don't worry if you didn't quite catch the answer...

If you've heard a track twice, and you're still not sure of the answer, scribble one down anyway — you never know, it might be the right one. You may as well write something sensible just in case — it's worth a shot.

The Speaking Exam

The important thing to remember for the Speaking Exam is that no one is trying to catch you out.

The Speaking Exam has three parts

During your preparation time, you can make notes to take in with you for the first two tasks. You can't keep the notes for the general conversation.

1) Your <u>speaking exam</u> will be conducted and recorded by your <u>teacher</u>.

2) The exam is in <u>three parts</u>. Before you start, you'll get <u>12 minutes</u> to prepare for the <u>first two sections</u>:

① Role-play (2 min.)	② Photo Card (3 min.)	③ Conversation (5-7 min.)
You'll get a <u>card</u> with a <u>scenario</u> on it. It'll have <u>five bullet points</u> — <u>three</u> will be <u>notes</u> on what to say, in French. The '<u>!</u>' means you'll be asked an <u>unknown question</u>, and '<u>?</u>' shows you have to ask a question about the words next to it. See <u>p.5</u> for an example.	Before the exam, you'll receive a <u>photo</u> and <u>three questions</u> relating to it (look at the example on <u>p.20</u>). Your teacher will ask you the three questions that are on the photo card, as well as <u>two questions you haven't seen</u>.	You and your teacher will have a <u>conversation</u>. The conversation will be based on the theme that <u>you've</u> chosen, and the other theme that <u>hasn't been covered</u> on the photo card. You'll have to ask your teacher at least <u>one question</u>.

3) The role-play card will <u>tell you</u> if you should use 'tu', but <u>otherwise</u>, use '<u>vous</u>' to talk to your teacher.

Try to be imaginative with your answers

You need to find ways to <u>show off</u> the full extent of your <u>French knowledge</u>. You should try to:

1) Use a <u>range of tenses</u> — e.g. for a question on daily routine, think of when <u>something different</u> happens.

> Mais demain ce sera différent car je jouerai au snooker après les cours.   *But tomorrow it will be different because I will play snooker after lessons.*

If you can't remember a word, just say something suitable that you do know instead, e.g. swap 'snooker' for 'hockey', or 'mum' for 'sister'.

2) Talk about <u>other people</u>, not just yourself — it's fine to <u>make people up</u> if that helps.

> J'aime le foot, mais ma mère le déteste.   *I like football, but my mum hates it.*

3) Give loads of <u>opinions</u> and <u>reasons</u> for your opinions.

> À mon avis, il faut faire plus de recyclage parce qu'on produit trop de déchets.   *In my opinion, we must do more recycling because we produce too much rubbish.*

If you're really struggling, ask for help in French

1) If you get <u>really stuck</u> trying to think of a word or phrase, you can <u>ask for help</u> — as long as it's <u>in French</u>.

2) For example, if you <u>can't remember</u> how to say 'homework' in French, <u>ask</u> your teacher. You <u>won't</u> get any marks for <u>vocabulary</u> your teacher's <u>given</u> you though.

> Comment dit-on 'homework' en français?   *How do you say 'homework' in French?*

3) If you <u>don't hear something clearly</u>, just ask:

> Pouvez-vous répéter, s'il vous plaît?   *Could you repeat that, please?*

You could also ask this if you're desperately in need of time to think of an answer.

Making mistakes isn't the end of the world...

Don't panic if you make a mistake in the speaking exam — what's important is how you deal with it. You won't lose marks for correcting yourself, so show the examiner that you know where you went wrong.

The Reading Exam

The Reading Exam is split into three parts, so make sure you know what to do for each one.

Read the questions and texts carefully

1) The <u>higher tier</u> reading paper is <u>1 hour long</u>, and has <u>three sections</u>.

2) In Sections A and B, you'll be given a <u>variety of French texts</u> and then asked questions about them. The texts could include blog posts, emails, newspaper reports, adverts and literary texts. <u>Section A</u> has questions and answers <u>in English</u>, and <u>Section B</u> has questions and answers <u>in French</u>.

3) <u>Section C</u> is a <u>translation</u> question — you'll have to translate a short passage of text from French <u>into English</u>. See p.156 for more tips on tackling translation questions.

4) In Sections A and B, <u>scan through the text</u> first to <u>get an idea</u> of what it's about. Then read the <u>questions</u> that go with it carefully, making sure you understand <u>what information</u> you should be looking out for.

5) Next, <u>go back through the text</u>. You're not expected to understand every word, so don't get distracted by trying to work out what everything means — <u>focus</u> on finding the <u>information you need</u>.

The inside front cover of this book has a list of common French question words, phrases and instructions.

Don't give up if you don't understand something

1) Use the <u>context</u> of the text to help you understand what it might be saying. You might be able to find some clues in the <u>title of the text</u> or the <u>type of text</u>.

2) Knowing how to spot <u>different word types</u> (e.g. nouns, verbs) can help you work out what's happening in a sentence. See the <u>grammar section</u> (p.108-150) for more.

3) You can <u>guess</u> some French words that look or sound the <u>same as English</u> words, e.g. le problème — *problem*, la musique — *music*, dangereux — *dangerous*.

Look for words that look like ones you know, e.g. 'le sac de couchage'. 'Le sac' means 'bag', and 'se coucher' means 'to sleep', so you can guess it means 'sleeping bag'.

4) Be careful though — you might come across some '<u>false friends</u>'. These are French words that look like an English word, but have a <u>completely different meaning</u>:

sensible	*sensitive*	mince	*slim*	la journée	*day*	le car	*coach*	les affaires (f)	*things*
grand(e)	*big*	joli(e)	*pretty*	la cave	*cellar*	le médecin	*doctor*	les baskets (f)	*trainers*
large	*wide*	le genre	*type / kind*	la veste	*jacket*	le crayon	*pencil*	attendre	*to wait*

Keep an eye on the time

1) There are quite a few questions to get through in the reading exam, so you need to work at a <u>good speed</u>.

2) If you're having trouble with a particular question, you might want to <u>move on</u> and <u>come back to it later</u>.

3) Don't forget that the <u>last question</u> in the paper (Section C) is a <u>translation</u> — this is worth <u>more marks</u> than any other question, so you should leave <u>plenty of time</u> to tackle it.

4) Make sure you put an answer down for <u>every question</u> — lots of the questions are multiple choice, so even if you can't work out the answer, it's always worth putting down one of the options.

Familiarise yourself with the structure of the exam...

Don't forget, the questions in Section B will be in French. Don't panic if you don't understand them — search for any familiar vocabulary and use any answer lines or boxes to help you guess what you have to do.

The Writing Exam

The Writing Exam is a great way of showing off what you can do — try to use varied vocabulary, include a range of tenses, and pack in any clever expressions that you've learnt over the years.

There'll be three tasks in the Writing Exam

1) The <u>higher tier</u> writing paper is <u>1 hour and 15 minutes long</u> and has <u>three tasks</u>.

2) Each task is worth a <u>different number of marks</u>, so you should spend more time on the higher-mark tasks.

① Structured Task (16 marks)

There will be <u>two tasks</u> to choose from. You'll be asked to write <u>about 90 words</u> in French, based on <u>four bullet points</u>. Make sure you write about each bullet point and give some <u>opinions</u>.

② Open-ended Task (32 marks)

There will also be <u>two tasks</u> to choose from. You'll need to write <u>about 150 words</u> in French, based on <u>two bullet points</u>. This task is more creative — make sure you include some <u>opinions</u> with <u>reasons</u>.

③ Translation (12 marks)

You'll be given an <u>English passage</u> to translate <u>into French</u>. The passage could be on <u>any topic</u> you've studied. There's more advice for doing translations on p.156.

Read the instructions carefully, and spend some time planning

1) Read the instructions for questions 1 and 2 carefully — you'll need to make sure you cover <u>all of the bullet points</u>. You can often use <u>words from the question</u> in your answer too.

2) Spend a few minutes for each question <u>planning out</u> your answer. Decide <u>how</u> you're going to cover everything that's required and <u>in what order</u> you're going to write things.

Try to use varied vocab and a range of tenses.

3) Write the <u>best answer</u> you can, using the French <u>that you know</u> — it doesn't matter if it's not true.

Check through your work thoroughly

Checking your work is <u>really important</u> — even small mistakes can cost marks. Take a look at this checklist:

- Are all the <u>verbs</u> in the <u>right tense</u>?
  Demain, je travaillais dans le jardin. ✖   Demain, je travail**lerai** dans le jardin. ✓

- Are the <u>verb endings</u> correct?
  Tu n'aime pas les framboises? ✖   Tu n'aime**s** pas les framboises? ✓

- Do your <u>adjectives agree</u> with their nouns?
  La cuisine est grand. ✖   La cuisine est grand**e**. ✓

- Are your <u>adjectives</u> in the <u>right place</u>?
  Il porte une rose chemise. ✖   Il porte une chemise rose. ✓

- Do your <u>past participles</u> agree?
  Ils sont parti. ✖   Ils sont parti**s**. ✓

- Have you <u>spelt</u> everything correctly, including using the right <u>accents</u>?
  Ele ecoute de la music avec ma mere. ✖   E**ll**e **é**coute de la musi**que** avec ma m**è**re. ✓

All of the points on this checklist are covered in the grammar section — see p.108-150.

Make sure you cover every aspect of the tasks...

When you're nervous and stressed, it's easy to miss out something the question has asked you to do. For tasks one and two, try to write about the bullet points in order, and tick them off as you go along.

The Translation Tasks

When you're studying French, you do little bits of translation in your head all the time. For the translation questions, you just need to apply those skills — one sentence at a time — to a couple of short passages.

In the Reading Exam, you'll translate from French to English

1) The final question of the reading paper will ask you to translate a <u>short French passage</u> (about 50 words) <u>into English</u>. The passage will be on a <u>topic you've studied</u>, so most of the vocabulary should be familiar.

2) Here are some <u>top tips</u> for doing your translation:

   • Read the whole text <u>before you start</u>. Make some <u>notes in English</u> to remind you of the main ideas.

   • Translate the text <u>one sentence at a time</u>, rather than word by word — this will avoid any of the French word order being carried into the English.

Elle achète la pomme rouge.	*She buys the apple red.* ✘	*She buys the red apple.* ✔
Thomas l'a mangée.	*Thomas it ate.* ✘	*Thomas ate it.* ✔

   • Keep an eye out for <u>different tenses</u> — there will definitely be a variety in the passage.

   • <u>Read through</u> your translation to make sure it sounds <u>natural</u>. Some words and phrases don't translate literally, so you'll need to make sure that your sentences sound like <u>normal English</u>:

   Watch out for adverbs that might suggest a change in tense, e.g. hier — *yesterday*, demain — *tomorrow*, à l'avenir — *in the future*.

La semaine dernière, elle a fait du camping.	*The week last, she did some camping.* ✘	*Last week, she went camping.* ✔

3) Make sure you've translated <u>everything</u> from the original text — you'll lose marks if you miss something.

In the Writing Exam, you'll translate from English to French

1) In the writing paper, you will have to translate <u>a short English passage</u> (about 50 words) <u>into French</u>.

2) Here are <u>some ideas</u> for how you could approach the translation:

   • <u>Read</u> through the <u>whole text</u> before you get started so you know exactly what the text is about.

   • Tackle the passage <u>one sentence at a time</u> — work slowly and carefully through each one.

   • <u>Don't</u> translate things <u>literally</u> — think about what each English sentence means and try to write it in the <u>most French way</u> you know. Don't worry — the translation is likely to include similar sentences to the ones you've learnt.

   • Work on the <u>word order</u> — remember that most French adjectives follow the noun. If the sentence is <u>negative</u>, check you've got 'ne' in the <u>right place</u> (see p.143).

   Don't try to write a perfect translation first time — do it roughly first, and then write it up properly, crossing out any old drafts. Remember to keep an eye on the time.

3) Once you've got something that you're happy with, go back through and <u>check that you've covered everything</u> that was in the English.

4) Now <u>check</u> your French text thoroughly using the <u>list from p.155</u>.

Thankfully, none of that got lost in translation...

There's no set way of translating a text, but following these ideas is a good place to start. Now you've taken all this advice on board, it's time to test it out — have a go at tackling the practice papers.

Practice Exam

Once you've been through all the questions in this book, you should be starting to feel prepared for the final exams. As a last piece of preparation, here's a practice exam for you to have a go at. It's been designed to give you the best exam practice possible for the AQA Higher Tier papers. Good luck!

General Certificate of Secondary Education

GCSE French
Higher Tier

Listening Paper

Centre name						*CGP*
Centre number						**Practice Exam Paper**
Candidate number						**GCSE French**

Surname	
Other names	
Candidate signature	

Time Allowed: 40 minutes approximately
+ 5 minutes reading before the test.

Instructions:
- Write in black ink.
- You have 5 minutes at the start of the test during which you may read through the questions and make notes. Then start the recording.
- Answer **all** questions in the spaces provided.
- Answer the questions in Section A in **English**.
- Answer the questions in Section B in **French**.
- Give all the information you are asked for, and **write neatly**.

Advice:
- Before each new question, read through all the question parts and instructions carefully.
- Listen carefully to the recording. There will be a pause to allow you to reread the question, make notes or write down your answers.
- Listen to the recording again. There will be a pause to allow you to complete or check your answers.
- You may write at any point during the exam.
- Each item on the recording is repeated once.
- You are **not** allowed to ask questions or interrupt during the exam.

Information:
- The maximum mark for this paper is **50**.
- The number of marks for each question is shown in brackets.
- You are **not** allowed to use a dictionary.

Section A   Questions and answers in **English**

Restaurants

While listening to French radio, you hear these advertisements for restaurants.

Choose the correct answer and write the letter in the box.

1   When is the fixed-price menu available?

A	Saturdays
B	Every day except Saturday
C	In the evening

[1 mark]

2   What does the bistro claim about its service?

A	It's friendly.
B	It's excellent.
C	It's fast.

[1 mark]

3   What type of food does the restaurant serve?

A	French
B	Italian
C	Spanish

[1 mark]

4   What does the advert say about dining at the tapas bar?

A	You have to reserve a table.
B	You can't bring children.
C	Dogs are welcome.

[1 mark]

School Subjects

Whilst in a small café in France, you overhear a group of students talking about the subjects they study at school.

What is their opinion of the subjects?

Write **P** for a positive attitude. Write **N** for a negative attitude.
Write **P+N** for a positive and a negative attitude.

5

Subject 1	Subject 2

[2 marks]

6

Subject 1	Subject 2

[2 marks]

7

Subject 1	Subject 2

[2 marks]

Sport

You listen to a documentary about young people and their various sporting activities.

Complete the following sentences with the correct details in **English**.

8   Marc plays football for ....   *[1 mark]*

9   At the beach, Marc goes ....   *[1 mark]*

10   Sylvie is ....   *[1 mark]*

11   Lisa doesn't cycle anymore because ....   *[1 mark]*

Voluntary Work

You attend a charity fundraising event at your French partner school where a group of students has been asked to discuss their experiences of voluntary work with different organisations.

Complete the sentences in **English**.

Example   Florian worked with a charity in .... *the USA* ....

He spent .... *two months* .... working at a summer camp.

12   Sandrine spent a year in ....

She worked on a project that ....   *[2 marks]*

13   Zayna went to Peru to ....

She enjoyed the experience, but ....   *[2 marks]*

14   Kassim chose to volunteer ....

He said many of the residents ....   *[2 marks]*

Social Media

Your cousin sends you a podcast in French about how people use social media.

Answer the questions in **English**.

Example   According to Paul, why is social media so popular?

It's the easiest way to contact people.

15   How do Paul's friends use social media?

Give **two** details.

1. ....

2. .... *[2 marks]*

16   Why does Paul use his phone to send messages on social media?

Give **two** details.

1. ....

2. .... *[2 marks]*

17   Why is social media important for Paul's mother?

.... *[1 mark]*

Turn over

Healthy Lifestyle

Listen to this advice from a doctor speaking on French radio about exercise.

Choose the correct answer and write the letter in the box.

Answer **both** parts of the question.

18.1 The doctor says that people don't exercise because...

A	they find it boring.
B	they are too busy.
C	they need to rest.

[1 mark]

18.2 The doctor advises...

A	daily exercise.
B	joining a gym.
C	rethinking your daily routine.

[1 mark]

Answer **both** parts of the question.

19.1 Instead of driving to work, the doctor suggests...

A	walking or cycling.
B	jogging.
C	finding a new route.

[1 mark]

19.2 People who take the bus to work could...

A	alternate this with walking.
B	get off one stop earlier.
C	stop taking the bus and walk.

[1 mark]

School Life

During a video call with your pen friend, Chantal, you ask about her life at school.

Answer the questions in **English**.

20   What does Chantal say her school could improve?

    ....   *[1 mark]*

21   Who would this change benefit?

    ....   *[1 mark]*

Music

Two members of a well-known Swiss band have agreed to take part in an international radio debate to discuss their views on online music streaming.

For each speaker, write down **one** advantage and **one** disadvantage.

Answer in **English**.

22   Alain

Advantage	Disadvantage

[2 marks]

23   Michelle

Advantage	Disadvantage

[2 marks]

Christmas

You've asked your French classmate, Amélie, about her plans for Christmas.

Choose the correct answer and write the letter in the box.

24   Next week, Amélie is going to...

A	go into town to see the Christmas lights.
B	decorate the Christmas tree.
C	stay with her aunt for a few days.

[1 mark]

25   The present that Amélie hasn't bought yet is...

A	a horse figurine for her stepmother.
B	a train set for her little brother.
C	a necklace for her grandmother.

[1 mark]

A Story

Your teacher has asked you to listen to an extract from 'La Terre' by Émile Zola as part of a group project.

Choose the correct answer and write the letter in the box.

26.1   How many floors does the Baillehache house have?

A	One
B	Two
C	Three

[1 mark]

26.2   When is the street busy?

A	Weekdays
B	Saturdays
C	Everyday

[1 mark]

26.3   What does the narrator say about the study?

A	It's to the left of the hallway.
B	It's very spacious.
C	It overlooks the road.

[1 mark]

Section B   Questions and answers in **French**

Futures carrières

Quelques étudiants dans un programme d'échange ont enregistré un interview sur leurs projets pour l'avenir.

Choisissez **deux** phrases qui sont **vraies** et écrivez les bonnes lettres dans les cases.

27   Jamil veut être journaliste pour quelles raisons ?

A	Il aime écrire.
B	Les journalistes sont bien payés.
C	Ce métier lui permettra de voyager.
D	Il s'intéresse aux actualités.
E	Son cousin est journaliste.

[2 marks]

28   Pourquoi Marie a-t-elle changé d'avis à propos de ses projets pour l'avenir ?

A	Elle a perdu sa passion pour la peinture.
B	Ses parents n'aimaient pas son choix de métier.
C	Sa sœur est devenue avocate.
D	Elle voudrait un travail important.
E	Elle est douée pour les langues.

[2 marks]

Turn over

La météo

Écoutez la météo pour ces villes en Belgique.

Pour chaque bulletin, choisissez le temps correct de la liste et écrivez la lettre dans la case.

A	Ciel sans nuages
B	Pluie
C	Sec
D	Brume
E	Froid avec des vents forts

29	Bruges	
30	Bruxelles	
31	Charleroi	

[1 mark]

[1 mark]

[1 mark]

La Bretagne

Écoutez cette publicité faite par un office de tourisme en Bretagne.

Répondez aux questions en **français**.

32   Qu'est-ce qu'on peut faire aux Sept-Îles ?

....   *[1 mark]*

33   Citez **une** attraction historique mentionée par la publicité.

....   *[1 mark]*

34   Qu'est-ce que c'est qu'un kouign-amann ?

....   *[1 mark]*

END OF QUESTIONS

General Certificate of Secondary Education

GCSE French
Higher Tier

Speaking Paper

Centre name				
Centre number				
Candidate number				

CGP

Practice Exam Paper
GCSE French

Surname	
Other names	
Candidate signature	

Time Allowed: 10-12 minutes
+ 12 minutes of supervised preparation time.

Instructions to candidates
* Find a friend or parent to read the teacher's part for you.
* You will have **12 minutes** to prepare the Role-play and Photo Card tasks.
* You may make notes on a separate piece of paper during the preparation time.
* You must not use any notes during the General Conversation.
* The General Conversation will be on the following themes: Local, national, international and global areas of interest; Current and future study and employment.
* You must ask at least one question in the General Conversation.

Instructions to teachers
* It is essential that you give the student every opportunity to use the material they have prepared.
* You may alter the wording of the questions in response to the candidate's previous answers. However you must remember **not** to provide students with any key vocabulary.
* The candidate **must** ask you at least **one** question during the General Conversation.
* Candidates who have not yet asked you a question towards the end of the test must be prompted in **French** with the following question: 'Is there anything you want to ask me?'

Information
* The test consists of **3** tasks.
* You may only prepare the Role-play and Photo Card tasks during the preparation time.
* The Role-play task will last approximately 2 minutes.
* The Photo Card task will last approximately 3 minutes.
* The General Conversation will last between 5 and 7 minutes.
* You are **not** allowed to use a dictionary at any time during the preparation time or the test.

In the actual exam, you will nominate one theme to be asked about in the General Conversation. This will determine your Photo Card theme and the remaining theme for the General Conversation. For this practice paper, you don't need to nominate a theme as there's only one Photo Card, so the General Conversation will use the two themes not covered by the Photo Card.

ROLE-PLAY
CANDIDATE'S MATERIAL

Instructions to candidate

- Your teacher will play the role of your French friend. They will speak first.

- You should use *tu* to address your friend.

- **!** – means you will have to respond to something you have not prepared.

- **?** – means you will have to ask your friend a question.

Tu parles d'où tu habites avec ton ami(e) français(e).

- Description de ta maison (**deux** détails)

- **!**

- **?** Maison idéale

- Opinion de ta ville et **une** raison

- Habiter où dans le futur (**deux** détails)

PHOTO CARD
CANDIDATE'S MATERIAL

Instructions to candidate

- You should look carefully at the photo during the preparation time.

- You can make notes on a separate piece of paper.

- Your teacher will ask you questions about the photo and about topics related to **free-time activities**.

© iStock.com/Chad McDermott

You will be asked the three questions below and then **two more questions** which you haven't seen in the preparation time.

- Qu'est-ce qu'il y a sur la photo ?

- Est-ce que tu aimes le sport ? ... Pourquoi / pourquoi pas ?

- Quel serait ton week-end de rêve ?

Turn over

ROLE-PLAY
TEACHER'S MATERIAL

Instructions to teacher

- You begin the role-play.

- You should address the candidate as *tu*.

- You may alter the wording of the questions in response to the candidate's previous answers.

- Do not supply the candidate with key vocabulary.

Begin the role-play by using the introductory text below.

Introductory text: *Tu parles d'où tu habites avec ton ami(e) français(e). Moi, je suis ton ami(e).*

1 Ask the candidate what their house is like. (Elicit **two** details.)

Comment est ta maison ?

2 Allow the candidate to give **two** details about what their house is like.

! Ask the candidate who they live with.

Tu habites avec qui ?

3 Allow the candidate to say who he / she lives with.

Très bien.

? Allow the candidate to ask you a question about your ideal home.

Give an appropriate answer.

4 Ask the candidate what they think of their town and why.

Qu'est-ce que tu penses de ta ville ? ... Pourquoi ?

5 Allow the candidate to say what he / she thinks about their town and why.

Ask the candidate where they'd like to live in the future. (Elicit **two** details.)

Où voudrais-tu habiter dans le futur ?

PHOTO CARD & GENERAL CONVERSATION
TEACHER'S MATERIAL

Photo Card

Theme: Identity and culture   **Topic**: Free-time activities

This part of the test should last for a maximum of **three minutes**. It may be less than that for some candidates. Candidates can use any notes they made during the preparation time.

Begin the conversation by asking the candidate the first question from the list below. Then ask the remaining four questions in order. You can adapt the questions, but make sure they still have the same meaning. You can repeat or reword any questions that the candidate does not understand. Allow the candidate to develop their answers as much as possible.

- Qu'est-ce qu'il y a sur la photo ?

- Est-ce que tu aimes le sport ? ... Pourquoi / pourquoi pas ?

- Quel serait ton week-end de rêve ?

- Est-ce que tu penses que tu as assez de temps libre ? ... Pourquoi ?

- Qu'est-ce que tu as fait hier soir ?

General Conversation

The General Conversation follows the Photo Card task. It should last between **five** and **seven minutes**, and a similar amount of time should be spent on each theme. Sample questions for a range of topics within each theme have been provided below, but these lists are not exhaustive.

Themes and sample questions for the General Conversation:

Local, national, international and global areas of interest

1) Quel type de travail bénévole voudrais-tu faire ? Pourquoi ?

2) À ton avis, pourquoi le travail des associations caritatives est-t-il important ?

3) Qu'est-ce qu'on pourrait faire pour aider les sans-abri ?

4) Qu'est-ce qui se passera si on ne peut pas empêcher le réchauffement de la Terre ?

5) Que fais-tu pour rester en bonne forme ?

6) Qu'est-ce que tu as fait l'année dernière pendant les grandes vacances ?

Current and future study and employment

1) Qu'est-ce que tu penses des pressions scolaires ?

2) Comment est ton collège ?

3) Qu'est-ce que tu fais pendant une journée typique au collège ?

4) Aimerais-tu prendre une année sabbatique ? ... Pourquoi / pourquoi pas ?

5) Est-ce que tu voudrais travailler à l'étranger ? ... Pourquoi / pourquoi pas ?

6) Quel est ton travail de rêve ? Pourquoi ?

Remember — the candidate must ask you at least one question during the General Conversation. If, towards the end of the task, the candidate has not asked you a question, you must prompt them by asking, « Est-ce qu'il y a quelque chose que tu veux me demander ? »

General Certificate of Secondary Education

GCSE French
Higher Tier

Reading Paper

Centre name					
Centre number					
Candidate number					

Surname	
Other names	
Candidate signature	

CGP

Practice Exam Paper GCSE French

Time Allowed: 1 hour

Instructions
* Write in black ink.
* Answer **all** questions in the spaces provided.
* Answer the questions in Section A in **English**.
* Answer the questions in Section B in **French**.
* In Section C, translate the passage into **English**.
* Give all the information you are asked for, and **write neatly**.
* Cross out any rough work that you do not want to be marked.

Information
* The maximum mark for this paper is **60**.
* The number of marks for each question is shown in brackets.
* You are **not** allowed to use a dictionary.

Section A   Questions and answers in **English**

1   Directions

You have texted your French friend, Émile, to ask for directions to his house.

Read his reply and answer the questions in **English**.

Salut,

Ma maison n'est pas trop difficile à trouver, c'est près du parc au centre-ville. Va à l'école, et puis prends la première rue à droite. Après, prends la deuxième rue à gauche et continue tout droit. Passe devant la boulangerie et tourne à gauche. Ma maison est au bout de la rue Serpentine.

À bientôt !

Émile

< Messages   Options

1.1 After reaching the school, what is the next direction?

.... *[1 mark]*

1.2 What should you do when you pass the bakery?

.... *[1 mark]*

1.3 Where exactly is Émile's house on rue Serpentine?

.... *[1 mark]*

Turn over

2   **Unhealthy living**

A French newspaper has published the results of a survey which asked parents about their concerns surrounding young people and their lifestyle choices.

Read the summary of the results.

LES CHOIX DE MODE DE VIE & LES JEUNES

Aujourd'hui, il y a beaucoup d'inquiétudes concernant les jeunes et leurs choix de mode de vie. Les parents sentent fréquemment que leurs efforts pour aider leurs enfants sont arrêtés par la pression des camarades.

Selon un sondage qui a été fait par ce journal l'année dernière :

•   Environ 46% des parents savent que leurs enfants boivent de l'alcool régulièrement.
•   23% sont certains qu'ils fument.
•   17% ont des inquiétudes en ce qui concerne la consommation des drogues.
•   Seulement 8% ont dû consulter un médecin pour obtenir des conseils.

Suite aux résultats, une organisation caritative a décidé de collaborer avec certains collèges pour conseiller aux jeunes de s'occuper de leur santé.

What percentage of parents made the following statements?

2.1   They have been to a doctor to ask for advice.   ☐ %   *[1 mark]*

2.2   They are sure that their child smokes.   ☐ %   *[1 mark]*

2.3   They have concerns about drug-taking.   ☐ %

[1 mark]

2.4   What did parents say about their attempts to help their children?
Answer in **English**.

.... *[1 mark]*

3 **TV**

Read what these two people say in an online forum about a new Belgian TV programme where people are sent on blind dates.

Identify the people and write **E** (Étienne), **S** (Susi) or **E+S** (Étienne and Susi) in the boxes.

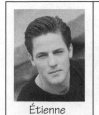
Étienne

J'ai regardé cette émission hier soir, et elle m'a beaucoup plu — tu dois la regarder ! Ce n'était pas une émission sérieuse, et pour moi les rendez-vous avec les femmes différentes étaient drôles. Malheureusement, aucune d'entre elles n'a choisi l'homme comme petit ami — c'était très triste pour lui.

Susi

Je pense que cette émission est complètement stupide. Il s'agit d'un homme qui dîne avec trois femmes pendant une semaine, mais elles sont présentées de manière très négative. Je n'ai aucune intention de la regarder à nouveau. Cependant, je suis désolée pour l'homme principal — je crois qu'il ne trouvera jamais de petite amie !

3.1 Who thought the programme was sexist? ☐ *[1 mark]*

3.2 Who found it funny? ☐ *[1 mark]*

3.3 Who felt sorry for the man in the programme? ☐ *[1 mark]*

3.4 Who would recommend the programme? ☐ *[1 mark]*

Turn over

4   **Poverty and homelessness**

You find an article online while researching for a school project on poverty in France.

Read the text and answer the questions in **English**.

La pauvreté en France a fortement augmenté à partir de 2008, et on estime que le pays compte environ 4,9 millions de pauvres. On est décrit comme 'pauvre' quand on gagne moins de 50% du revenu moyen national.

Le nombre de sans-abri à Paris est estimé à 28.000, et la plupart sont des hommes. L'approche de l'hiver est un souci majeur et le conseil municipal a permis aux deux associations caritatives d'ouvrir 20 centres de refuge — un dans chaque arrondissement — pour éviter le pire. Cependant, il reste beaucoup à faire pour trouver la meilleure solution à long terme.

4.1   What has happened to the number of poor people since 2008?

.... *[1 mark]*

4.2   What does the article say about the majority of homeless people in Paris?

.... *[1 mark]*

4.3   What is being done to help them?

.... *[1 mark]*

5 **Education post-16**

Your French friend has sent you an email about his plans for after his exams.

Read what he has to say, and write the correct letter in each box.

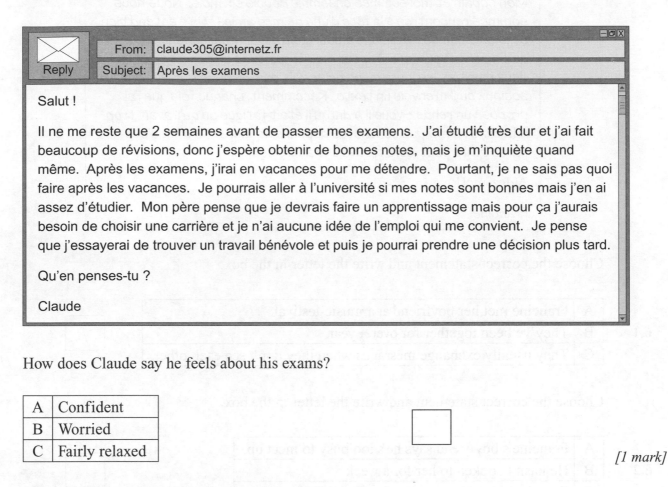

From: claude305@internetz.fr
Subject: Après les examens

Salut !

Il ne me reste que 2 semaines avant de passer mes examens. J'ai étudié très dur et j'ai fait beaucoup de révisions, donc j'espère obtenir de bonnes notes, mais je m'inquiète quand même. Après les examens, j'irai en vacances pour me détendre. Pourtant, je ne sais pas quoi faire après les vacances. Je pourrais aller à l'université si mes notes sont bonnes mais j'en ai assez d'étudier. Mon père pense que je devrais faire un apprentissage mais pour ça j'aurais besoin de choisir une carrière et je n'ai aucune idée de l'emploi qui me convient. Je pense que j'essayerai de trouver un travail bénévole et puis je pourrai prendre une décision plus tard.

Qu'en penses-tu ?

Claude

5.1 How does Claude say he feels about his exams?

A	Confident
B	Worried
C	Fairly relaxed

[1 mark]

5.2 Why doesn't Claude want to go to university?

A	He doesn't know which subject to study.
B	His marks won't be good enough.
C	He is fed up of studying.

[1 mark]

5.3 Why is Claude reluctant to do an apprenticeship?

A	He has no idea which career would suit him.
B	He wants to go back to school after summer.
C	It's what his father wants.

[1 mark]

5.4 What does Claude say he thinks he will do?

A	Find a job
B	Go to college later
C	Find some voluntary work

[1 mark]

Turn over

6 Relationships

You read this letter on the problem page in a French magazine.

> Mon copain et moi sommes ensemble depuis six mois. Nous nous sommes rencontrés à la fête d'une de mes amies. On s'entend bien et je suis tombée vraiment amoureuse de lui. Pourtant, je crois qu'il a perdu tout intérêt pour moi. D'habitude on se voit tous les deux jours, et les jours où on ne se voit pas, on parle sur les réseaux sociaux ou il m'envoie un texto. Récemment, chaque fois que j'ai proposé un rendez-vous il a dit qu'il était fatigué ou qu'il avait trop à faire. Il ne m'a pas contactée depuis cinq jours. Je m'inquiète parce qu'il a peut-être trouvé une autre copine.
>
> Aidez-moi !
>
> Francine

Choose the correct statement and write the letter in the box.

6.1

A	Francine met her boyfriend at a music festival.
B	They've been together for over a year.
C	They usually exchange messages when they don't see each other.

[1 mark]

Choose the correct statement and write the letter in the box.

6.2

A	Francine's boyfriend says he's too busy to meet up.
B	He hasn't spoken to her for a week.
C	Francine thinks he wants to break up with her.

[1 mark]

7   **A wedding**

Read this extract from 'Un Mariage' by Ernest Laut in which the narrator is talking about a wedding procession.

Answer the questions in **English**.

> Tout de suite, j'ai supposé qu'on allait célébrer le mariage du chef de quelque grosse industrie, et j'ai pensé que tous les ouvriers de l'usine s'étaient rassemblés là pour faire honneur au patron.
>
> Mais j'étais surpris lorsque, au lieu des brillants équipages que j'attendais, j'ai vu apparaître, au bout de la rue de la Mairie, le cortège* nuptial, cortège pédestre et simple s'il en a été : en tête les deux époux, derrière les quatre témoins — c'était tout !
>
> L'enthousiasme des spectateurs n'en a été pas moins bouillant, je dois le dire.
>
> Ils se sont rangés de chaque côté de la rue, et quand les époux ont passé entre ces deux haies** humaines, une immense clameur s'est élevée :
>
> — Vive la mariée !
>
> *cortège — procession
> **haies — hedges

7.1   Whose marriage did the narrator originally assume was taking place?

Write the correct letter in the box.

A	A local chef
B	The owner of the factory
C	A head of industry

[1 mark]

7.2   How many people were in the wedding procession?

.... [1 mark]

7.3   Where were the spectators standing?

.... [1 mark]

Turn over

8 Film reviews

While on holiday in Switzerland, you decide to go to the cinema.

Read the reviews of the films you could see.

La femme en blanc	J'ai beaucoup aimé ce film. C'est un film d'horreur qui raconte l'histoire d'une femme qui est morte le jour de son mariage. La tension était incroyable et je l'ai trouvé très effrayant.
Julian et Fabien	Le film explore le voyage de deux vrais jumeaux qui sont séparés à la naissance. Après leur première rencontre, ils s'embarquent dans beaucoup d'aventures ensemble. Le film est inspiré de faits réels mais c'était difficile de suivre l'histoire.
Bataille extra-terrestre	Il s'agit d'une armée de soldats extra-terrestres super-méchants qui essaye d'envahir la Terre, et d'un homme et sa famille qui dirigent la résistance. En général, je ne regarde pas les films de science fiction, mais ce film est spectaculaire avec beaucoup d'effets spéciaux.
Le crépuscule	Ce film décrit l'histoire d'une femme qui cherche l'homme qu'elle avait aimé quand elle était très jeune — son premier amour. Malheureusement, l'actrice principale m'a énervé parce qu'elle était trop sentimentale. Je ne le recommande pas.

Complete the grids below in **English** to indicate whether the opinions of the films were positive or negative and why.

Example

La femme en blanc	Opinion	Reason
	positive	very scary

8.1

Julian et Fabien	Opinion	Reason

[2 marks]

8.2

Bataille extra-terrestre	Opinion	Reason

[2 marks]

8.3

Le crépuscule	Opinion	Reason

[2 marks]

9 **Smartphones**

Your French friend sends you a link to this blog post on smartphones.

> Merci aux progrès technologiques, presque tout le monde possède un téléphone intelligent : un smartphone. Un smartphone n'est pas seulement un téléphone : on peut l'utiliser pour accéder à Internet, écouter de la musique, regarder les films, prendre des photos et même pour trouver son chemin — la liste est infinie. Pourtant, nous commençons à nous attacher trop à nos portables. Tout le monde connaît au moins une personne dans son entourage qui est 'accro' à son portable — une personne qui ne peut pas s'empêcher d'envoyer des messages pendant un repas et qui doit afficher chaque détail de leur vie sur les réseaux sociaux.
>
> Les scientifiques disent que les conséquences de cette addiction sont inquiétantes. Certaines personnes se sentent anxieux s'ils sont séparés de leur smartphone, et si on passe trop de temps à regarder les portables, la lumière de l'écran peut perturber le sommeil. La recommandation : nous devrions essayer de séparer la vie virtuelle et la vie réelle.

9.1   According to the blog post, a smartphone can also be used as...

A	a games console.
B	a torch.
C	a map.

[1 mark]

9.2   What actions does the blog post suggest are typical of smartphone addicts?
Give **two** details.

1. ....

2. .... *[2 marks]*

9.3   What do scientists say about smartphone screens?

.... *[1 mark]*

Turn over

Section B   Questions and answers in **French**

10   **Un email**

Lisez l'email de votre amie qui parle de sa journée dans les magasins.

Répondez aux questions en **français**.

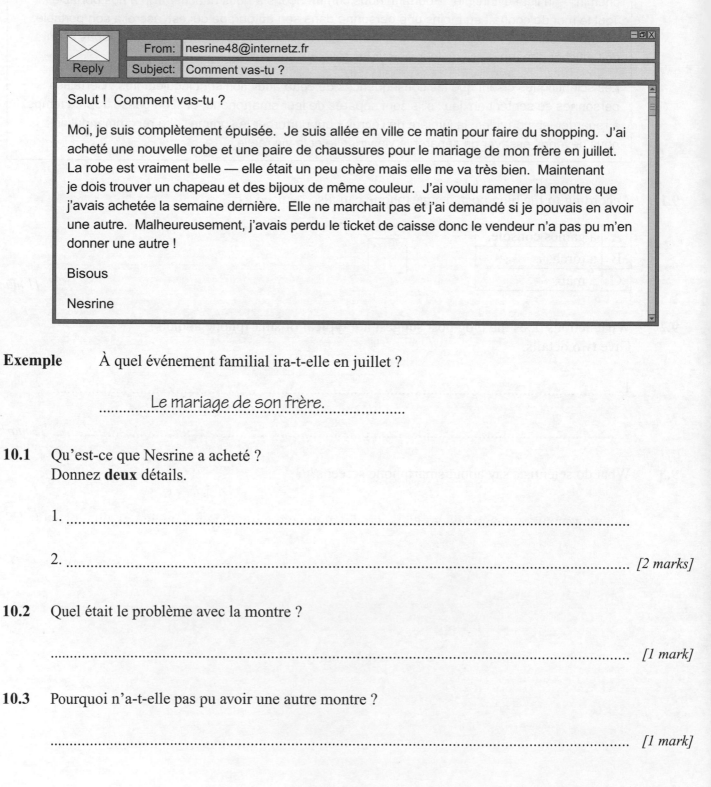

> From: nesrine48@internetz.fr
>
> Subject: Comment vas-tu ?
>
> Salut ! Comment vas-tu ?
>
> Moi, je suis complètement épuisée. Je suis allée en ville ce matin pour faire du shopping. J'ai acheté une nouvelle robe et une paire de chaussures pour le mariage de mon frère en juillet. La robe est vraiment belle — elle était un peu chère mais elle me va très bien. Maintenant je dois trouver un chapeau et des bijoux de même couleur. J'ai voulu ramener la montre que j'avais achetée la semaine dernière. Elle ne marchait pas et j'ai demandé si je pouvais en avoir une autre. Malheureusement, j'avais perdu le ticket de caisse donc le vendeur n'a pas pu m'en donner une autre !
>
> Bisous
>
> Nesrine

Exemple   À quel événement familial ira-t-elle en juillet ?

.... *Le mariage de son frère.* ....

10.1   Qu'est-ce que Nesrine a acheté ?
Donnez **deux** détails.

1. ....

2. .... *[2 marks]*

10.2   Quel était le problème avec la montre ?

.... *[1 mark]*

10.3   Pourquoi n'a-t-elle pas pu avoir une autre montre ?

.... *[1 mark]*

11   **L'environnement**

Ces jeunes ont écrit à une revue française pour faire des suggestions pour aider les gens à être plus écologiques.

Répondez aux questions en **français**.

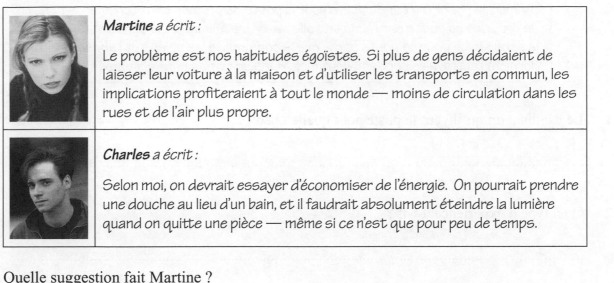

Martine a écrit :

Le problème est nos habitudes égoïstes. Si plus de gens décidaient de laisser leur voiture à la maison et d'utiliser les transports en commun, les implications profiteraient à tout le monde — moins de circulation dans les rues et de l'air plus propre.

Charles a écrit :

Selon moi, on devrait essayer d'économiser de l'énergie. On pourrait prendre une douche au lieu d'un bain, et il faudrait absolument éteindre la lumière quand on quitte une pièce — même si ce n'est que pour peu de temps.

11.1   Quelle suggestion fait Martine ?

.... *[1 mark]*

11.2   Qu'est-ce que Charles dit qu'il faut faire pour conserver de l'énergie ?
Donnez **deux** détails.

1. ....

2. .... *[2 marks]*

12 Demande d'emploi

Lisez ces demandes d'emploi.

Répondez aux questions en **français**.

> J'aimerais poser ma candidature pour le poste de promeneur de chiens. Je voudrais ce poste car j'aime travailler avec les animaux. Je pense que je serais idéal pour ce poste parce que je comprends les chiens et l'année dernière j'ai travaillé pendant deux mois dans un refuge pour animaux.

12.1 Le candidat dit qu'il veut le poste pour quelle raison ?

.... *[1 mark]*

12.2 Quel type d'expérience a-t-il ?

.... *[1 mark]*

> J'ai lu votre annonce et je voudrais poser ma candidature pour le poste de vendeuse dans le nouveau magasin de vêtements. Je m'intéresse beaucoup à la mode et je pense que je serais parfaite pour ce poste. Je suis travailleuse et j'ai déjà deux ans d'expérience comme vendeuse dans un petit magasin à Nantes.

12.3 Pourquoi veut-elle ce poste ?

.... *[1 mark]*

12.4 Quelle qualité possède-t-elle qui l'aiderait dans ce poste ?

.... *[1 mark]*

13   Pâques

Lisez cet article sur Pâques dans le magazine *Fêtes chouettes*.

Écrivez la bonne lettre dans chaque case.

> Pâques est une fête très importante en France. C'est la fête religieuse la plus importante de l'Église catholique mais de nombreuses coutumes destinées à célébrer le retour du printemps s'y attachent donc c'est important même pour les gens qui ne sont pas religieux. On offre des œufs de Pâques : un symbole de la naissance et du retour du printemps. Mais en France la légende dit que les œufs sont apportés par les cloches de Pâques. Le jeudi avant le dimanche de Pâques, les cloches des églises sont silencieuses et on dit aux enfants que les cloches sont parties pour Rome mais elles reviennent le jour de Pâques avec des œufs.

13.1   Pourquoi Pâques est-il aussi important pour les gens qui ne sont pas religieux ?

A	Ils peuvent manger beaucoup d'œufs.
B	La fête représente le retour du printemps.
C	Ils aiment les coutumes.

[1 mark]

13.2   D'où viennent les œufs de Pâques en France ?

A	Les cloches
B	Le lapin de Pâques
C	L'église

[1 mark]

13.3   Qu'est-ce qui se passe dans les églises avant le dimanche de Pâques ?

A	Les cloches sont nettoyées.
B	Les cloches sont rendues silencieuses.
C	On sonne les cloches.

[1 mark]

14 **Les trois mousquetaires**

Lisez cet extrait du livre '*Les trois mousquetaires*' d'Alexandre Dumas.

Complétez le texte suivant avec les mots de la liste ci-dessous.

Écrivez la bonne lettre dans chaque case.

Mon fils, avait dit le gentilhomme gascon, mon fils, ce cheval est né dans la maison de votre

père, il y a treize ans, et y est resté depuis ce temps-là, ce qui doit vous porter à l'aimer. Ne le

[E] jamais, laissez-le mourir tranquillement et [ ] de vieillesse.

À la cour, a continué M. d'Artagnan père, si toutefois vous avez l'honneur d'y aller, soutenez

dignement votre [ ] de gentilhomme, qui a été porté dignement par vos ancêtres depuis

plus de cinq cents ans. C'est par son courage qu'un gentilhomme fait son chemin aujourd'hui.

Quiconque tremble une seconde laisse peut-être échapper la chance que la fortune lui tendait.

Vous êtes [ ] , vous devez être brave pour deux raisons : la première, c'est que vous

[ ] Gascon, et la seconde, c'est que vous êtes mon fils. Ne craignez pas les occasions et

cherchez les aventures.

A	chemin
B	honorablement
C	jeune
D	êtes
E	**vendez**
F	nom
G	carrière

[4 marks]

Section C   Translation into **English**

15   You see this post on a website for holiday reviews.

Translate it into **English**.

> Quelles terribles vacances ! Je viens de revenir de mon voyage en Allemagne et c'était vraiment affreux. Je suis allé à Berlin avec mes cousins. La ville était incroyable, mais l'hôtel où nous sommes restés était désagréable. Il n'y avait pas d'eau chaude ! Si je retournais un jour à Berlin, je trouverais un autre logement.

[9 marks]

....

....

....

....

....

....

....

....

....

....

END OF QUESTIONS

General Certificate of Secondary Education

GCSE French
Higher Tier

Writing Paper

Centre name					
Centre number					
Candidate number					

Surname
Other names
Candidate signature

CGP

Practice Exam Paper
GCSE French

Time Allowed: 1 hour 15 minutes

Instructions
* Write in black ink.
* Give all the information you are asked for, and **write neatly**.
* You must answer **three** questions.
* Answer **either** Question 1.1 **or** Question 1.2. Do **not** answer both questions.
* Answer **either** Question 2.1 **or** Question 2.2. Do **not** answer both questions.
* You **must** answer Question 3.
* All questions must be answered in **French**.
* In the actual exam, you must write your answers in the spaces provided. Do **not** write on blank pages.
* You may plan your answers in the exam booklet. Make sure you cross through any work you do
  not want to be marked.

Information
* This paper contains **3** writing tasks.
* The maximum mark for this paper is **60**.
* The number of marks for each question is shown in brackets.
* For Questions 1 and 2, the highest marks will be awarded for answers that make reference to each
  bullet point and include a variety of vocabulary, structures and opinions with reasons.
* You are **not** allowed to use a dictionary.

Answer **either** Question 1.1 **or** Question 1.2

1.1 Vous décrivez vos projets pour l'avenir pour votre blog.

Décrivez :

- vos projets pour après les examens
- votre travail idéal
- les avantages et les désavantages de ce travail
- votre expérience professionnelle dans le passé.

Écrivez environ **90** mots en **français**. Répondez à chaque aspect de la question.

[16 marks]

1.2 Vous décrivez les problèmes environnementaux pour votre blog.

Décrivez :

- les problèmes environnementaux causés par les voitures
- les avantages des transports en commun
- une activité récente que vous avez faite pour sauvegarder l'environnement
- vos idées pour sauvegarder l'environnement dans l'avenir.

Écrivez environ **90** mots en **français**. Répondez à chaque aspect de la question.

[16 marks]

Answer **either** Question 2.1 **or** Question 2.2

2.1 Vous écrivez un article sur les problèmes sociaux dans votre ville pour un magazine français.

Décrivez :

- les problèmes sociaux dans votre ville
- un problème que vous avez remarqué récemment.

Écrivez environ **150** mots en **français**. Répondez aux deux aspects de la question.

[32 marks]

2.2 Vous écrivez un article sur les réseaux sociaux pour un magazine français.

Décrivez :

- les avantages et les désavantages des réseaux sociaux
- une expérience récente qui vous est arrivée sur les réseaux sociaux.

Écrivez environ **150** mots en **français**. Répondez aux deux aspects de la question.

[32 marks]

You **must** answer Question 3

3 Translate the following passage into **French**.

> Yesterday, I went to the supermarket to do the shopping. I bought fruit, vegetables and some bread. Usually, I prefer to do online shopping because it is faster. However, I want some new shoes and I will have to go to the shops to buy them because I will need to try them on.

[12 marks]

Vocabulary

Section One — General Stuff

Conjunctions (p.127)

à cause de	because of
à part	apart from
ainsi	therefore / so
alors	so / therefore / then
aussi	also
car	because
cependant	however
c'est-à-dire	that is to say
comme	as / like
d'un côté / de l'autre côté	on the one hand / on the other hand
donc	therefore / so
ensuite	then / next
et	and
évidemment	obviously
lorsque	when / as soon as
mais	but
même si	even if
ni...ni	neither...nor
ou	or
ou bien	or else
par contre	on the other hand
parce que	because
par exemple	for example
pendant que	while
pourtant	however
puis	then
puisque	seeing that / since
quand	when
sans doute	undoubtedly / without doubt
si	if
y compris	including

Comparisons (p.113 & 118)

aussi...que	as...as
plus / moins	more / less
plus que / moins que	more than / less than
bon(ne) / meilleur(e) / le/la meilleur(e)	good / better / the best
mauvais(e) / pire / le/la pire	bad / worse / the worst
bien / mieux / le/la mieux	well / better / the best
mal / plus mal / le/la plus mal	badly / worse / the worst
beaucoup / plus / le/la plus	lots / more / the most
peu / moins / le/la moins	few / less / the least

Prepositions (p.128-129)

à	to / in / at
à côté de	next to
à travers	across / through
après	after
au bord de	at the side / edge of
au bout de	at the end of (length, rather than time)
au-dessous de	beneath / below
au-dessus de	above / over
au fond de	at the back of / at the bottom of
au lieu de	instead of
au milieu de	in the middle of
autour de	around
avant	before
avec	with
chez	at the house of
contre	against
dans	in
de	of / from
depuis	since / for
derrière	behind
devant	in front of
en	in / to
en dehors de	outside (of)
en face de	opposite
entre	between
jusqu'à	up to / until
malgré	despite / in spite of
parmi	amongst
pendant	during
pour	for / in order to
près de	near
sans	without
selon	according to
sous	under
sur	on
vers	towards

Negatives (p.143)

ne...aucun(e)	not any / not a single
ne...jamais	never
ne...ni...ni	neither...nor
ne...pas	not
ne...personne	nobody / no-one
ne...plus	no more / no longer
ne...que	only / nothing but
ne...rien	nothing
pas encore	not yet

Numbers (p.1)

zéro	zero
un	one
deux	two
trois	three
quatre	four
cinq	five
six	six
sept	seven
huit	eight
neuf	nine
dix	ten
onze	eleven
douze	twelve
treize	thirteen
quatorze	fourteen
quinze	fifteen
seize	sixteen
dix-sept	seventeen
dix-huit	eighteen
dix-neuf	nineteen
vingt	twenty
vingt et un	twenty-one
vingt-deux	twenty-two
trente	thirty
quarante	forty
cinquante	fifty
soixante	sixty
soixante-dix	seventy
soixante et onze	seventy-one
soixante-douze	seventy-two
quatre-vingts	eighty
quatre-vingt-un	eighty-one
quatre-vingt-dix	ninety
quatre-vingt-onze	ninety-one
quatre-vingt-dix-huit	ninety-eight
cent	one hundred
cent cinquante	one hundred and fifty
six cent vingt-trois	six hundred and twenty-three
mille	one thousand
mille neuf cent quarante-sept	one thousand nine hundred and forty-seven
dix mille	ten thousand
cent mille	one hundred thousand
un million	one million
premier / première	first
deuxième	second
troisième	third
quatrième	fourth
cinquième	fifth
sixième	sixth
septième	seventh
huitième	eighth
neuvième	ninth
dixième	tenth
quatre-vingt-dix-neuvième	ninety-ninth
une dizaine	about ten
des dizaines	lots / dozens
une douzaine	a dozen
une vingtaine	about twenty
un nombre de	a number of

① ② ③ ④ ⑤ ⑥ ⑦

Times and Dates (p.2-3)

lundi	Monday
mardi	Tuesday
mercredi	Wednesday
jeudi	Thursday
vendredi	Friday
samedi	Saturday
dimanche	Sunday
janvier	January
février	February
mars	March
avril	April
mai	May
juin	June
juillet	July
août	August
septembre	September
octobre	October
novembre	November
décembre	December
l'hiver (m)	winter
le printemps	spring
l'été (m)	summer
l'automne (m)	autumn
à la fois	at the same time
à l'avenir	in the future
à l'heure	on time
à temps partiel	part-time
à temps plein	full-time
l'an (m)	year
l'année (f)	year
après	after
après-demain	the day after tomorrow
l'après-midi (m / f)	afternoon
l'aube (f)	dawn
aujourd'hui	today
auparavant	formerly / in the past
avant	before
avant-hier	the day before yesterday
bientôt	soon
le coucher du soleil	sunset
d'abord	at first / firstly
d'habitude	usually
de bonne heure	early
de l'après-midi	in the afternoon
de nouveau	again
de temps en temps	from time to time
le début	start
déjà	already
demain	tomorrow
dernier / dernière	last
du matin	in the morning
du soir	in the evening
en attendant	whilst waiting (for)
en avance	in advance
en ce moment	at the moment
en retard	late
en train de (faire...)	in the process of (doing)
en même temps	at the same time
encore une fois	once more
enfin	at last / finally
environ	about
et quart	quarter past
et demie	half past
la fin	end
hier	yesterday
il y a	ago
le jour	day
la journée	day
le lendemain	the next day
longtemps	for a long time
maintenant	now
le matin	morning
moins le quart	quarter to
le mois	month
normalement	normally
la nuit	night
parfois	sometimes
le passé	past
pendant	during
plus tard	later
presque	almost / nearly
prochain(e)	next
quelquefois	sometimes
rarement	rarely
récemment	recently
la semaine	week
seulement	only
le siècle	century
le soir	evening
soudain	suddenly
souvent	often
suivant(e)	following
(être) sur le point de	(to be) about to
tard	late
tôt	early
toujours	always / still
tous les jours	every day
tout à coup	suddenly / all of a sudden
tout de suite	immediately
vite	quickly
le week-end	weekend

Colours and Shapes

blanc / blanche	white
bleu(e)	blue
châtain	light brown
clair(e)	light
foncé(e)	dark
gris(e)	grey
jaune	yellow
marron	brown
noir(e)	black
noisette	hazel
orange	orange
pourpre	purple
rose	pink
rouge	red
vert(e)	green
carré(e)	square
rond(e)	round

Weights and Measures

assez	enough / quite
bas(se)	low
la boîte	box / tin / can
la bouteille	bottle
court(e)	short
le demi	half
un demi-litre	half a litre
encore de	more
étroit(e)	narrow
un gramme	a gram
gros	fat
haut(e)	high
un kilogramme	a kilogram
large	wide
un litre	a litre
maigre	skinny / thin
mince	slim / thin
la moitié	half
le morceau	piece
moyen / moyenne	medium / average
le nombre	number
le paquet	packet
pas mal de	quite a few
peser	to weigh
plein de	full of / lots of
la pointure	size (for shoes)
la portion	portion
le quart	quarter
suffisamment	sufficiently
la taille	size (for clothes)
tout(e)	all
la tranche	slice
tranché(e)	sliced
les trois-quarts (m)	three-quarters
trop	too much

Materials

l'argent (m)	silver
le béton	concrete
le bois	wood
le cuir	leather
le fer	iron
la laine	wool
l'or (m)	gold
la soie	silk
le verre	glass

Access

complet / complète	full
l'entrée (f)	entry / entrance
fermé(e)	closed
fermer	to close
interdit(e)	forbidden
libre	free / vacant / unoccupied
occupé(e)	taken / occupied / engaged
ouvert(e)	open
ouvrir	to open
la sortie	exit

Vocabulary

Questions (p.4-5)

Combien ?	How much / How many?
Comment ?	How?
Est-ce que ?	expression put before a verb that makes a sentence into a question
Où ?	Where?
Pourquoi ?	Why?
Quand ?	When?
Que ?	What?
Quel / Quelle ?	Which?
Qu'est-ce que ?	What?
Qu'est-ce qui ?	What?
Qu'est-ce que c'est ?	What is it?
Qui ?	Who?
quoi ?	What?
À quelle heure ?	At what time?
Ça s'écrit comment ?	How is that written?
C'est combien ?	How much is it?
C'est quelle date ?	What is the date?
C'est quel jour ?	What day is it?
De quelle couleur ?	What colour?
D'où ?	From where?
Pour combien de temps ?	For how long?
Que veut dire... ?	What does... mean?
Quelle heure est-il ?	What time is it?

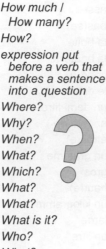

Being Polite (p.6-7)

à bientôt	see you soon
à demain	see you tomorrow
à tout à l'heure	see you soon / later
allô	hello (on phone)
amitiés	best wishes
au revoir	goodbye
Au secours !	Help!
bien sûr	of course, certainly
bienvenue	welcome
Bon anniversaire !	Happy birthday!
Bon appétit !	Have a good meal!
Bon voyage !	Have a good trip!
bonjour	hello
Bonne année !	Happy New Year!
Bonne chance !	Good luck!
bonne idée	good idea
bonne nuit	good night
bonnes vacances	have a good holiday
bonsoir	good evening
ça va bien, merci	(I am) fine, thanks
ça ne va pas bien	(I am) not well
comme ci, comme ça	so-so / OK
Comment ça va ?	How are you? (informal)
Comment allez-vous ?	How are you? (formal)
d'accord	OK / fine
de rien	you're welcome
désolé(e)	sorry
enchanté(e)	pleased to meet you
Et toi ?	And you? (informal)
Et vous ?	And you? (formal)
excusez-moi	excuse me (formal)

Félicitations !	Congratulations!
j'aimerais...	I would like...
je me sens...	I feel...
je ne sais pas	I don't know
je voudrais...	I would like...
Joyeux Noël !	Merry Christmas!
meilleurs voeux	best wishes
merci (beaucoup)	thank you (very much)
pardon	excuse me (informal)
pas mal	not bad
Puis-je... ?	may I... ?
Puis-je te présenter... ?	May I introduce... ? (informal)
Puis-je vous présenter... ?	May I introduce... ? (formal)
quel dommage	what a shame
salut	hi
Santé !	Cheers!
s'il te plaît	please (informal)
s'il vous plaît	please (formal)
Super !	Great!
voici...	this is...

Opinions (p.8-10)

à mon avis	in my opinion
absolument	absolutely
adorer	to love
aimer	to like / to love
aimer bien	to like
affreux / affreuse	awful
agréable	pleasant
amical(e)	friendly
amusant(e)	funny
l'avantage (m)	advantage
barbant(e)	boring
beau / bel / belle	handsome / beautiful
bien entendu	of course
bien sûr	of course
bon(ne)	good
ça dépend	it depends
ça m'énerve	it gets on my nerves
ça me fait rire	it makes me laugh
ça me fait pleurer	it makes me cry
ça me plaît	I like it
ça m'est égal	I don't care
ça ne me dit rien	it means nothing to me / I don't fancy that / I don't feel like it
ça suffit	that's enough
car	because
casse-pieds	annoying
certainement	certainly
cher / chère	expensive
chouette	great
compliqué(e)	complicated
content(e)	happy
croire	to believe
désagréable	unpleasant
désirer	to want
détester	to hate
dire	to say / to tell

doué(e)	gifted / talented
drôle	funny
embêtant(e)	annoying
en général	in general
enchanté(e)	delighted
ennuyeux / ennuyeuse	boring
espérer	to hope
Es-tu d'accord ?	Do you agree?
étonné(e)	astonished / amazed
facile	easy
faible	weak
fantastique	fantastic
formidable	great
franchement	frankly
généralement	generally
génial(e)	brilliant
grâce à	thanks to
grave	serious
habile	clever
l'inconvénient (m)	disadvantage
intéressant(e)	interesting
s'intéresser à	to be interested in
inutile	useless
incroyable	incredible
inquiet / inquiète	worried
marrant(e)	funny
en avoir marre (de)	to be fed up (with)
mauvais(e)	bad
merveilleux / merveilleuse	marvellous
mignon / mignonne	cute
moche	ugly
(moi) non plus	(me) neither
nouveau / nouvelle	new
nul / nulle	rubbish
par contre	on the other hand
parfait(e)	perfect
passionnant(e)	exciting
la peine	the bother
penser	to think
personnellement	personally
peut-être	perhaps
pourtant	however
pratique	practical
préférer	to prefer
promettre	to promise
Quel est ton avis sur... ?	What is your opinion of...?
ridicule	ridiculous
rigolo / rigolote	funny
sage	well-behaved
selon moi...	in my opinion...
sembler	to seem
sensass	sensational
super	great
supporter	to put up with
sympa / sympathique	nice (person)
utile	useful
vouloir	to wish / to want
vraiment	really / truly

Correctness

avoir raison	*to be right*
avoir tort	*to be wrong*
corriger	*to correct*
l'erreur (f)	*error / mistake*
la faute	*fault / mistake*
faux / fausse	*false*
il (me) faut	*you (I) must*
juste	*correct*
obligatoire	*compulsory*
parfait(e)	*perfect*
sûr(e)	*certain / sure*
se tromper	*to make a mistake*
vrai(e)	*true*

Abbreviations

le CDI (centre de documentation et d'information)	*resource centre*
le CES (collège d'enseignement secondaire)	*secondary school*
l'EPS (éducation physique et sportive) (f)	*PE (physical education)*
l'HLM (habitation à loyer modéré) (f)	*council / social housing*
le SAMU (service d'aide médicale d'urgence)	*emergency medical services*
le SDF (sans domicile fixe)	*homeless person*
la SNCF (société nationale des chemins de fer français)	*National Rail Service*
le TGV (train à grande vitesse)	*high-speed train*
la TVA (taxe sur la valeur ajoutée)	*VAT (Value Added Tax)*
le VTT (vélo tout terrain)	*mountain bike*

Section Two — Me, My Family and Friends

You and Your Family (p.16-17)

aîné(e)	*elder*
l'anniversaire (m)	*birthday*
s'appeler	*to be called*
avoir...ans	*to be...years old*
le beau-père	*step-father*
la belle-mère	*step-mother*
le cousin / la cousine	*cousin*
le demi-frère	*half-brother / step-brother*
la demi-sœur	*half-sister / step-sister*
divorcé(e)	*divorced*
d'origine...	*of... origin*
la famille proche	*close relatives*
la famille élargie	*extended family*
la fille	*daughter / girl*
le fils	*son*
le fils / la fille unique	*only child*
le frère	*brother*
la grand-mère	*grandmother*
le grand-père	*grandfather*
les grands-parents (m)	*grandparents*
le jumeau / la jumelle	*twin*
la mère	*mother*
mort(e)	*dead*
mourir	*to die*
la naissance	*birth*
naître	*to be born*
né(e) le...	*born on the...*
le neveu	*nephew*
la nièce	*niece*
le nom	*surname*
nous sommes...	*there are... of us*
l'oncle (m)	*uncle*
le / la partenaire	*partner*
le père	*father*
le / la petit(e) ami(e)	*boyfriend / girlfriend*
la petite-fille	*granddaughter*
le petit-fils	*grandson*
plus âgé(e)	*older*
plus jeune	*younger*
le prénom	*first name*
la sœur	*sister*
la tante	*aunt*
vivre ensemble	*to live together*

Describing People (p.18-19)

aimable	*kind*
l'apparence (f)	*appearance*
la barbe	*beard*
bavard(e)	*chatty / talkative*
beau / bel / belle	*handsome / beautiful*
bête	*stupid / silly*
les bijoux (m)	*jewellery*
blond(e)	*blonde*
bouclé(e)	*curly*
le bouton	*spot / pimple*
brun(e)	*brown*
le caractère	*personality*
les cheveux (m)	*hair*
la cicatrice	*scar*
clair(e)	*light*
compréhensif / compréhensive	*understanding*
court(e)	*short (hair)*
de mauvaise humeur	*bad-tempered*
de taille moyenne	*of medium height*
égoïste	*selfish*
l'esprit (m)	*mind*
étonnant(e)	*amazing*
étrange	*strange*
fâché(e)	*angry*
fier / fière	*proud*
foncé(e)	*dark*
fou / fol / folle	*mad, crazy*
frisé(e)	*curly*
gêner	*to annoy*
généreux / généreuse	*generous*
gentil / gentille	*kind, nice*
le grain de beauté	*mole (on skin)*
grand(e)	*tall*
gros / grosse	*fat*
heureux / heureuse	*happy*
jaloux / jalouse	*jealous*
jeune	*young*
la jeunesse	*youth*

joli(e)	*pretty*
laid(e)	*ugly*
long / longue	*long*
les lunettes (f)	*glasses*
méchant(e)	*naughty*
mi-long / mi-longue	*medium length*
mince	*slim*
ondulé(e)	*wavy*
paresseux / paresseuse	*lazy*
pénible	*annoying*
la personnalité	*personality*
petit(e)	*short*
raide	*straight*
roux / rousse	*ginger*
le sens de l'humour	*sense of humour*
sensible	*sensitive*
sportif / sportive	*sporty*
sympa	*kind / nice*
timide	*shy*
tranquille	*quiet / calm*
travailleur / travailleuse	*hard-working*
triste	*sad*
vieux / vieil / vieille	*old*
vif / vive	*lively*
les yeux (m)	*eyes*

Relationships (p.20-21)

l'amour (m)	*love*
la bague	*ring*
casse-pieds	*a pain in the neck*
célibataire	*single*
compréhensif / compréhensive	*understanding*
la confiance	*trust*
connaître	*to know (a person)*
le copain / la copine	*friend / mate*
se disputer	*to argue*
ensemble	*together*
s'entendre (avec)	*to get on (with)*
épouser	*to marry*
être fâché(e)	*to be angry*
se faire des amis	*to make friends*
la femme	*wife / woman*

les fiançailles (f)	engagement
gâter	to spoil
gâté(e)	spoilt
injuste	unfair
le mari	husband
le mariage	marriage
se marier	to get married / to marry

le / la meilleur(e) ami(e)	best friend
mépriser	to despise
se mettre en colère	to get angry
les noces (f)	wedding
partager	to share
le / la partenaire	partner
le petit ami	boyfriend

la petite amie	girlfriend
les rapports (m)	relationships
se rendre compte	to realise
(se) séparer	to separate
séparé(e)	separated
sortir	to go out

Section Three — Free-Time Activities

Music, Cinema and TV (p.27-29)

s'abonner	to subscribe
l'acteur (m) / l'actrice (f)	actor / actress
les actualités (f)	news
l'ado (m / f)	adolescent
apprendre à	to learn to
l'argent (m)	money
la bande-annonce	trailer
le billet	ticket
célèbre	famous
la chaîne de télé	TV channel
la chanson	song
chanter	to sing
le chanteur / la chanteuse	singer
la chorale	choir
les clips (m)	music videos
commencer	to start
le concert	concert
la dance	dance music
débuter	to begin
le dessin animé	cartoon
diffuser	to broadcast
divertissant(e)	entertaining
le documentaire	documentary
écouter de la musique	to listen to music
les (m) effets spéciaux	special effects
l'émission (f)	programme
entraînant(e)	catchy
faire partie de	to take part in
féliciter	to congratulate
le feuilleton	soap opera
le film d'action	action film
le film d'amour	romantic film
le film d'animation	animated film
le film comique	comedy film
le film de guerre	war film
le film d'horreur	horror film
le film policier	detective film
le genre	genre / type / kind
le groupe	band
l'histoire (f)	storyline
les informations (f)	news
s'intéresser à	to be interested in
l'intrigue (f)	plot
le jeu télévisé	game show
jouer (d'un instrument)	to play (an instrument)

le musicien / la musicienne	musician
la musique pop	pop music
la musique rock	rock music
l'orchestre (m)	orchestra
le passe-temps	hobby
le personnage	character
la publicité	advert(s)
regarder	to watch
relaxant(e)	relaxing
rencontrer	to meet
répéter	to rehearse
se reposer	to rest
la séance	performance
la série	series
la série historique	period drama
le tarif réduit	reduced price
la télé réalité	reality TV
le temps libre	free time
la vedette	film star
voir	see
vouloir	to wish / to want

Food and Eating Out (p.30-31)

avoir faim	to be hungry
avoir soif	to be thirsty
l'addition (f)	the bill
l'agneau (m)	lamb
l'ail (m)	garlic
allergique à	allergic to
amer / amère	bitter
l'ananas (m)	pineapple
l'assiette (f)	plate / dish
le beurre	butter
bien cuit(e)	well cooked
la bière	beer
le bœuf	beef
boire	to drink
la boisson	drink
le café	coffee
le canard	duck
la carte	menu
la cerise	cherry
le champignon	mushroom
choisir	to choose
le chou	cabbage
le chou-fleur	cauliflower
le citron	lemon
commander	to order
la confiture	jam
coûter	to cost

la crêpe	pancake
le croque-monsieur	toasted ham and cheese sandwich
les crudités (f)	raw chopped vegetables
la cuisine	kitchen / cooking
cuisiner	to cook
dégoûtant(e)	disgusting
le déjeuner	lunch
le dessert	dessert
la dinde	turkey
le dîner	evening meal
l'eau (f) minérale	mineral water
l'eau (f) plate / gazeuse	still / fizzy water
emporter	to take away
épicé(e)	spicy
l'escargot (m)	snail
l'espèce (f)	type / kind
essayer	to try
la fraise	strawberry
la framboise	raspberry
le fromage	cheese
les frites (f)	chips
les fruits (m)	fruit
les fruits (m) de mer	seafood
la glace	ice cream
le goût	taste
goûter	to taste
les haricots (m) verts	green beans
le hors d'œuvre	starter
le jambon	ham
le lait	milk
les légumes (m)	vegetables
manger	to eat
la noix	nut
nourissant(e)	nourishing
la nourriture	food
l'œuf (m)	egg
l'oie (f)	goose
l'oignon (m)	onion
le pain	bread
le pamplemousse	grapefruit
les pâtes (f)	pasta
payer	to pay (for)
prendre	to take
la pêche	fishing / peach
le petit-déjeuner	breakfast
les petits pois (m)	peas
piquant(e)	spicy
se plaindre	to complain

le plat principal	main meal / dish	un verre de...	a glass of...	le lieu (avoir lieu)	place (to take place)
la poire	pear	la viande	meat	marquer un but / un essai	to score a goal / a try
le poisson	fish	le vin	wine		
le poivre	pepper	le yaourt	yoghurt	se motiver	to motivate oneself
la pomme	apple			nager	to swim
la pomme de terre	potato	**Sport (p.32-33)**		la natation	swimming
le potage	soup	l'aviron (m)	rowing	le netball	netball
le poulet	chicken	le badminton	badminton	passionnant(e)	exciting
le pourboire	tip	le basket	basketball	le patin à glace	ice skating
la prune	plum	captivant(e)	engaging	la patinoire	ice rink
les raisins (m)	grapes	le centre sportif	sports centre	la pêche	fishing
le repas	meal	le cheval	horse	perdre	to lose
le restaurant	restaurant	le club des jeunes	youth club	la piscine	swimming pool
le riz	rice	compétitif / compétitive	competitive	la planche à voile	wind-surfing
salé(e)	salty			pratiquer un sport	to do a sport
la saucisse	sausage	courir	to run	la promenade	walk
le saumon	salmon	la course	race	régulièrement	regularly
le sel	salt	les échecs (m)	chess	le rugby	rugby
le serveur / la serveuse	waiter / waitress	l'entraînement (m)	sports practice	le skate	skateboarding
		s'entraîner	to train	le ski (nautique)	(water) skiing
le steak haché	burger	l'équipe (f)	team	sportif / sportive	sporty
le sucre	sugar	l'équitation (f)	horse riding	les sports (m) d'hiver	winter sports
sucré(e)	sweet	l'escalade (f)	rock climbing	le stade	stadium
la tasse	cup	l'événement (m)	event	le tennis	tennis
le thé	tea	faire du vélo	to cycle	le terrain du sport	sports field
le thon	tuna	faire une randonnée	to go on a walk / hike	la tournée	tour
la truite	trout	gagner	to win	le tournoi	tournament
le veau	veal	fana de	a fan of	tricher	to cheat
végétalien(ne)	vegan	le foot / football	football	la voile	sailing
végétarien(ne)	vegetarian	le hockey	hockey	le volley	volleyball

Section Four — Technology in Everyday Life

Technology (p.39-42)

à cause de	because of	enregistrer	to record	l'ordinateur (m)	computer
l'abonné (m) / l'abonnée (f)	subscriber	envoyer	to send	l'ordinateur (m) portable	laptop
		être accro à	to be addicted to		
acheter	to buy	faire attention	to be careful	la page d'accueil	welcome page
afficher	to post	facile	easy	partager	to share
au lieu de	instead of	faire des achats (en ligne)	to shop (online)	passer du temps	to spend time
l'avantage (m)	advantage			la pile	battery
le bloggeur	blogger	faire des recherches	to do research	le portable	mobile (phone)
le caméscope	camcorder	le fichier	file	pratique	practical
chercher	to look for	le forum	chat room	recevoir	to receive
le clavier	keyboard	la fraude	fraud	remplir	to fill (in)
cliquer	to click	le genre	type / kind	le réseau social	social network
le compte	account	grâce à	thanks to	rester en contact	to stay in contact
la console de jeux	games console	l'imprimante (f)	printer	sauvegarder	to save
le courrier électronique	email	imprimer	to print	le site internet / web	website
		l'inconvénient (m)	disadvantage / drawback	les sites sociaux	social media sites
la cyber-intimidation	cyber-bullying			la souris	mouse
dangereux / dangereuse	dangerous	l'internaute (m)	internet user	surfer sur Internet	to surf the internet
		Internet (m)	Internet	la tablette	tablet
le désavantage	disadvantage	le jeu	game	taper	to type
les détails (m) personnels	personal details	le lecteur DVD	DVD player	tchatter	to talk online
		le lecteur MP3	MP3 player	télécharger	to download
l'écran (m)	screen	le logiciel	software	le texto	text message
l'écran (m) tactile	touch screen	mettre	to put	la touche	key
l'écrivain (m)	author	mettre en ligne	to upload	le traitement de texte	word processing
effacer	to delete	le moniteur	monitor		
l'email (m)	email	le mot de passe	password	utiliser	to use
en ligne	online	naviguer (sur)	to browse	la vie privée	private life
		numérique	digital		

Vocabulary

Section Five — Customs and Festivals

Customs and Festivals (p.48-50)

l'Aïd (f) al-Fitr	Eid al-Fitr
athée	atheist
Bonne année !	Happy New Year!
Bon anniversaire !	Happy birthday!
Bonne chance !	Good luck!
la bougie	candle
la bûche de Noël	yule log
le cadeau	present
célébrer	to celebrate
chanter	to sing
chrétien(ne)	Christian
commercial(e)	commercial
la couronne	crown
la danse	dance
le défilé	procession
la dinde	turkey
l'église (f)	church
l'événement (m)	event
Félicitations !	Congratulations!
la fête	festival / celebration / party
la fête des mères / pères	Mother's / Father's Day
la fête des rois	Epiphany / Twelfth Night
la fête du travail	May Day
la fête nationale	Bastille Day
fêter	to celebrate
les feux (m) d'artifice	fireworks
la fève	charm
la foi	faith
la galette des rois	cake for Epiphany
le gâteau des rois	cake for Epiphany
la Hanoukka	Hanukkah
historique	historical
impressionant(e)	impressive
jouer un tour	to play a trick
le Jour de l'An	New Year's Day
le jour férié	bank holiday
Joyeux Noël !	Merry Christmas!
juif / juive	Jewish
la messe	mass
la mosquée	mosque
musulman(e)	Muslim
l'oie (f)	goose
le pain calendal	Christmas loaf
Pâques	Easter
la Pentecôte	Whitsuntide
la plaisanterie	joke
le poisson d'avril	April Fools' Day
Poisson d'avril !	April Fool!
prier	to pray
le ramadan	Ramadan
la reine	queen
religieux / religieuse	religious
la réunion	meeting
le réveillon	meal eaten after midnight in France
le roi	king
la Saint Valentin	Valentine's Day
la Saint-Sylvestre	New Year's Eve
le sapin de Noël	Christmas tree
sentimental(e)	sentimental
la synagogue	synagogue
la Toussaint	All Saints Day
les vacances	holidays
la veille de Noël	Christmas Eve

Section Six — Where You Live

Where You Live (p.56-57)

à la montagne	in the mountains
au bord de la mer	by the sea
au premier / deuxième étage (m)	on the first / second floor
animé	lively
l'appartement (m)	flat
l'arbre (m)	tree
l'armoire (f)	wardrobe
la banlieue	suburb
la banque	bank
le bâtiment	building
la bibliothèque	library
la bijouterie	jeweller's shop
la boucherie	butcher's
la boulangerie	bakery
le bruit	noise
bruyant	noisy
le bureau	office / study / desk
calme	quiet
à la campagne	in the countryside
la cave	cellar
célèbre	famous
le centre commercial	shopping centre
le centre-ville	town centre
la chaise	chair
la chambre	bedroom
le champ	field
la charcuterie	delicatessen
le cinéma	cinema
la circulation	traffic
la colline	hill
les commerces (m)	shops
le commissariat	police station
la cuisine	kitchen / cooking
déménager	to move house
démodé	old-fashioned
les distractions (f)	things to do
l'embouteillage (m)	traffic jam
emménager	to move in
l'endroit (m)	place
l'escalier (m)	staircase
l'étage (m)	floor / storey
la fenêtre	window
la ferme	farm
la fermeture	closure
le four	oven
le foyer	home
la gare	railway station
la gare routière	bus station
les gens (m)	people
la grande ville	city
l'habitant (m)	inhabitant
l'HLM (f)	council housing
l'hôtel (m) de ville	town hall
l'immeuble (m)	block of flats
la librairie	bookshop
le lit	bed
le loyer	rent
la lumière	light
la mairie	town hall
la maison (individuelle / jumelée / mitoyenne)	house (detached / semi-detached / terraced)
le marché	market
les meubles (m)	furniture
le mur	wall
le musée	museum
tout(e) neuf / neuve	brand new
le parc	park
la pâtisserie	cake shop
pauvre	poor
la pièce	room
pittoresque	picturesque
le placard	cupboard
la place	square
la poste	post office
le quartier	area
quitter	to leave
le rez-de-chaussée	ground floor
le risque	risk
sale	dirty
la salle à manger	dining room
la salle de bains	bathroom
le salon	living room / lounge
la sécurité	safety
le sous-sol	basement
la station-service	service station
le supermarché	supermarket
surchargé	overcrowded
le tabac	newsagent's
le théâtre	theatre
les transports (m) en commun	public transport
travailler	to work
se trouver	to be situated
l'usine (f)	factory

la vie	life	les courses (f)	shopping	la veste	jacket
la ville	town	la cravate	tie	les vêtements (m)	clothes
vivre	to live	défectueux /	faulty	la vitrine	shop window
le voisin / la voisine	neighbour	défectueuse			
la zone piétonne	pedestrian zone	dépenser	to spend (money)		

What You Do at Home (p.58)

aider	to help	endommagé(e)	damaged	**Directions (p.62)**	
l'argent (m) de poche	pocket money	en espèces	with cash	à droite	on / to the right
le bricolage	DIY (do it yourself)	l'écharpe (f)	scarf	à gauche	on / to the left
se brosser les dents	to brush your teeth	en ligne	online	le carrefour	crossroads
se coucher	to go to bed	essayer	to try on	C'est loin d'ici ?	Is it far from here?
les courses (f)	shopping	l'étiquette (f)	label	chez	at the house of
cuisiner	to cook	se faire rembourser	to get a refund	de chaque côté	on each side
devoir	to have to	le foulard	scarf	de l'autre côté	on the other side
se doucher	to shower	les gants (m)	gloves	en bas	down(stairs)
économiser	to save	le gilet	waistcoat	en face de	opposite
faire le lit	to make the bed	le grand magasin	department store	en haut	up(stairs)
la fleur	flower	la grande surface	superstore	environ	about
garder	to look after	gratuit(e)	free (of charge)	l'est (m)	east
s'habiller	to get dressed	l'imperméable (m)	raincoat	les feux (m) (de signalisation)	(traffic) lights
le jardinage	gardening	le jean	jeans	l'hôpital (m)	hospital
laver	to wash	la jupe	skirt	ici	here
se laver	to wash (yourself)	un kilogramme	a kilogram	juste à côté de	right next to
la lessive	laundry	le lèche-vitrine (faire du)	window shopping (to go window shopping)	jusqu'à	until
se lever	to get up			là	there
mettre la table	to lay the table	un litre	litre	là-bas	over there
nettoyer	to clean	livrer	to deliver	loin de	far from
passer l'aspirateur	to vacuum	le magasin	shop	le nord	north
la pelouse	lawn	le manteau	coat	nulle part	nowhere
poser	to put down	la marque	make / label / brand	Où est...?	Where is...?
prendre le petit-déjeuner	to eat breakfast	la mode	fashion	l'ouest (m)	west
propre	clean, tidy	la moitié	half	le panneau	sign
ranger	to tidy	le morceau	piece	par	by
la tâche	task	le pantalon	trousers	partout	everywhere
la vaisselle	washing-up	un paquet	packet	le péage	toll
		le parfum	perfume	le pont	bridge

Shopping (p.59-61)

abîmé(e)	damaged	perdre	to lose	la place	square
les baskets (f)	trainers	peser	to weigh	près de	near to
besoin (m) (avoir... de)	need (to need)	le portefeuille	wallet	quelque part	somewhere
la boîte	box / tin / can	le porte-monnaie	purse	le rond-point	roundabout
le bijou	jewel, jewellery	la portion	portion	la rue	street
le blouson	coat / jacket	pouvoir	to be able	situé(e)	situated
bon marché	cheap	pratique	convenient	le sud	south
Ça me va.	It suits me.	le prix	price	tout droit	straight ahead
la caisse	till	le pull	jumper	tout près	very near
la carte bancaire	bank card	le pull à capuche	hoodie	toutes directions	all directions
la ceinture	belt	le pyjama	pyjamas	traverser	to cross
le centre commercial	shopping centre	le quart	quarter	le trottoir	pavement
C'est combien, s'il vous plaît ?	How much is it, please?	le rayon	department	se trouver	to be situated
le chapeau	hat	réduire	to reduce	**Weather (p.63)**	
les chaussettes (f)	socks	réduit(e)	reduced	agité(e)	turbulent
les chaussures (f)	shoes	je regarde	I'm browsing	l'averse (f)	shower
la chemise	shirt	rembourser	to refund	briller	to shine
cher / chère	expensive	la robe	dress	le brouillard	fog
le choix	choice	les soldes (m)	sale	la brume	mist
la chose	thing	le supermarché	supermarket	la chaleur	heat
		la taille	size	chaud(e)	hot
		le ticket de caisse	receipt	le ciel	sky
		la tranche	slice	le climat	climate
		tranché(e)	sliced	couvert(e)	overcast
		le vendeur / la vendeuse	shop assistant	doux / douce	mild
				l'éclair (m)	lightning
		vendre	to sell	l'éclaircie (f)	bright spell

ensoleillé(e)	*sunny*	mouillé(e)	*wet*	la pluie	*rain*
faire beau	*to be fine (weather)*	neiger	*to snow*	sec / sèche	*dry*
faire mauvais	*to be bad (weather)*	le nuage	*cloud*	le soleil	*sun*
froid(e)	*cold*	nuageux / nuageuse	*cloudy*	la tempête	*storm*
geler	*to freeze*	l'ombre (m)	*shade, shadow*	le temps	*weather*
la glace	*ice*	l'orage (m)	*storm*	le tonnerre	*thunder*
humide	*humid / wet*	orageux / orageuse	*stormy*	tremper	*to soak*
la météo	*weather forecast*	pleuvoir	*to rain*	le vent	*wind*

Section Seven — Lifestyle

Health (p.69-70)

à pied	*on foot*	faire de l'exercice	*to exercise*	le tabac	*tobacco*
accro (à)	*addicted (to)*	faire un régime	*to be on a diet*	le tabagisme	*addiction to smoking*
agir (il s'agit de)	*to act (it's a question of)*	le fast-food	*fast food*	le tatouage	*tattooing / tattoo*
		fatigué(e)	*tired*	tenter	*to attempt*
l'alcool (m)	*alcohol*	le foie	*liver*	tousser	*to cough*
alcoolique	*alcoholic*	la forme	*fitness*	le / la toxicomane	*drug addict*
l'alimentation (f)	*food*	fort(e)	*strong*	valoir mieux	*to be better*
aller bien	*to be well*	fumer	*to smoke*	vide	*empty*
aller mieux	*to be better*	garder	*to look after*	vivre sainement	*living healthily*
s'amuser	*to enjoy oneself*	garder la forme	*to stay in shape*	la voix	*voice*
arrêter	*to stop*	le gras	*fat*	vomir	*to be sick*
avertir	*to warn*	gras(se)	*fatty*		
avoir sommeil	*to be sleepy*	l'habitude (f)	*habit*	## Illnesses (p.71)
boire	*to drink*	hors d'haleine	*out of breath*	le cancer (du poumon)	*(lung) cancer*
le bonbon	*sweet*	ivre	*drunk*		
le bonheur	*happiness*	la maladie (grave)	*(serious) illness*	se conformer	*to conform*
cacher	*to hide*	malsain(e)	*unhealthy*	la crise cardiaque	*heart attack*
le casse-croûte	*snack*	le mannequin	*model*	le docteur	*doctor*
le chocolat	*chocolate*	les matières grasses (f)	*fats*	le doigt	*finger*
la cigarette électronique	*e-cigarette*			le dos	*back*
		mener	*to lead*	l'estomac (m)	*stomach*
combattre	*to combat*	la musculation	*weight training*	la gorge	*throat*
le conseil	*advice*	nocif / nocive	*harmful (for your health)*	la grippe	*flu*
la consommation	*consumption / usage*			guérir	*to cure / treat*
		la nourriture bio	*organic food*	la main	*hand*
dégoûtant(e)	*disgusting*	l'obésité (f)	*obesity*	malade	*ill / sick*
le déjeuner	*lunch*	l'odeur (f)	*smell*	la maladie	*illness*
la dépendance	*addiction*	la peau	*skin*	le médecin	*doctor*
déprimé(e)	*depressed*	le petit déjeuner	*breakfast*	le médicament	*medicine*
désintoxiquer	*to detox*	pressé(e)	*in a hurry / rushed / squeezed*	le nez	*nose*
se détendre	*to relax*			l'obésité (f)	*obesity*
devenir	*to become*	quotidien(ne)	*daily*	l'œil (m)	*eye*
le dîner	*evening meal*	se relaxer	*to relax*	l'ordonnance (f)	*prescription*
dormir	*to sleep*	renoncer	*to give up*	l'oreille (f)	*ear*
la douleur	*pain*	le repas	*meal*	l'orteil (m)	*toe*
la drogue	*drug*	respirer	*to breathe*	les pays en voie de développement	*under-developed countries*
se droguer	*to take drugs*	rester	*to stay*		
l'eau potable (f)	*drinking water*	réussir	*to succeed*	le pied	*foot*
l'égalité (f)	*equality*	sain(e)	*healthy*	la pression	*pressure*
en bonne forme	*fit*	salé(e)	*salty*	le poids	*weight*
en bonne santé	*in good health*	la santé	*health*	un rhume	*a cold*
en vélo	*by bike*	(se) sentir	*to feel*	se sentir mal	*to feel unwell*
s'enivrer	*to get drunk*	le sida	*AIDS*	le sida	*AIDS*
l'entraînement (m)	*training*	soigner	*to care for*	la tête	*head*
s'entraîner	*to train*	le soin	*care*	tomber malade	*to fall ill*
épuiser	*to exhaust*	le sommeil	*sleep*	tousser	*to cough*
équilibré(e)	*balanced*	sortir en boîte	*to go clubbing*	le ventre	*tummy*
essoufflé(e)	*breathless*	le sucre	*sugar*	vomir	*to vomit*
éviter	*to avoid*	sucré(e)	*sugary*	les yeux (m)	*eyes*
faible	*weak*	suivre	*to follow*		
		surveiller	*to watch*		

Section Eight — Social and Global Issues

Environmental Problems (p.77-78)

allumer	to switch on
améliorer	to improve
augmenter	to increase
le bain	bath
la boîte (en carton)	(cardboard) box
le boîte (en aluminium)	(aluminium) can
la campagne	campaign
le centre de recyclage	recycling centre
le charbon	coal
le chauffage central	central heating
la couche d'ozone	ozone layer
croire	to believe
cultiver	to grow
le déboisement	deforestation
les déchets (m)	rubbish
décomposer	to decompose
détruire	to destroy
disparaître	to disappear
la douche	shower
économiser	to save
écologique	environmentally friendly
l'effet (m) de serre	greenhouse effect
effrayant(e)	frightening
l'emballage (m)	packaging
empêcher	to prevent
en danger	in danger
endommager	to damage
les énergies (f) fossiles	fossil fuels
l'énergie (f) renouvelable	renewable energy
l'ennui (m)	problem, worry
l'environnement (m)	environment
l'éolienne (f)	wind turbine
l'espace (m) vert	green area
l'état (m)	state
éteindre	to switch off
faire du recyclage	to recycle
gaspiller	to waste
le gaz carbonique	carbon dioxide
le gaz d'échappement	exhaust fumes
les habitats (m)	habitats
jeter	to throw (away)
s'inquiéter	to worry
la marée	tide
les matières (f) premières	raw materials
menacé(e)	threatened
mener à	to lead to

mondial(e)	worldwide
le niveau	level
les ordures (f)	rubbish
le papier	paper
le paysage	countryside / landscape
le pétrole	oil
la piste cyclable	cycle lane
pollué(e)	polluted
la pollution	pollution
potable	drinkable
la poubelle	dustbin
les produits (m) bio	green products
protéger	to protect
ramasser	to pick up
le réchauffement de la Terre	global warming
recyclable	recyclable
les ressources (f) naturelles	natural resources
le risque sanitaire	health hazard
le robinet	tap
le sac en plastique	plastic bag
sauver	to save
le souci	worry / concern
le trou	hole
utiliser	to use
la vague	wave
le verre	glass

Problems in Society (p.79-81)

agresser	to attack
améliorer	to improve
l'association (f) caritative	charity
l'attaque (f)	attack
avoir besoin de	to need
la bande	gang
battu(e)	hit
les biens	possessions
blessé(e)	injured
la catastrophe naturelle	natural disaster
le chômage	unemployment
combattre	to combat
coupable	guilty
un défi	a challenge
déprimé(e)	depressed
la dette	debt
effrayant(e)	frightening
égal(e)	equal
l'égalité (f)	equality
l'émeute (f)	riot
l'enquête (f)	enquiry
entouré(e)	surrounded
éteindre	to turn off

gratifiant(e)	rewarding
la guerre	war
le harcèlement	bullying / harassment
harceler	to bully / harass
Il vaut la peine.	It's worthwhile.
l'immigration (f)	immigration
l'immigré (m)	immigrant
l'incendie (m)	fire
l'inégalité (f) sociale	social inequality
l'inondation (f)	flood
inonder	to flood
lourd(e)	heavy / serious
lutter	to struggle
la manifestation	demonstration
mener une campagne	to lead a campaign
mentir	to lie
mondial(e)	worldwide
se moquer de	to make fun of
les morts (f)	deaths / fatalities
la paix	peace
les pauvres	the poor
la pauvreté	poverty
les personnes (f) défavorisées	disadvantaged people
se plaindre	to complain
le / la politicien(ne)	politician
prioritiser	to prioritise
produire	to provide / to produce
reconnaissant(e)	grateful
le réfugié	refugee
le / la sans-abri	homeless person
les SDF	homeless people
socialement exclu(e)	socially excluded
se souvenir de	to remember
supporter	to tolerate / put up with
supprimer	to suppress / eliminate
le témoin	witness
le travail bénévole	voluntary work
le tremblement de terre	earthquake
tuer	to kill
la victime	victim
voler	to steal
le voyou	yob / hooligan
vulnérable	vulnerable

Section Nine — Travel and Tourism

Where to Go (p.87)

à la montagne	in the mountains
à l'étranger	abroad
l'Afrique (f)	Africa
africain(e)	African
l'Algérie (f)	Algeria
algérien(ne)	Algerian
l'Allemagne (f)	Germany
allemand(e)	German
les Alpes (f)	the Alps
l'Amérique (f) du Sud	South America
américain(e)	American
l'Angleterre (f)	England
anglais(e)	English
l'Asie (f)	Asia
asiatique	Asian
la Belgique	Belgium
belge	Belgian
le Brésil	Brazil
brésilien(ne)	Brazilian
la Chine	China
chinois(e)	Chinese
la côte	coast
Douvres	Dover
l'Écosse (f)	Scotland
écossais(e)	Scottish
l'Espagne (f)	Spain
espagnol(e)	Spanish
les États-Unis (m)	USA
l'Europe (f)	Europe
européen(ne)	European
la France	France
français(e)	French
la frontière	border / frontier
la Grande-Bretagne	Great Britain
britannique	British
l'île (f)	island
l'Inde (f)	India
indien(ne)	Indian
le Japon	Japan
japonais(e)	Japanese
Londres	London
la Manche	English Channel
le Maroc	Morocco
marocain(e)	Moroccan
la Méditerranée	Mediterranean
la mer	sea
monde	world
le pays de Galles	Wales
gallois(e)	Welsh
Paris	Paris
la plage	beach
la Russie	Russia
russe	Russian
la Suisse	Switzerland
suisse	Swiss
la Tunisie	Tunisia
tunisien(ne)	Tunisian

Preparation (p.88-89)

l'accueil (m)	welcome / reception
l'agence (f) de voyages	travel agency
l'aire (f) de jeux	play area
l'ascenseur (m)	lift
l'auberge (f) de jeunesse	youth hostel
les bagages (m)	luggage
le camping	campsite
le camping-car	campervan
la caravane	caravan
casser	to break
la chambre	room
la chambre d'hôte	bed and breakfast
la chambre de famille	family room
chercher	to look for
la clé	key
la climatisation	air conditioning
la colonie de vacances	holiday / summer camp
déranger	to disturb
descendre	to go down
donner sur	to overlook
le dortoir	dormitory
dresser	to put up (tent)
durer	to last
l'échange (m)	exchange
l'emplacement (m)	pitch
en plein air	in the open air
expliquer	to explain
héberger	to lodge / accommodate
l'hôtel (m) (de luxe)	(luxury) hotel
inconnu(e)	unknown
jumelé(e)	twinned
le lavabo	wash basin
lever	to lift
le lit	bed
le lit à deux places	double bed
les lits (m) jumeaux	twin beds
les lits (m) superposés	bunk beds
le logement	accommodation
loger	to stay / to lodge
la moquette	carpet
le passeport	passport
la pièce d'identité	ID
les préparatifs (m)	preparations
prêt(e)	ready
le projet	plan
le / la propriétaire	owner
remercier	to thank
réserver	to book / to reserve
rester	to stay
le sac de couchage	sleeping bag
la salle de séjour	lounge
le séjour	stay / visit
la station balnéaire	seaside resort
la tente	tent
les vacances (f)	holidays
la valise	suitcase
la vue de mer	sea view

Getting There (p.90)

l'aéroport (m)	airport
l'arrivée (f)	arrival
s'asseoir	to sit down
attendre	to wait (for)
atterrir	to land
l'auto (f)	car
l'autobus (m)	bus
l'autoroute (f)	motorway
l'avion (m)	plane
le bateau	boat
le car	coach
la carte	map
le chemin	way / path
le chemin de fer	railway
conduire	to drive
décoller	to take off
le départ	departure
en retard	late
s'enregistrer	to check in
l'essence (f)	petrol
l'horaire (m)	timetable
laisser	to leave
lentement	slowly
la location de voitures	car rental
louer	to rent / to hire
manquer	to miss
se mettre en route	to set off
la moto	motorbike
partir	to leave
le permis de conduire	driving licence
ralentir	to slow down
le retour	return
retourner	to return
revenir	to come back
la route	way / road
le train	train
le trajet	journey
la traversée	crossing
la voiture	car
le vol	flight
voler	to fly
le voyage	journey / trip
voyager	to travel

What to Do (p.91)

l'aventure (f)	adventure
l'avis (m)	opinion
se baigner	to bathe, swim
le bord de la mer	seaside
la carte postale	postcard
la cathédrale	cathedral
le château	castle

Vocabulary

le concours	*competition*	se lever	*to get up*	se promener	*to go for a walk*
se coucher	*to go to bed*	le loisir	*free time (activity)*	la randonnée	*walk / hike*
la crème solaire	*sun cream*	les lunettes (f) de soleil	*sun glasses*	remarquer	*to notice*
la culture	*culture*	le maillot de bain	*swimming costume*	le rendez-vous	*meeting*
se débrouiller	*to get by*	marcher	*to walk*	les renseignements (m)	*information*
l'événement (m)	*event*	la montagne	*mountain*	se réveiller	*to wake up*
l'étranger (m) / l'étrangère (f)	*stranger / foreigner*	monter	*to go up / ascend*	la rivière	*river*
explorer	*to explore*	le musée	*museum*	le sable	*sand*
se faire bronzer	*to sunbathe*	nager	*to swim*	le site touristique	*tourist attraction*
faire du camping	*to go camping*	la nature	*nature*	le sommet	*summit*
faire la connaissance	*to get to know*	l'office (m) de tourisme	*tourist office*	le spectacle	*show*
faire la grasse matinée	*to lie in / sleep in*	paraître	*to seem*	le tour	*tour*
la foire	*fair*	le parc d'attractions	*theme park*	le tour en bateau	*boat tour*
se garer	*to park*	la perte	*loss*	le tourisme	*tourism*
s'habituer à	*to get used to*	la plage	*beach*	tourner	*to turn*
l'herbe (f)	*grass*	plaire	*to please*	traduire	*to translate*
le jardin zoologique	*zoo*	le plan de ville	*town plan*	la visite guidée	*guided tour*
le lac	*lake*	la plongée sous-marine	*underwater diving*	le zoo	*zoo*
laver	*to wash*	se présenter	*to introduce oneself*		
se laver	*to wash (yourself)*				

Section Ten — Current and Future Study and Employment

School Subjects (p.97)

affreux / affreuse	*awful*
l'allemand (m)	*German*
apprendre	*to learn*
la chimie	*chemistry*
chouette	*great*
la couture	*sewing*
le dessin	*art*
ennuyeux / ennuyeuse	*boring*
l'espagnol (m)	*Spanish*
l'EPS (éducation physique et sportive) (f)	*PE (physical education)*
le français	*French*
il ne sert à rien	*it's useless*
l'informatique (f)	*IT (information technology)*
l'instruction (f) civique	*citizenship*
s'intéresser à	*to be interested in*
la langue	*language*
les langues vivantes (f)	*modern languages*
la littérature anglaise	*English literature*
la physique	*physics*
la religion	*religious studies*
la matière	*subject*
passionnant(e)	*engaging*
préféré(e)	*favourite*

School Life (p.98-100)

à la mode	*fashionable*
aller à pied	*to go on foot*
l'ambiance (f)	*atmosphere*
apprendre	*to learn*
bien équipé(e)	*well equipped*
le bulletin scolaire	*school report*
la calculette	*calculator*
la cantine	*canteen*
le car de ramassage	*school bus*
le collège	*secondary school*
comprendre	*to understand*
le couloir	*corridor*
le cours	*lesson*
de bonne heure	*early*
demander	*to ask*
les devoirs (m)	*homework*
la difficulté	*difficulty*
le diplôme	*qualification*
le directeur	*headmaster*
la directrice	*headmistress*
discuter	*to discuss*
distribuer	*to give out*
doué(e)	*gifted / talented*
le droit	*right*
échouer	*to fail*
l'école (f) confessionnelle	*religious school*
l'école (f) primaire	*primary school*
l'école (f) privée	*private school*
l'école (f) publique	*state school*
l'école (f) secondaire	*secondary school*
l'élève (m / f)	*pupil*
l'emploi (m) du temps	*timetable*

en retard	*late*
en seconde	*in year 11*
enseigner	*to teach*
l'erreur (f)	*error / mistake*
les études (f)	*study*
l'étudiant (m)	*student*
l'examen (m)	*examination*
l'expérience (f)	*experiment*
faire attention	*to pay attention*
fatigant(e)	*tiring*
le gymnase	*sports hall*
les incivilités (f)	*rudeness*
l'injure (f)	*insult*
l'instituteur (m) / l'institutrice (f)	*primary school teacher*
interdit(e)	*forbidden*
l'internat (m)	*boarding school*
une journée typique	*a typical day*
le laboratoire	*laboratory*
la leçon	*lesson*
la lecture	*reading*
lire	*to read*
le lycée	*sixth form college*
mal équipé(e)	*badly equipped*
le maquillage	*make up*
la maternelle	*nursery school*
la note	*mark*
oublier	*to forget*
passer un examen	*to sit an exam*
la pause	*break / pause*
penser	*to think*
permettre	*to allow / permit*
la piscine	*swimming pool*
porter	*to wear / carry*
la pression	*pressure*
le / la professeur	*teacher*
le proviseur	*head teacher*

la récré(ation)	break
redoubler	to resit the year
la règle	rule
le règlement	school rules
la rentrée	return to school (after the holidays)
répéter	to repeat
la réponse	reply
le résultat	result
la retenue	detention
réussir un examen	to pass an exam
la salle de classe	classroom
savoir	to know
scolaire	school (adj)
la semaine	week
le tableau	board
le terrain de sport	sports ground
le trimestre	term
trouver	to find
l'uniforme (m) scolaire	school uniform
les vacances (f)	holidays
la vie scolaire	school life

Education Post-16 (p.101)

l'année (f) sabbatique	gap year
l'apprenti(e) (m / f)	apprentice
l'apprentissage (m)	apprenticeship
l'avenir (m)	future
avoir envie de	to want to
avoir l'intention de	to intend to
le bac(calauréat)	A-levels
le conseiller / la conseillère d'orientation	careers adviser
en première	in year 12
en terminale	in year 13
l'enseignement (m) postscolaire	further education
l'épreuve (f)	test
l'établissement (m)	establishment
étudier	to study
la faculté	university / faculty
former	to train
laisser tomber	to drop
la liberté	freedom
la licence	degree
le lycée	sixth form college / grammar school
le lycée professionnel	technical college
le travail bénévole	voluntary work
l'université (f)	university

Career Choices (p.102)

à peine	scarcely
à temps partiel	part-time
à temps plein	full-time
l'agent de police (m)	police officer
assis(e)	sitting
l'avenir (m)	future
l'avocat(e) (m / f)	lawyer
le babysitting	babysitting
le boucher	butcher
le boulanger	baker
le boulot	job (informal)
le candidat	candidate
le coiffeur / la coiffeuse	hairdresser
le commerce	business
le / la comptable	accountant
compter (sur)	to count (on)
la croisière	cruise
le débouché	job opportunity / prospect
debout	standing
le dessinateur de mode	fashion designer
disponible	available
élargir	to widen
l'emploi (m)	job (formal)
l'employé(e) (m / f)	employee
l'employeur (m) / l'employeuse (f)	employer
enrichissant(e)	enriching / rewarding
l'entreprise (f)	firm / enterprise
l'entretien (m)	interview
espérer	to hope
l'espoir (m)	hope
le facteur / la factrice	postman / postwoman
le fermier / la fermière	farmer
gagner	to earn / win
l'idée (f)	idea
l'infirmier (m) / l'infirmière (f)	nurse
l'informaticien(ne) (m / f)	IT worker
l'ingénieur (m / f)	engineer
l'instituteur (m) / l'institutrice (f)	primary school teacher
l'interprète (m / f)	interpreter
le journal	newspaper
le / la journaliste	journalist
la livre (sterling)	pound (sterling)

le maçon	builder
le mécanicien / la mécanicienne	mechanic
le médecin	doctor
mettre de l'argent de côté	to save money
le monde du travail	the world of work
l'outil (m)	tool
le patron / la patronne	boss
le petit job	part-time job
le plombier	plumber
le policier (m) / la policière (f)	police officer
le / la professeur	teacher
recevoir	to receive
la retraite	retirement
le rêve	dream
rêver	to dream
le salaire	salary
le traducteur / la traductrice	translator
le travailleur social / la travailleuse sociale	social worker
varié(e)	varied
le vendeur / la vendeuse	shop assistant
venir de	to have just
le / la vétérinaire	vet

Answers

The answers to the translation questions are sample answers only, just to give you an idea of one way to translate them. There may be different ways to translate these passages that are also correct.

Section One — General Stuff

Page 1: Numbers
1) Il a trois sœurs. (Il n'a pas de frère.)
2) la première maison de la rue Phillipe
3) C'est la troisième rue après le parc.
4) une vingtaine

Page 3: Times and Dates
1) 6.45 am
2) 8.30 am
3) Tuesdays and Thursdays
4) 1996

Page 9: Opinions
1) Maurice le Pain is not very funny.
2) He is really talented.
3) They are always great.
4) Because he is handsome.
5) He is great.

Page 10: Putting it All Together
1) A. true B. false
2) A. false B. false
3) A. true B. false

Page 11: Listening Questions
1 a) 2 b) about 10 c) €256 d) 5 e) about 20
2 a) true b) false c) false d) false e) true f) false

Page 13: Reading Questions
1 a) 73 b) 20 c) 17 d) 14 e) 47 f) 16
2 a) le mardi soir, à sept heures
b) un concours
c) le lundi soir et le samedi matin
d) la semaine prochaine

Page 14: Writing Questions
1) Le lundi, je vois mes ami(e)s. La semaine dernière, nous avons regardé un film d'action. Ce week-end, je vais faire les magasins avec mes cousin(e)s.
2) Mon sport préféré, c'est le rugby parce que c'est très passionnant. Je joue au rugby depuis sept ans. Le week-end, j'aime regarder le sport à la télévision avec mes amis, mais je ne m'intéresse pas au football. Je pense que les joueurs sont arrogants. Dans le futur / À l'avenir, je voudrais être prof.

Section Two — Me, My Family and Friends

Page 17: My Family
In my family, there are three people — my mother, my father and me. Unfortunately, I don't have any brothers or sisters, so I'm an only child. On the other hand, I have lots of cousins and I see them often. Last weekend, for example, we went to the cinema together and we really enjoyed ourselves.

Page 18: Describing People
1) A and D 2) C and D

Page 21: Partnership
1) C 2) B

Page 22: Listening Questions
1 a) true b) false c) true d) true
2 a) vivre seul b) célibataire
c) (penser à) se marier et (à) avoir des enfants

Page 24: Reading Questions
1 a) Two from: Elle est assez grande. / Elle a les cheveux blonds et courts. / Elle a les yeux verts. / Elle est sportive.
b) Il est (déjà) plus grand que leur père.
c) Elle aime jouer au football. *[1 mark]*
Elle joue au football tous les samedis. *[1 mark]*

2 a) Sylvie b) Louis c) Étienne

Page 25: Writing Questions
2) J'ai rencontré mes deux meilleures amies au club des jeunes. Edith est très amusante / drôle et bavarde, comme moi. Delphine est timide mais gentille et généreuse. Elles sont très différentes mais elles sont très sympathiques et nous passons beaucoup de temps ensemble. Nous nous entendons bien. Quelquefois il est difficile de se faire des amis.

Section Three — Free-Time Activities

Page 27: Music
1) professeur 2) ambiance / atmosphère 3) répéter

Page 28: Cinema
Mon ami(e) et moi sommes allé(e)s au cinéma le week-end dernier. Nous avons regardé un film d'horreur. Je n'avais pas peur, mais mon ami(e) a crié pendant le film. J'aime aller au cinéma. C'est toujours divertissant. Le mois prochain, j'irai voir le nouveau film d'action.

Page 29: TV
1) false 2) true 3) true 4) true

Page 30: Food
1) B 2) A 3) A 4) B

Page 34: Listening Questions
1 a) It allows people to watch films. b) 38 seconds
c) Two from: It took place on 28th December 1895. / It took place in the basement of the Grand Café in Paris. / It lasted around 20 minutes. / Ten films were shown.
2 a) meat / burgers b) beef
c) She is allergic to egg. *[1 mark]*
She has to wash her hair. *[1 mark]*

Page 36: Reading Questions
1 a) A b) B c) A+B
2) I love music. I like all types / genres of music. I listen to music all the time, normally on my mobile (phone). Yesterday, I was listening to music while walking to school when I started to sing with the music. My friends were looking at me but I didn't know why!

Page 37: Writing Questions
2) Mon sport préféré c'est le basket. Je joue au basket depuis trois ans. Je m'entraîne deux fois par semaine après le collège et quelquefois il y a un tournoi le week-end. La semaine dernière mon équipe a gagné. Je joue aussi au tennis le samedi. À l'avenir, je voudrais / j'aimerais apprendre à faire du ski.

Section Four — Technology in Everyday Life

Page 40: Technology
J'ai reçu / eu un nouveau portable pour mon anniversaire. Ma mère me l'a acheté. C'est très utile parce que je peux contacter mes parents et mes amis quand je veux. Je peux aussi télécharger de la musique et des jeux d'Internet. Demain, je l'utiliserai pour acheter un livre en ligne.

Page 41: Social Media
1) Elle tchatte avec ses amis.
2) Ils sont indispensables.
3) Elle regarde ses photos.

Page 43: Listening Questions
1 a) send messages. b) learn Spanish.
c) spend too much time in front of a screen.
2 a) C and D b) B and D c) B and C

Page 45: Reading Questions
1 a) M b) A c) L d) A
2) I am addicted to social networks. I want to know what my friends are doing, and I think that it's a good way to communicate and to meet others. Last year, for example, I got to know a boy in Canada and we talk online every week.

Page 46: Writing Questions

2) Mes parents ne veulent pas que j'utilise les réseaux sociaux. Ils pensent que ça peut être très dangereux mais je ne suis pas d'accord. Je ne mets pas mes photos en ligne et je ne partage jamais mes vidéos. Nous discutons des problèmes comme le harcèlement au collège. Cependant, je pense que les professeurs devraient nous donner plus d'informations.

Section Five — Customs and Festivals

Page 48: Festivals in French-Speaking Countries

1 a) 34% b) 18% c) 16% 2) 20%

Page 49: Festivals in French-Speaking Countries

1) A 2) B 3) B

Page 51: Listening Questions

1) A, E
2 a) A b) C c) B d) C

Page 53: Reading Questions

1 a) Two from: Bastille Day / Easter / Christmas
   b) to help people learn more about the country's past
   c) One from: There is music outdoors. / The atmosphere is superb. / Musicians from around the world are invited. / It is very international.
2) F, D, C, A

Page 54: Writing Questions

2) Le 14 juillet est la Fête nationale en France. Beaucoup de touristes vont à Paris pour voir les défilés. Cette année, je suis allé(e) à un parc près de la tour Eiffel pour regarder les feux d'artifice. C'était une expérience formidable / chouette / géniale. Mes ami(e)s aimeraient visiter Paris l'année prochaine, donc nous célébrerons ensemble.

Section Six — Where You Live

Page 56: Talking About Where You Live

1) by the second year
2) one for men and one for women
3) He gave them a job and bread.
4) unemployment and poverty

Page 58: What You Do at Home

I get ten euros of pocket money per / a week. But I have to work to earn this money. I do household chores every day to help my parents. In addition, last Saturday I babysat. I buy lots of music online, but I'm going to try to save up because I would like to go on holiday with my friends.

Page 61: More Shopping

Sara — disadvantage: You can't ask the assistant for advice.
Pierre — advantage: You don't have to queue. **or**: You save time.
or: The supermarkets deliver your shopping.
Pierre — disadvantage: You can't try on the clothes.

Page 62: Giving and Asking for Directions

1) Get off at the **bus station** and change buses.
2) After turning left, carry on until **the library**.
3) Cross the road, and after about 100 m the Belle Époque will be **on the left**.

Page 63: Weather

1) true 2) true 3) false

Page 64: Listening Questions

1 a) Likes: cooking (for his family) Dislikes: washing the car
   b) Likes: doing the laundry Dislikes: washing up
2 a) a strawberry cake [1 mark] a bottle of red wine [1 mark]
   b) She had forgotten her purse. c) go window shopping

Page 66: Reading Questions

1 a) One from: The traffic was frightening. / There was a traffic jam on every street. / The air pollution was unbearable. / The noise was unbearable.
   b) the most beautiful city in the world

c) show him the wonders of Paris

2) I live with my parents, my brother and my sister. When I was younger, we lived in a flat in the town centre. Now we live in a big house which is near the park. I like my house because there is lots of space for all the family. However, the house is very old.

Page 67: Writing Questions

2) C'est l'anniversaire de ma petite amie cette semaine, donc je dois acheter un cadeau. Hier je suis allé(e) au grand magasin. J'ai trouvé une jolie robe mais le magasin n'avait pas sa taille. J'ai vu un chapeau aussi, mais c'était trop cher. J'achèterai des fleurs pour ma petite amie, mais je pense que c'est barbant.

Section Seven — Lifestyle

Page 71: Illnesses

I often go to the hospital to visit my grandmother, who has been ill since last year. At the beginning, I was sad, but she's starting to get better. In the future, I would like to be a doctor to help people who are suffering. I would like to find new medicines to cure them and do research on serious illnesses.

Page 72: Listening Questions

1 a) C b) D c) A
2 a) disgusting ... she finds the smell really unpleasant
   b) relax ... smoke less often
   c) she gave up (a year ago) ... it is really antisocial

Page 74: Reading Questions

1) There are lots of people who would like to be skinny / thin like the celebrities you see on television. It is often a problem among young people. Last year, my best friend wanted to be thinner and she went on a diet. She was tired all the time. It was really sad.
2) Tomorrow there will be an important match for my football team. However, I am worried because the players have had a lot of health problems. Chloé has broken her arm and will not be able to play tomorrow. Michelle has ear ache and her mother won't let her leave the house. In addition, two other girls are ill.

Page 75: Writing Questions

2) J'aimerais / je voudrais être en bonne forme, donc j'essaie / j'essaye de bien manger. Je pense qu'il est important d'être sain(e) quand on est jeune. Je mangeais beaucoup de glace, mais maintenant je préfère manger des repas équilibrés. Je fais aussi de l'exercice trois fois par semaine. Je vais au collège à pied au lieu de prendre l'autobus / le car de ramassage.

Section Eight — Social and Global Issues

Page 78: Environmental Problems

La pollution a causé des problèmes graves pour l'environnement. Elle a détruit beaucoup d'habitats. Je pense que les gens ne font pas assez pour protéger la planète. Tous les jours, nous jetons des matières recyclables et gaspillons des ressources naturelles. À l'avenir, nous devrons utiliser l'énergie renouvelable, au lieu du charbon et du pétrole.

Page 80: Problems in Society

1) A 2) F 3) B 4) C

Page 82: Listening Questions

1 a) Natural resources aren't infinite / are limited.
   b) recycle their rubbish [1 mark] buy products with recyclable packaging [1 mark]
   c) Two from: cardboard boxes, plastic bottles, glass bottles, plastic bags
2 a) B b) A c) A

Page 84: Reading Questions

1) B and D
2) I live in a city where there is a lot of violence, and I'm really scared of the gangs in my area. In the evening, there are places which I avoid, especially as I was once attacked on my way home. It was frightening. We need to do something but I don't know what.

Page 85: Writing Questions

2) Je pense qu'il est très important de protéger l'environnement. Il y a beaucoup qu'on pourrait faire à la maison. Par exemple, en hiver j'éteins toujours le chauffage central pendant la journée. Hier, j'ai pris une douche au lieu d'un bain parce que ça utilise moins d'eau.

Answers

Section Nine — Travel and Tourism

Page 87: Where to Go
1) Elle veut aller en Angleterre. Elle veut voir un match de football.
2) Elle veut passer les vacances au bord de la mer. Elle veut aller chaque jour à la plage.
3) Il veut rester en France. Il veut faire du camping.

Page 88: Accommodation
B and E

Page 90: How to Get There
Next week, I'm going to go on holiday to the United States. In particular, I would like to see New York. I've reserved / booked a luxury hotel there with a big swimming pool. However, the journey worries me a lot. I'm scared of flying, and I will be on the plane for seven hours.

Page 92: Listening Questions
1 a) 1
  b) more information about the different types of room (available)
  c) Two from: your name; your telephone number; the dates of your stay
2 a) C and D   b) C and D   c) A and C

Page 94: Reading Questions
1 a) It is too expensive to go alone or with friends.
  b) a holiday camp / in another European country
  c) You will learn another language.
    You will earn a bit of money.
2)   E, A, F, B

Page 95: Writing Questions
2) L'année dernière, ma famille a logé / est restée dans un petit hôtel en Angleterre. Quel désastre ! Notre chambre était très petite. La salle de bains était vraiment sale, c'était dégoûtant. La nourriture au restaurant était affreuse et le serveur était impoli. L'année prochaine, nous irons en Chine et visiterons un parc d'attractions.

Section Ten — Current and Future Study and Employment

Page 98: School Routine
1)   son petit frère   2)   mardi   3)   basket

Page 99: School Life
1)   K   2)   A   3)   K

Page 101: Education Post-16
Pour célébrer la fin des examens, j'ai regardé des films avec mes amis. Nous sommes très heureux / heureuses parce que c'est les vacances. En septembre prochain, j'irai au lycée pour faire le bac(calauréat) et j'aimerais / je voudrais obtenir de bons résultats. Cependant, mon / ma meilleur(e) ami(e) veut / a envie de faire un apprentissage.

Page 102: Career Choices and Ambitions
When I was younger, I wanted to be a baker because I loved to make cakes. Today, I'm still interested in cooking, and I would like to be a chef when I leave school. I have a part-time job in a restaurant kitchen. I don't earn a lot of money, but I hope that the experience will be useful in the future.

Page 103: Listening Questions
1 a) A   b) C   c) A   2 a) C and D   b) A and D

Page 105: Reading Questions
1) I am going to go to the sixth form college near my home. The building is very modern and the classrooms are big. Also, / In addition, I will be able to sing in the choir and play in the orchestra. Unfortunately, my best friend will not go to sixth form college with me, because she wants to go to technical college.
2) a) M   b) L   c) A

Page 106: Writing Questions
2) J'en ai marre du collège parce qu'il y a beaucoup de pression. Les cours sont barbants / ennuyeux et je ne les aime pas. Hier, mon / ma professeur s'est mis(e) en colère / s'est fâché(e) et j'ai eu une retenue pendant la pause de midi. Aussi / En plus, nous devons porter un uniforme scolaire mais je préférerais choisir mes vêtements moi-même.

Section Eleven — Grammar

Page 108: Words for People and Objects
1) le cadeau — les cadeaux   4) le cheval — les chevaux
2) la piscine — les piscines   5) la voiture — les voitures
3) le citron — les citrons   6) la pâtisserie — les pâtisseries

Page 109: 'The', 'A' and 'Some'
1) L'homme a un peu **de** pain.   4) Nous avons **des** bananes.
2) Les étudiants viennent **du** Maroc.   5) Ils n'ont pas **de** raisins.
3) Je vais **au** pays de Galles.   6) Il va **à la** bibliothèque.

Page 110: Words to Describe Things
1) La mère fière.   5) Les chiens vifs.
2) Une fille triste.   6) Les voitures blanches.
3) Le chat lent.   7) Une femme gentille.
4) Une maison bleue.   8) Une veste chère.

Page 111: Words to Describe Things
3 and 6 are correct. The others should be:
1) C'est un jeune chien.   4) Tu as lu un livre ennuyeux.
2) Le train long est bleu.   5) J'ai une nouvelle voiture rouge.

Page 112: Words to Describe Things
1) **Mon** père n'aime pas **sa** nouvelle voiture.
2) **Tes** amis ne vont pas à **notre** lycée.
3) **Cet** hôtel est grand.
4) **Cette** cuisinière a **quelques** légumes.

Page 113: Words to Compare Things
1) Navid et Pauline sont les plus forts.
2) Ta / Votre grand-mère est plus vieille que mon grand-père.
3) Ce magasin est le moins cher.
4) Julie est aussi active que Thérèse.
5) Ses idées sont les pires.
6) Le français est le meilleur.

Pages 114-115: Quick Questions
1 a) m   c) f   e) f   g) m   i) f   k) f   m) f   o) f
  b) m   d) f   f) m   h) m   j) m   l) f   n) m
2 a) f   c) m   e) f   g) m   i) m   k) m   m) f   o) m
  b) m   d) f   f) f   h) f   j) f   l) f   n) f
3 a) la maison   c) le professeur   e) la robe   g) l'abricot
  b) le jardin   d) l'orange   f) l'hôpital   h) l'hiver
4 a) des   c) de l'   e) de   g) du
  b) de   d) de la   f) de   h) des
5 a) facile   c) vieux   e) triste   g) bonne
  b) amusants, gentils   d) belle   f) grande   h) long, ennuyeux
6 a) Alexandre a les yeux **bleus**.
  b) J'habite dans une maison **moderne**.
  c) La **première** question est très **difficile**.
  d) Susanna porte un chapeau **rouge** et des chaussures **orange**.
  e) Mes frères sont assez **sportifs**.
  f) Le cochon d'Inde est **heureux** et **mignon**.
7 a) longues   b) nouvelle   c) toute   d) rigolo
8 a) blanche   b) étrangers   c) dernières   d) chère   e) sèches
9 a) J'ai une chemise **bleue**.
  b) Nous sommes au **premier** étage.
  c) Loïc habite dans un **petit** appartement.
  d) Il chante des chansons **étrangères**.
  e) C'est une **bonne** peinture.
10 a) mon chien   e) ses chaussures
   b) leur voiture   f) son frère
   c) ta / votre maison   g) nos parents
   d) mon copain / ma copine   h) ton / votre cheval
11 a) Mon vélo est rouge.
   b) Est-ce que ton manteau est bleu ?
   c) Sa mère habite en Irlande.
   d) Avez-vous parlé à votre grand-mère ?
   e) Ils n'ont pas fait leurs devoirs.
   f) Est-ce que tu as vu son argent ?

12 a) Je joue au rugby **chaque** week-end.

  b) Eric a acheté **quelques** légumes.

  c) **Chaque** élève doit faire des devoirs.

  d) Il a trouvé **quelques** livres intéressants.

13 a) ce   b) Cet   c) ce   d) Ces   e) cette

14 a) Cette fête est la plus passionnante.

  b) Je suis étrange / bizarre, mais il est le plus étrange / bizarre.

  c) Ces arbres sont les plus verts.

Page 116: Words to Describe Actions

1)	tristement	4)	fièrement	7)	mauvais
2)	négativement	5)	absolument	8)	constamment
3)	sérieusement	6)	lentement		

Page 117: Words to Describe Actions

1) Je joue au tennis là-bas.

2) Tu chantes tous les jours.

3) Normalement, je vais en ville en bus.

4) Elles vont là-bas.

5) Par conséquent, j'aime mes matières.

6) J'aime ce nouveau professeur maintenant.

Page 118: Words to Compare Actions

1) Thomas joue du piano **le mieux**.

2) François va à l'étranger **le plus fréquemment**.

3) Lucie court **plus que** Emmanuel.

4) Je regarde la télévision **le moins souvent**.

5) Tu ris **autant que** moi.

6) Je chante **pire que** toi.

Page 119: Words to Say How Much

1) Elle est **très** vive.

2) Ils ont **un peu d'**eau.

3) Le musicien est **vraiment** doué.

4) C'est **assez** intéressant.

  'Assez' (quite) isn't followed by 'de' here because it's an intensifier.

5) Tu as beaucoup **de** chaussettes.

6) L'homme a trop **de** chocolat.

Page 120: Quick Questions

1 a) facilement   e) gentiment   i) deuxièmement

  b) précisément   f) complètement   j) calmement

  c) heureusement   g) clairement   k) incroyablement

  d) évidemment   h) stupidement   l) honnêtement

2 a) Zanna écrit autant qu'Étienne.

  b) Le chien noir est le plus âgé / vieux.

  c) Les gâteaux au chocolat sont les meilleurs.

  d) Je joue au tennis mieux que ma sœur.

3 a) Julian joue du banjo **mieux** que Claude.

  b) Ayesha nage **le pire** dans la mer.

  c) Lucie écrit **le moins** au collège.

  d) Mathieu cuisine **plus** à la maison que Charles.

4 a) Hier   b) souvent   c) Normalement   d) demain   e) déjà

5 a) Je l'ai vu **là-bas**.

  b) Elle a perdu son portable **quelque part**.

  c) Mon père a ses papiers **partout**.

  d) L'aéroport est assez **loin** de la ville.

  e) Venez **ici**, s'il vous plaît.

6 a) in general / generally   d) next year   g) last week

  b) absolutely   e) late   h) at the same time

  c) from time to time   f) in any case

7 a) a little bit / a little bit of / a little

  b) enough   d) little / not much / not many

  c) too much / too many   e) lots of / many / a lot of

8 a) Elles ont **assez de** poissons.

  b) Elle a **trop d'**argent.

  c) Mon ami a **beaucoup de** serpents.

  d) Le magicien a eu **peu de** succès.

Page 121: I, Me, You, We, Them

1) Hélène **lui** donne le livre.

2) **Elle** aime les chiens.

3) Tu peux **les** voir?

4) Avez-vous le livre? Non, elle **l'**a.

5) **Nous** allons au cinéma.

6) Non, **elles** ne sont pas ici.

Page 122: Something, There, Any

1, 4 and 6 are correct. The others should be:

2) **Tout** le monde sait que c'est vrai.

3) A-t-elle des livres? Oui, elle **en** a.

5) Tu connais le château? J'**y** suis allé(e).

Page 123: Position and Order of Object Pronouns

1) Il le lui donne. *He gives it to him / her.*

2) C'est moi qui l'ai écouté. *It's me who listened to him.*

3) Tu l'as écrit toi-même. *You wrote it yourself.*

4) Vous y êtes allés avec nous. *You went there with us.*

5) Elle t'a dit. *She told you.*

6) Je vais lui en parler. *I'm going to talk to him / her about it.*

Page 124: Relative and Interrogative Pronouns

1) L'homme qui est sportif.

2) La pizza que j'aime manger.

3) J'ai cinq crayons qui sont rouges.

4) Tu cours avec qui? / Avec qui cours-tu?

5) La voiture qu'elle conduit est lente.

6) À quoi penses-tu?

Page 125: Possessive and Demonstrative Pronouns

1) Le stylo là est **le tien**.

2) Celle-là est **la sienne**.

3) **Cela** n'est pas drôle!

4) Ces chiens sont **les nôtres**.

5) Où as-tu vu **ça / cela**?

6) C'est **le / la vôtre**.

Page 126: Quick Questions

1 a) **Elle** aime le chocolat.   d) **Il** joue au football.

  b) **Il** a mangé mes chaussures.   e) **Elle** est sous la table.

  c) **Ils** détestent les filles.   f) **Elles** sont allées au cinéma.

2 a) Je **la** regarde.   b) Paul **le** lit.   c) Je **les** déteste.

3 a) quelque chose   c) tout le monde   e) plusieurs

  b) quelqu'un   d) chacun(e)

4 a) On **y** va s'il fait beau.

  b) Est-ce que tu peux m'**en** acheter ?

  c) Je n'**y** vais pas à cause des monstres.

  d) Les vacances, parlons-**en**.

  e) Tu **y** es déjà allée ?

  f) On ne s'**en** sortira jamais !

5 a) Nous pouvons le leur donner.

  b) Mon père t'y attend.

  c) Vous lui en achetez.

  d) Elle les y rencontre.

  e) Je la lui avais offerte.

  f) Il leur a téléphoné hier.

6 a) Le lapin **que** tu as tué était délicieux.

  b) C'est un homme **qui** aime le poulet.

  c) Les sandales **qu'**il porte avec des chaussettes sont laides.

  d) Le gendarme **qui** a volé ma voiture était vieux.

7 a) The farmer has a hen whose eggs are perfect.

  b) He had three cakes, two of which were filled with fruit.

  c) The illness from which she suffers gives her a blue nose.

8 a) le nôtre   b) la sienne   c) les miennes   d) la sienne

9 a) I don't like this dress. I prefer that one.

  b) Have you read these books? This one is very good, but that one is boring.

  c) I like dogs, but those ones are really nasty.

Page 127: Joining Words

1) d   2) b   3) e   4) a   5) c   6) f

Answers

Page 128: Prepositions

1) Je joue au foot.
2) Elle rend visite à Manu.
3) Il s'agit d'un jeune garçon.
4) un pull en laine
5) Je joue de la clarinette.
6) Ils / Elles habitent en France.
7) Il va à la banque.
8) Tu viens du pays de Galles.

Page 129: Prepositions

1) Je suis **chez** Paul avec Dima.
2) Le magasin est **sous** le pont.
3) Je vais aller en vacances **pour** deux semaines.
4) Je travaille à la pharmacie **depuis** six mois.

Page 130: Quick Questions

1 a) but
b) neither...nor
c) when / as soon as
d) like, as
e) or
f) when
g) since
h) while
i) because
j) or else
k) after
l) then

2 a) Je voudrais une pomme **et** une poire.
b) C'est mon anniversaire **mais** je ne sors pas.
c) **Si** tu manges le champignon, je te tuerai.
d) Je me douche, **puis** je m'habille.
e) **Comme** j'étais en retard, j'ai manqué le bus.

3 a) à   c) dans   e) en   g) dans
b) aux   d) à   f) en   h) aux

4 a) sous   c) sans   e) chez   g) avec
b) sur   d) après   f) vers   h) avant

5 a) My father is very tired because he works all the time.
b) Take a chocolate if you want.
c) I'm tired so I'm going to go to bed.
d) What are you going to do during the holidays?
e) I play football with my brother.

6 a) de la   c) à la   e) du   g) à la   i) du
b) aux   d) au   f) de   h) de la   j) à

7 a) L'école est en face de la piscine.
b) Je suis resté(e) à la maison / chez moi à cause de la pluie.
c) Il y a un supermarché à côté du parc.
d) Aix-en-Provence est / se trouve près de Marseille.

Page 131: Verbs in the Present Tense

1) je parle
2) il établit
3) nous remplissons
4) tu réponds
5) elles entendent
6) vous commencez
7) vous perdez
8) ils grossissent
9) j'allume
10) on vend

Page 132: Irregular Verbs in the Present Tense

1) nous **devons**
2) je **veux**
3) vous **êtes**
4) tu **dois**
5) elle **va**
6) ils **font**
7) elles **peuvent**
8) on **sait**
9) ils **ont**
10) nous **faisons**

Page 133: More About the Present Tense

1) Je commence à comprendre.
2) Je veux manger de la pizza.
3) J'étudie le français depuis deux ans.
4) Je joue au foot depuis 1999.
5) Aimes-tu / Aimez-vous les prunes?
6) Joues-tu / Jouez-vous du piano?

Page 134: Quick Questions

1 a) je parle
b) tu écoutes / vous écoutez
c) nous jouons
d) ils / elles détestent
e) il écoute

2 a) agis
b) achetez
c) finis
d) choisissent
e) partagez
f) punissent
g) bat
h) attendez
i) mord
j) vends

3 a) e, e   b) ons, es   c) e, ent   d) ez, e

4 a) boit
b) disent
c) lis
d) ouvrez
e) ferme
f) pouvons

5 a) fais   c) veut   e) faites   g) allons   i) doivent
b) vas   d) devons   f) fait   h) voulez   j) vais

6 a) Nous sommes heureux.
b) Mon père est ingénieur.
c) Les devoirs sont ennuyeux.

d) Vous êtes anglais.
e) Je suis fatigué.
f) Elle est belle.

7 a) J'apprends à jouer de la guitare.
b) Je n'arrive jamais à manger mon petit-déjeuner.
c) Il commence à pleuvoir.
d) J'arrive toujours à faire mes devoirs.

8 a) (j') ai   c) a   e) avez
b) as   d) avons   f) ont

9 a) Mange-t-elle de la viande ?
b) Vas-tu en ville ce matin ?
c) Aime-t-il le chocolat ?
d) A-t-elle un petit ami ?
e) Savez-vous parler chinois ?
f) Devons-nous partir bientôt ?

Page 135: Talking About the Future

1) il va aller / il ira
2) je vais avoir / j'aurai
3) nous allons finir / nous finirons
4) tu vas regarder / tu regarderas
5) elles vont dire / elles diront
6) vous allez faire / vous ferez
7) tu vas pouvoir / tu pourras
8) elle va venir / elle viendra
9) ils vont être / ils seront
10) on va vendre / on vendra

Page 136: Talking About the Past

1) j'ai parlé
2) il a élargi
3) nous avons fini
4) tu as vendu
5) on a grandi
6) elles ont mangé
7) j'ai répondu
8) vous avez cherché

Page 137: Talking About the Past

1) elles ont mis
2) nous avons lu
3) tu as dit
4) je suis allé(e)
5) elle est arrivée
6) nous avons dû
7) ils sont retournés
8) je me suis lavé(e)

Page 138: Talking About the Past

The imperfect verb phrases are:
1) nous venions
3) elle faisait
4) vous veniez
8) tu étais

Page 139: Talking About the Past

1) J'ai couru. (perfect)
2) Ils / elles ont mangé. (perfect)
3) Tu riais. (imperfect)
4) Il était pénible / embêtant. (imperfect)
5) C'était terrifiant. (imperfect)
6) Elle a pleuré. (perfect)
7) Je jouais au basket. (imperfect)
8) Je rangeais (imperfect) quand elle est arrivée. (perfect)

Pages 140-141: Quick Questions

1 a) je vais choisir
b) tu vas manger
c) ils vont finir
d) vous allez prendre

2 a) elles arriveront
b) on dansera
c) il jouera
d) nous vendrons

3 a) demanderez
b) donnerai
c) écriront
d) finirai
e) entendra

4 a) I will go
b) we will be
c) you will be able to
d) they will say
e) he will have to
f) she will want
g) you will have
h) I will do

5 a) j'ai joué
b) tu as vendu
c) vous avez regardé
d) elles ont dormi
e) il a écouté
f) j'ai mangé
g) nous avons fini
h) on a choisi

6 a) lu
b) eu
c) été
d) mort
e) craint
f) dû
g) conduit
h) mis
i) pris
j) voulu
k) su
l) né

7 a) Hier soir mon frère **est sorti** avec ses amis et il **est rentré** très tard.
b) J'**ai voulu** te téléphoner mais j'**ai dû** faire mes devoirs.

Answers

c) Le film **a fini** à huit heures, donc nous **avons pu** en voir un autre.

d) Quand vous **êtes allée** à la discothèque, est-ce que vous **avez mis** votre robe rouge ?

8 a) s   b) e   c) es   d) —

9 a) a lu   b) as mis   c) ont écrit   d) avez vécu

10 a) je suis allé(e)   e) nous sommes monté(e)s

b) vous êtes devenu(s)   f) ils sont partis

c) elle est sortie   g) tu es tombé(e)

d) il est arrivé   h) elle est entrée

11 a) Il y avait un concert au théâtre.

b) C'était trop facile.

c) Dans ma chambre, il y avait un lit et une armoire.

12 a) Les moutons faisaient du bruit au centre-ville.

b) Nous étions bronzées après nos vacances.

c) Tu avais la grippe.

d) Tu étais très content de recevoir le paquet.

e) Je faisais la vaisselle avec mes doigts de pied.

f) J'avais un melon et une courgette.

13 a) je dormais   d) tu devais

b) ils finissaient   e) vous écoutiez

c) il semblait   f) nous restions

14 a) Susie **a téléphoné** pendant que tu **faisais** tes devoirs.

b) J'**ai mangé** tout le gâteau pendant que ma mère **regardait** la télévision.

c) Il **s'est cassé** la jambe pendant que nous **jouions** au rugby.

d) Pendant que vous **rangiez** votre chambre, j'**ai pris** une douche.

15 a) I was watching television.

b) She was dancing in the dining room.

c) We were waiting for the postman.

d) They were making a lot of noise.

16 a) I used to play the piano.

b) We used to go to the park every day.

c) We used to watch the news.

d) You used to believe in Father Christmas.

e) You used to buy the newspaper.

f) He used to eat green beans.

Page 142: Reflexive Verbs and Pronouns

1) nous nous couchons   5) tu t'es amusé(e)

2) vous vous disputez   6) je vais me détendre

3) elles se lèvent   7) elle s'est sentie

4) il s'intéresse à   8) nous allons nous plaindre

Page 143: Negative Forms

1) Je ne mange jamais de viande.

2) Il n'a pas de chien.

3) Tu ne bois que de l'eau.

4) Ils n'aiment personne.

5) Nous ne vivons / habitons plus ensemble.

6) Vous n'y allez jamais.

Page 144: Would, Could and Should

1) tu améliorerais   6) vous viendriez

2) il élargirait   7) on serait

3) nous rendrions   8) elle aurait

4) je ferais   9) ils se laveraient

5) elles iraient   10) vous chercheriez

Page 145: Giving Orders

1) Finissez vos devoirs!   5) Ne va pas!

2) Organisons une fête!   6) Ne courez pas!

3) Écoute!   7) Couche-toi!

4) Mangeons!   8) Ne vous disputez pas!

Page 146: Quick Questions

1 a) m'excuse   c) vous amusez   e) se sent / se sentait

b) nous lavons   d) se trouvent   f) se couchent

2 a) e   b) s   c) —   d) es

3 a) Je ne mange pas de viande.

b) Elle n'aime pas faire les courses.

c) Tu n'as pas beaucoup d'argent.

d) Nous n'allons pas au cinéma ce soir.

4 a) Je ne mange ni petit pois ni carottes.

b) Elle ne porte que des chaussettes bleues.

c) Nous ne sommes jamais allé(e)s en Russie.

d) Elles ne parlent à personne.

5 a) préférerais   b) détesterions   c) jouerais   d) prendraient

6 a) J'irais au cinéma, mais je n'ai pas assez d'argent.

b) Nous aimerions aider.

c) Tu devrais arriver à onze heures.

7 a) Mange   b) Soyez   c) Allons   d) Finis

8 a) Prête-moi ton stylo !   d) Assieds-toi !

b) Couche-toi !   e) Asseyez-vous !

c) Taisez-vous !   f) Levons-nous !

9 a) Ne sors pas !   c) Ne te couche pas !

b) N'allons pas à la piscine !   d) Ne te lève pas !

Page 147: 'Had done' and '-ing'

1) j'avais joué   5) en aidant

2) nous nous étions disputé(e)s   6) en restant

3) vous étiez arrivé(e)s   7) après être parti(e)(s)

4) elles avaient été   8) après avoir détruit

Page 148: The Passive

The passive sentences are:

1) L'homme est heurté par la voiture.

4) La pomme sera mangée par mon oncle.

6) La tasse a été cassée.

Page 149: Impersonal Verbs and the Subjunctive

The phrases containing a verb in the subjunctive are:

3) avant que vous alliez   6) pour que nous puissions

4) bien qu'elles soient   8) bien qu'il puisse

Page 150: Quick Questions

1 a) il avait décrit   d) il avait vécu   g) nous étions allé(e)s

b) vous aviez fait   e) ils avaient dit   h) j'avais mangé

c) elles étaient parties   f) tu avais manqué

2 a) I had finished.

b) Mark had forgotten to close the window.

c) Michelle and Sharon had arrived.

d) She had got up at three o'clock.

e) We had lost the cow.

f) I had left by car.

3 a) voulant   d) finissant   g) perdant   j) allant

b) donnant   e) rendant   h) faisant   k) sachant

c) achetant   f) choisissant   i) disant   l) buvant

4 a) We entertain ourselves by reading comics.

b) He stays fit by playing tennis.

c) I do my homework while watching the TV.

5 a) Après avoir fait le gâteau, je l'ai mangé.

b) Après être parti, il est revenu.

6 a) She is knocked over by the snail.

b) I am watched by everyone at the theatre.

c) Louis and Carlo were punished by their teacher.

d) You have been found by the fire-fighters.

7 a) you / one must   d) it's about

b) it is necessary to   e) it's snowing

c) it seems   f) it's hot

8 a) iv   b) i   c) ii   d) iii

9 a) Il faut que tu <u>viennes</u> — tout le monde sera là !

You must come — everyone will be there!

b) Il semble qu'ils <u>aient</u> une maladie grave.

It seems that they have a serious illness.

c) Je veux qu'il me <u>dise</u> toute l'histoire.

I want him to tell me the whole story.

d) Il est possible que nous y <u>allions</u> ce soir.

It is possible that we will go there this evening.

Practice Exam — Listening Paper

Question Number	Answer	Marks
1	B	[1 mark]
2	C	[1 mark]
3	B	[1 mark]
4	A	[1 mark]
5	Subject 1 — N	[1 mark]
	Subject 2 — P + N	[1 mark]
6	Subject 1 — N	[1 mark]
	Subject 2— N	[1 mark]
7	Subject 1 — P + N	[1 mark]
	Subject 2 — P	[1 mark]
8	his school team.	[1 mark]
9	water skiing.	[1 mark]
10	a member of a tennis club.	[1 mark]
11	she injured herself / she can't.	[1 mark]
12	Madagascar	[1 mark]
	protected endangered species.	[1 mark]
13	help poor villages.	[1 mark]
	it was tiring.	[1 mark]
14	at on old people's home.	[1 mark]
	felt lonely.	[1 mark]
15	They post photos.	[1 mark]
	They organise parties.	[1 mark]
16	It's practical.	[1 mark]
	It lets him keep his conversations private.	[1 mark]
17	Keeping in touch with family who live abroad.	[1 mark]
18	B	[1 mark]
	C	[1 mark]
19	A	[1 mark]
	B	[1 mark]
20	The experience outside of lessons.	[1 mark]
21	Students who aren't sporty / have other interests.	[1 mark]
22	Advantage: Easy to find the music you want.	[1 mark]
	Disadvantage: Sound quality isn't as good as a CD.	[1 mark]
23	Advantage: Can listen to music straight away.	[1 mark]
	Disadvantage: Not good for new bands / New bands need to sell albums to make money.	[1 mark]
24	B	[1 mark]
25	B	[1 mark]
26	A	[1 mark]
	B	[1 mark]
	C	[1 mark]
27	A	[1 mark]
	D	[1 mark]
28	B	[1 mark]
	E	[1 mark]
29	B	[1 mark]
30	E	[1 mark]
31	D	[1 mark]
32	Observer les oiseaux	[1 mark]
33	Les châteaux médiévaux / Les cités fortifiées.	[1 mark]
34	Un gâteau / Un type de gâteau.	[1 mark]

Total marks for Listening Paper: 50

≡ You'll find mark schemes for the Speaking and Writing papers on p.212 & p.213. ≡

Practice Exam — Speaking Paper

Role-play sample answer

1) Ma maison est assez grande et elle a une porte rouge.
2) J'habite avec mon père, ma mère et mes deux frères.
3) Comment serait ta maison idéale ?
4) J'aime ma ville parce qu'il y a beaucoup d'activités pour les jeunes.
5) Je voudrais habiter à la campagne dans une ferme ou peut-être à l'étranger.

Photo Card sample answer

1) Sur la photo, il y a un groupe de gens qui font de la natation. C'est probablement une compétition où ils veulent tous gagner.
2) Oui, j'aime le sport parce que c'est bon pour la santé. Je joue au tennis deux fois par semaine. Mon sport préféré est le hockey car c'est très compétitif.
3) Mon week-end de rêve serait plein d'activités. J'aimerais lire et écouter de la musique. S'il faisait beau, j'aimerais faire de la randonnée avec ma famille.
4) À mon avis, je n'ai pas assez de temps libre pour me détendre car on nous donne trop de devoirs.
5) Je suis allé(e) au cinéma avec mon ami. Nous avons vu un film d'action, c'était passionnant mais un peu trop violent. Normalement, je préfère les films policiers.

General Conversation sample answers

Local, national, international and global areas of interest

1) Je voudrais faire du travail bénévole dans une école primaire pour aider les enfants à lire et à écrire. Je pense que c'est important d'encourager les élèves qui n'ont pas confiance en eux en classe.
2) Selon moi, le travail des associations caritatives est extrêmement important parce qu'il aide les gens défavorisés qui n'ont pas les moyens d'améliorer leurs situations. Quand on vit dans une situation difficile, c'est souvent impossible de s'en échapper sans l'aide des autres.
3) On pourrait construire des centres de refuge pour donner un lieu sûr aux sans-abri où ils pourraient manger et dormir. On pourrait aussi donner de la nourriture aux banques alimentaires.
4) Les conséquences du réchauffement de la Terre sont nombreuses. Les animaux qui habitent dans les zones froides doivent s'adapter à des températures plus chaudes. Les zones qui sont déjà très chaudes deviennent de plus en plus sèches, donc l'eau devient une ressource rare. Est-ce que vous vous inquiétez du réchauffement de la Terre ?
5) Au collège, je fais partie de l'équipe de squash. Le week-end, je vais au centre sportif avec mon oncle pour jouer au volley, et quelquefois on joue au badminton. Pour maintenir une alimentation saine, je mange beaucoup de légumes et j'évite les aliments qui sont pleins de sucre comme le chocolat.
6) L'année dernière, je suis allé(e) en Écosse pour rendre visite à ma grand-mère. Elle habite dans un petit village près du Loch Ness. Nous avons passé deux semaines avec elle, et puis nous sommes allés en Espagne pendant une semaine.

Current and future study and employment

1) Je crois qu'il y a trop de devoirs au collège. Quand j'étais plus jeune, on avait beaucoup moins à faire en dehors de la classe. Quelquefois, je m'inquiète de mes notes parce que je voudrais être médecin et j'ai besoin de très bonnes notes.
2) Mon collège est assez petit. Il y a environ cinq cents élèves, donc on connaît presque tout le monde. Nous avons deux terrains de foot et une piscine à côté de la cour. L'année prochaine, il y aura un nouveau proviseur du collège.
3) Une journée typique au collège est assez longue. On commence à neuf heures, et la journée scolaire termine à quinze heures trente. Normalement, on a cinq cours chaque jour — deux avant la récréation, un entre la récré et le déjeuner, puis deux leçons avant la fin de la journée.
4) Oui, j'aimerais prendre une année sabbatique pour faire le tour du monde. Je voudrais voir et expérimenter des choses différentes. En plus, je ne sais pas quoi faire après le lycée. Est-ce que vous avez pris une année sabbatique ?
5) Moi, non. Je voudrais rester près de ma famille car elle m'est très importante. Dans le passé, j'avais l'intention de travailler en Espagne, mais maintenant je ne veux plus le faire.
6) Mon travail de rêve serait de trouver des os de dinosaures. J'adore découvrir de nouvelles choses et je m'intéresse beaucoup à l'évolution. Selon moi, c'est le travail le plus passionnant et intéressant du monde !

Practice Exam — Writing Paper

Q1.1 — Sample answer

Après les examens, j'irai au lycée car je veux aller à l'université. Mon travail idéal serait d'être vétérinaire parce que j'adore les animaux. Je pense que ce serait un métier très intéressant car je pourrais travailler avec beaucoup d'animaux différents. Pourtant, c'est une carrière difficile parce que les animaux sont plus difficiles à traiter que les humains. Pour être vétérinaire, il faut avoir de l'expérience professionnelle. Il y a deux ans, j'ai travaillé dans une clinique vétérinaire pendant trois mois. J'ai fait beaucoup de tâches pour lesquelles j'avais besoin d'une bonne connaissance de la biologie.

Q1.2 — Sample answer

À mon avis, les voitures sont la cause principale du réchauffement de la Terre. Il y en a trop sur les routes et cela a augmenté les émissions de gaz d'échappement. Une stratégie pour réduire les émissions est d'utiliser plus les transports en commun. Un autobus peut transporter soixante personnes au lieu d'une voiture qui peut en transporter seulement cinq. Si tout le monde prenait l'autobus, on pourrait réduire la pollution. Le week-end dernier, je suis allé(e) au cinéma à vélo. À l'avenir, j'achèterai une voiture électrique parce qu'elles sont plus propres que les voitures normales.

Q2.1 — Sample answer

Il y a une abondance de problèmes sociaux dans ma ville. Premièrement, un grand nombre de gens sont au chômage. Dans le passé, il y avait beaucoup d'industries dans ma ville, mais maintenant les usines sont fermées. Trouver un autre emploi, c'est difficile, puisqu'une ville comme la mienne est assez petite et rurale. Un autre problème qui existe est que la plupart de gens fument. À mon avis, fumer, c'est mauvais pour la santé et ça coûte très cher. Il est interdit de fumer dans les lieux publics, mais certaines personnes ne respectent pas les règles. En plus, je pense que l'alcool cause le plus de problèmes. Par exemple, la semaine dernière, j'ai vu un groupe de gens qui buvait dans la rue. Deux d'entre eux ont commencé à se battre, et un homme est tombé et s'est blessé. Quand on voit des choses comme ça, c'est intimidant. On se sent vraiment anxieux.

Q2.2 — Sample answer

Les réseaux sociaux ont changé notre vie. Maintenant on peut rester en contact avec ses amis tout le temps — quand on est à la maison, au collège, dans le train, même au lit. Les familles et les amis qui vivent à l'étranger peuvent utiliser les réseaux sociaux pour rester en contact et pour partager des photos. Pourtant, un des risques des réseaux sociaux est qu'on pourrait les utiliser pour harceler les gens. En plus, certains choisissent de passer plus de temps en ligne qu'avec leurs amis. J'utilise les réseaux sociaux pour faire de la recherche. Par exemple, la semaine dernière j'ai voulu aller au cinéma mais je n'avais aucune idée quel film aller voir. J'ai posé la question sur les réseaux sociaux et mes amis ont décrit les films qu'ils ont vus et m'ont donné leur avis. Un ami a dit qu'il aimerait y aller avec moi. Donc j'utilise les réseaux sociaux pour améliorer ma vie sociale.

Q3 — Sample answer

Hier, je suis allé(e) au supermarché pour faire des courses. J'ai acheté des fruits, des légumes et du pain. D'habitude / Normalement / En général, je préfère faire des achats sur Internet / en ligne parce que c'est plus rapide. Cependant, je veux de nouvelles chaussures et je vais devoir aller aux magasins pour les acheter parce que j'aurai besoin de les essayer.

Practice Exam — Reading Paper

Question Number	Answer	Marks
1.1	Take the first street on the right.	*[1 mark]*
1.2	Turn left.	*[1 mark]*
1.3	at the end	*[1 mark]*
2.1	8%	*[1 mark]*
2.2	23%	*[1 mark]*
2.3	17%	*[1 mark]*
2.4	They are stopped by peer pressure.	*[1 mark]*
3.1	S	*[1 mark]*
3.2	E	*[1 mark]*
3.3	E + S	*[1 mark]*
3.4	E	*[1 mark]*
4.1	It has increased dramatically.	*[1 mark]*
4.2	They are male.	*[1 mark]*
4.3	20 refuge centres are being opened in the city.	*[1 mark]*
5.1	B	*[1 mark]*
5.2	C	*[1 mark]*
5.3	A	*[1 mark]*
5.4	C	*[1 mark]*
6.1	C	*[1 mark]*
6.2	A	*[1 mark]*
7.1	C	*[1 mark]*
7.2	six	*[1 mark]*
7.3	either side of the street	*[1 mark]*
8.1	negative; story was difficult to follow	*[2 marks]*
8.2	positive; lots of special effects	*[2 marks]*
8.3	negative; main actress was too sentimental	*[2 marks]*
9.1	C	*[1 mark]*
9.2	They send messages during meals.	*[1 mark]*
	They post every detail of their life on social media.	*[1 mark]*
9.3	The light can disturb sleep patterns.	*[1 mark]*
10.1	une robe	*[1 mark]*
	une paire de chaussure	*[1 mark]*
10.2	La montre ne marche pas.	*[1 mark]*
10.3	Elle avait perdu le reçu.	*[1 mark]*
11.1	utiliser les transports en commun / laisser la voiture à la maison.	*[1 mark]*
11.2	prendre une douche au lieu d'un bain	*[1 mark]*
	éteindre les lumières	*[1 mark]*
12.1	Il aime travailler avec les animaux.	*[1 mark]*
12.2	Il a travaillé dans un refuge pour animaux.	*[1 mark]*
12.3	Elle s'intéresse à la mode.	*[1 mark]*
12.4	Elle est travailleuse.	*[1 mark]*
13.1	B	*[1 mark]*
13.2	A	*[1 mark]*
13.3	B	*[1 mark]*
14	B, F, C, D	*[4 marks]*
15	What a terrible holiday! *[1 mark]* I have just returned *[1 mark]* from my trip to Germany *[1 mark]* and it was truly / really awful. *[1 mark]* I went to Berlin with my cousins. *[1 mark]* The city was incredible, but the hotel where we stayed was unpleasant. *[1 mark]* There wasn't any / there was no hot water! *[1 mark]* If I were to return / go back to Berlin one day, *[1 mark]* I would find different accommodation / somewhere else to stay. *[1 mark]*	*[9 marks]*

Total marks for Reading Paper: 60

Answers

Speaking Exam Mark Scheme

It's very difficult to mark the practice Speaking Exam yourself because there isn't one 'right' answer for most questions. To make it easier to mark, record the exam and use a dictionary, or get someone who's really good at French, to mark how well you did. Use the mark schemes below to help you, but bear in mind that they're only a rough guide. Ideally, you need a French teacher who knows the AQA mark schemes well to mark it properly.

Role-play (15 marks)

In the Role-play, you're marked separately on your communication and your use of language. There are 2 marks available for communication for each of the 5 bullet points (tasks) in the Role-play (10 marks in total), and then 5 marks are available for your use of language.

Marks	Communication (per task)
2	You complete the task clearly.
1	You complete part of the task clearly.
0	You don't complete the task correctly.

Marks	Knowledge and Use of Language (overall)
4-5	Your knowledge and use of vocabulary is good / very good.
2-3	Your knowledge and use of vocabulary is reasonable.
0-1	Your knowledge and use of vocabulary is very poor / poor.

Photo Card (15 marks)

You are scored out of 15 for the Photo Card, and the only criteria is the quality of your communication.

Marks	Communication
13-15	You reply clearly to all of the questions and develop most of your answers. You give and explain an opinion.
10-12	You reply clearly to all or most of the questions and develop some of your answers. You give and explain an opinion.
7-9	You give reasonable answers to most questions and develop one or more of your answers. You give an opinion.
4-6	You give reasonable answers to most questions, but some of your answers are short and / or a bit repetitive.
1-3	You reply to some of the questions, but your answers are short and / or repetitive.
0	You don't say anything that's relevant.

General Conversation (30 marks)

The General Conversation should last between five and seven minutes, and you are marked on four separate criteria.

Marks	Communication
9-10	You consistently give well-developed answers, present information clearly, and explain your opinions convincingly.
7-8	You regularly develop your answers, present information clearly, and give and explain your opinions.
5-6	You develop some of your answers, usually present information clearly, and often explain some of your opinions.
3-4	Your answers are generally short, but you present some information clearly and sometimes explain your opinions.
1-2	You give short answers, and there are some questions you can't answer or don't answer clearly. You give some opinions.
0	You don't say anything that's relevant to the questions.

You lose one mark for communication if you don't ask the examiner a question at some point during the General Conversation.

Marks	Range and Accuracy of Language
9-10	You use an excellent range of vocabulary and structures. You use the past, present and future tenses confidently and correctly. Any mistakes are small and only occur when you're attempting complex structures and / or vocabulary.
7-8	You use a good range of vocabulary and structures. You use past, present and future tenses correctly, with small mistakes.
5-6	Your vocabulary is good and you use some structures and tenses correctly. Your meaning is clear despite some mistakes.
3-4	You use simple vocabulary and structures well. You use some different tenses and your meaning is generally clear.
1-2	You use simple vocabulary and structures, with some repetition. Frequent mistakes can make your meaning unclear.
0	You don't say anything that makes sense or can be easily understood.

Marks	Pronunciation and Intonation
4-5	Your pronunciation and intonation are mostly / consistently good.
2-3	Your pronunciation and intonation are often good, but there are several mistakes.
1	Your pronunciation can generally be understood, and you attempt to use some intonation.
0	You don't pronounce anything clearly and you cannot be understood.

Marks	Spontaneity and Fluency
4-5	The conversation flows naturally and seems spontaneous. You answer promptly and your speech flows easily at times.
2-3	The conversation generally flows well, but at times it seems as though you're relying on pre-learnt answers. Sometimes you answer promptly, but you hesitate before answering some questions, and you may not be able to answer them all.
1	Lots of what you say seems as though it has been pre-learnt. You hesitate a lot and your answers don't flow.
0	You don't show any spontaneity and can't be easily understood.

Writing Exam Mark Scheme

Like the Speaking Exam, it's difficult to mark the writing exam yourself because there are no 'right' answers. Again, you ideally need a French teacher who knows the AQA mark schemes to mark your answers properly. Each of the writing tasks has a different mark scheme.

Question 1 (16 marks)

Marks	Content
9-10	You've completed the task fully, your meaning is always clear and you've expressed multiple opinions.
7-8	You've written a good answer covering all four bullet points. Your meaning is clear and you've used multiple opinions.
5-6	You've written a reasonable answer, covered most bullet points and given an opinion. Your meaning isn't always clear.
3-4	Your answer is quite basic, covering some of the bullet points. You've given an opinion, but your meaning can be unclear.
1-2	Your answer is limited, covering one or two bullet points. Your meaning is often unclear and you haven't given an opinion.
0	You haven't written anything relevant. If you score 0 for content, you automatically get 0 for the whole question.

Marks	Quality of Language
5-6	You've used a wide range of vocabulary, some complex sentences and structures, and at least three tenses. Errors are mostly minor, and any major errors occur only in complex sentences and structures, with the meaning remaining clear.
3-4	You've used a variety of vocabulary, some complex sentences and structures, and at least two tenses. There are frequent minor errors and some major errors, but the meaning is usually clear.
1-2	You've used a narrow range of vocabulary and your sentences are mainly short. There are frequent major errors.
0	You haven't written anything that's suitable for the task.

Question 2 (32 marks)

Marks	Content
13-15	You've written a relevant, detailed answer that clearly gives a lot of information, and you've justified your opinions.
10-12	Your answer is detailed, mostly relevant and it usually presents information clearly. You've justified your opinions.
7-9	Your answer is generally relevant and gives plenty of information. Some bits are unclear, but you have given opinions.
4-6	Your answer gives some relevant information, but at times your meaning is unclear. You have given an opinion.
1-3	Your answer is basic, contains limited relevant information and is often unclear. You may have given an opinion.
0	You haven't written anything relevant. If you score 0 for content, you automatically get 0 for the whole question.

Marks	Range of Language
10-12	You've used a wide range of vocabulary, some complex sentences and structures, and an appropriate style.
7-9	You've used a variety of vocabulary, attempted some complex sentences and structures, and used an appropriate style.
4-6	You've tried to use a variety of vocabulary and sentences. Your style of writing is not always appropriate for the task.
1-3	You've repeated some vocabulary, your sentences are mostly short and simple, and you haven't thought about your style.
0	You haven't written anything that's suitable for the task.

Marks	Accuracy
4-5	Your writing is mostly accurate and you've formed verbs and tenses correctly. There are only a few small errors.
2-3	Your writing is more accurate than inaccurate, and your verbs and tenses are mostly correct. There are some errors.
1	You have made some major errors, your verbs and tenses are often incorrect, and your meaning is not always clear.
0	You haven't written anything that makes sense or could be easily understood.

Question 3 (12 marks)

Marks	Conveying Key Messages	Marks	Use of Grammar, Language and Structures
5-6	You've conveyed nearly all / all of the key messages in your translation.	5-6	You've shown very good / excellent knowledge of vocabulary and structures, with very few mistakes.
3-4	You've conveyed most of the key messages in your translation.	3-4	You've shown a good / reasonable knowledge of vocabulary and structures, and the translation is more accurate than inaccurate.
1-2	You've conveyed very few / few of the key messages in your translation.	1-2	You've displayed limited knowledge of vocabulary and structures, and there are lots of mistakes.
0	You haven't written anything relevant. If you score 0 here, you get 0 for the whole task.	0	You haven't written anything that's suitable for the task.

Transcripts

Section One — General Stuff

Track 01 — p.3

E.g. **F1**: Et maintenant, écoutez le proviseur pendant cinq minutes, lorsqu'il fait des annonces.

1) **M1**: D'abord, nous avons les résultats de notre sondage sur les habitudes de nos élèves. Le sondage nous a montré que la plupart des élèves se lèvent à sept heures moins le quart.

2) **M1**: Les cours commencent à huit heures et demie. La plupart des élèves pensent qu'ils commencent trop tôt.

3) **M1**: Deuxièmement, il y a maintenant des cours de danse le mardi et le jeudi dans le gymnase — inscrivez-vous !

4) **M1**: Et pour finir, ce collège a été établi en mille neuf cent quatre-vingt-seize, donc cette année il y aura une fête pour célébrer son vingtième anniversaire.

Track 02 — p.10

E.g. **M1**: Qu'est-ce que tu aimes faire le week-end, Blandine ?

F1: Alors… ça dépend. Quelquefois j'aime faire du sport. J'adore jouer au foot car c'est bon pour la forme.

1) **F1**: Je m'amuse bien avec mon équipe. Mais je n'aime pas faire du sport quand je suis fatiguée. Et toi Marc — est-ce que tu aimes le sport ?

M1: Je ne m'intéresse pas trop au sport, mais la natation me plaît car c'est relaxant.

2) **M1**: Personnellement, je préfère les livres. En ce moment je lis un roman formidable. L'histoire est vraiment intéressante.

F1: Les livres sont ennuyeux. Je n'aime pas lire.

3) **F1**: Moi, j'adore les films. J'en regarde beaucoup — les films d'action, les films d'horreur… même les films romantiques. Quel est ton avis sur les films, Marc ?

M1: Les comédies m'énervent. Mais regarder un film me plaît si les acteurs sont bons. La semaine dernière, j'ai vu un film d'action. C'était formidable.

Track 03 — p.11

1a) **M1**: Mon week-end était génial ! Tout d'abord, j'ai fait du shopping et j'ai acheté plein de choses. J'avais besoin de nouveaux vêtements, donc j'ai acheté deux T-shirts et un jean.

1b) **M1**: J'adore regarder les films et heureusement j'ai trouvé beaucoup de DVD dans un magasin de disques — j'en ai acheté une dizaine.

1c) **M1**: Finalement, j'ai choisi trois nouvelles casquettes de base-ball. Elles sont chouettes. Tout ça m'a coûté deux cent cinquante-six euros.

1d) **M1**: J'ai passé le samedi soir avec cinq de mes copains. Nous avons regardé un film ensemble. C'était le seizième anniversaire de mon meilleur ami, donc il a reçu beaucoup de cadeaux.

1e) **M1**: Je pense qu'en tout, il a eu une vingtaine de cadeaux. Il a de la chance !

Track 04 — p.11

2a) **M1**: Salut Claire ! Comment ça va ?

F1: Salut Georges ! Ça va très bien, merci. Je viens d'assister à un concert chouette de ma chanteuse préférée, Lilette Laurent. C'est une chanteuse vraiment douée, es-tu d'accord avec moi ?

2b) **M1**: Bien sûr que non. Personnellement, je trouve qu'elle n'a pas de talent. Elle est riche et stupide. J'avoue qu'elle est assez belle, mais c'est tout. En plus elle n'écrit pas ses propres chansons. Toutes les vedettes sont ainsi : leur seul objectif, c'est de gagner de l'argent.

2c) **F1**: Tu as tort ! À mon avis, elle a beaucoup de talent et en plus elle est très sympathique. Elle travaille avec les enfants défavorisés. J'ai regardé une émission à son sujet et ça m'a vraiment impressionnée.

2d) **M1**: Ce n'est pas vrai ; elle veut simplement attirer l'attention du public. Elle en a besoin, car sa musique est affreuse !

2e) **F1**: Encore une fois je ne suis pas d'accord avec toi. Tu ne comprends rien. À mon avis, sa nouvelle chanson est géniale. Sa musique rend les gens heureux et moi, je crois que ça, c'est la chose la plus importante.

2f) **M1**: D'accord. Je ne vais pas me disputer avec toi ; ça ne sert à rien. Moi, j'aime le rock. La musique pop m'énerve, surtout les chanteurs gâtés comme Lilette Laurent.

F1: Tu es méchant, toi !

Section Two — Me, My Family and Friends

Track 05 — p.18

E.g. **F1**: Alors, Fabien, tu habites toujours à la maison. Parle-moi un peu de ta famille.

1) **M1**: Chez moi, il y a toujours du bruit — ma famille est très vive. J'ai deux sœurs et un frère qui sont tous plus jeunes que moi. Mes sœurs sont jumelles. Elles ont toutes les deux les cheveux roux et les yeux verts. J'ai aussi un demi-frère aîné qui n'habite plus à la maison.

2) **M1**: Ma mère est toujours calme et souriante. Elle a les yeux bleus et les cheveux blonds, courts et raides. Mon père est sympa. Il est grand et il a une barbe. Physiquement, je ressemble plus à ma mère qu'à mon père.

Track 06 — p.22

1a) **F1**: Pourriez-vous décrire l'homme que vous avez vu, s'il vous plaît ?

F2: Pas de problème : je l'ai vu très clairement. C'était un petit homme. On pourrait dire qu'il était un peu gros aussi.

M1: Mais non ma chérie, ce n'est pas vrai. Il était très grand — on l'a remarqué même de loin.

1b) **M1**: En plus, je ne suis pas convaincu qu'il soit gros. Je crois qu'il était assez maigre.

F2: Tu ne sais pas ce que tu as vu, mon cher. Il me semble que tu ne portais pas tes lunettes. C'était un petit homme gros.

F1: Merci, c'est… très utile.

1c) **F1**: Est-ce que vous vous rappelez son visage ou ses cheveux ?

F2: Je m'en souviens très bien ! Il s'agissait d'un homme laid au grand nez. En plus, il avait les cheveux noirs et longs.

1d) **M1**: Attends Patricia, tu imagines des choses. Il avait les cheveux blonds et courts. Je n'ai pas vu son visage.

Track 07 — p.22

2a) **F1**: Bonjour et bienvenue à cette édition de « L'heure des jeunes ». Aujourd'hui, nos invités vont parler du mariage. Armand, qu'en penses-tu ?

M1: Je pense que le mariage c'est très important mais je peux très bien vivre seul — je n'ai pas l'intention de me marier tout de suite.

2b) **M1**: En fait, je préférerais rester célibataire — c'est plus facile et je pourrais faire tout ce que je voudrais.

2c) **F1**: Et toi, Zoé, qu'est-ce que tu en penses ?

F2: À l'avenir je voudrais me marier et avoir des enfants. Je sors avec mon copain depuis trois ans mais il n'est pas prêt à y penser.

Section Three — Free-Time Activities

Track 08 — p.27

E.g. **F1**: Bonjour Joël. Merci d'avoir accepté de répondre à nos questions. Depuis quel âge joues-tu d'un instrument de musique ?

M1: J'ai appris à jouer de la guitare quand j'avais 12 ans, mais mon premier amour, c'est le violon. J'ai commencé à en jouer à cinq ans, et à l'âge de sept ans, je jouais déjà dans un orchestre.

1) **F1**: C'était difficile d'apprendre à jouer d'un instrument ?

M1: Oui, au début ce n'était pas facile car je ne m'entendais pas avec mon professeur. Il était trop strict. Heureusement, ma mère m'a trouvé un nouveau professeur.

2) **F1:** Et pourquoi l'envie de faire partie d'un groupe plutôt que de faire une carrière solo ?

   M1: À l'âge de 15 ans, j'ai assisté à mon premier concert. J'ai trouvé l'ambiance géniale et j'adorais la musique du groupe. Au concert j'ai compris que faire partie d'un groupe était plus amusant que jouer tout seul.

3) **F1:** Et qu'est-ce qu'il faut faire pour réussir à devenir un musicien célèbre ?

   M1: Naturellement il faut aimer la musique. Mais le plus important c'est de répéter régulièrement et de toujours essayer de faire de son mieux.

   F1: Merci Joël, et bonne continuation.

Track 09 — p.30

E.g. **F1:** Comme je suis musulmane, je ne peux pas manger de porc parce que ma religion me l'interdit. Je mange souvent du poisson, et j'aime bien l'agneau aussi. Et toi, Ahmed ?

1) **M1:** J'adore les légumes, en particulier les petits pois et les champignons. Je mange aussi du chou-fleur de temps en temps. Qu'est-ce que tu aimes, Élodie ?

2) **F2:** J'aime beaucoup la nourriture épicée, mais ma petite sœur déteste ça ! Elle mange beaucoup de nourriture sucrée. Ce n'est pas bon pour la santé !

3) **M1:** Moi, je suis végétarien. Je ne mange jamais de viande. Ma mère me cuisine des plats avec des légumes. J'aime manger des pommes de terre avec des tomates et des petits pois.

4) **F1:** Je préfère les fraises aux framboises, et je déteste l'ananas : c'est trop acide. Je ne peux pas manger les noix car je suis allergique.

Track 10 — p.34

1a) **F1:** En 1895, les frères Lumière ont inventé le cinématographe, et grâce à cet appareil, l'art du cinéma est né. Le cinématographe était une caméra qui permettait aux gens de regarder des films.

1b) **F1:** Leur premier film s'appelait 'La Sortie de l'usine Lumière' et ça durait seulement 38 secondes.

1c) **F1:** Ils ont organisé la première représentation publique payante des films le 28 décembre 1895 au sous-sol du Grand Café à Paris. La séance a duré environ 20 minutes et on y a projeté dix films.

Track 11 — p.34

2a) **F1:** Allô ?

   M1: Salut Juliette, c'est Leo à l'appareil.

   F1: Leo ! Quelle surprise… Ça va ?

   M1: Ça va bien merci. Je t'appelle car je voulais te demander si tu avais envie de dîner avec moi ce soir. Il y a un nouveau restaurant en ville où on prépare des plats délicieux. La viande là-bas est superbe, surtout les steaks hachés.

2b) **F1:** Ben… en fait, je suis végétarienne. Quel dommage !

   M1: Tu es devenue végétarienne ?

   F1: Oui, c'est vrai. Avant, j'aimais bien manger du bœuf mais je trouve que la viande est très mauvaise pour la planète.

   M1: Pas de problème, je suis sûr que nous pouvons trouver un restaurant qui te plaira. Est-ce que tu aimes le fromage ?

   F1: Ben… malheureusement je ne mange pas de fromage.

2c) **M1:** Ben… et si nous allions manger des crêpes ?

   F1: Je suis allergique aux œufs. Je l'ai découvert hier. Et en plus, il faut que je me lave les cheveux ce soir. Au revoir !

Section Four — Technology in Everyday Life

Track 12 — p.43

E.g. **M1:** Je trouve que c'est un peu dangereux. On ne sait jamais ce qu'on va trouver.

1a) **F1:** Moi, je trouve Internet super. J'aime le fait qu'on peut rester en contact avec tout le monde quelle que soit l'heure. J'adore communiquer avec mes amies, donc j'utilise mon smartphone pour envoyer des messages.

1b) **F2:** Moi, j'aime assez la technologie, parce qu'on peut s'en servir pour découvrir de nouvelles choses. Il y a une application pour tout et j'apprends beaucoup. Par exemple, j'utilise une application pour apprendre l'espagnol.

1c) **M1:** J'aime Internet, mais il me semble que les jeunes passent trop de temps devant un écran en raison des appareils comme les tablettes et les smartphones. On est toujours connecté.

Track 13 — p.43

2a) **M1:** Tu utilises les réseaux sociaux, Cho ?

   F1: Oui, j'aime utiliser les réseaux sociaux. Cependant, je sais que cela peut être dangereux et il faut faire attention à ce qu'on partage. Je pense qu'on échange trop de renseignements personnels en ligne. Au collège on nous donne des conseils pour nous protéger, surtout du cyber-harcèlement. Une copine a été victime du cyber-harcèlement, c'était affreux.

2b) **F1:** Et toi, Jules ?

   M1: Moi, j'utilise les médias sociaux pour partager des photos et des vidéos. Je pense que c'est génial de pouvoir montrer aux autres ce qu'on fait. Par exemple, si on sort le soir, on peut mettre des images en ligne, pour que tout le monde sache que tu t'amuses. En outre, on peut voir les photos que les autres ont mises en ligne, ce qui est toujours intéressant parce qu'on sait ce qu'ils font.

2c) **M1:** Et toi, Clara : est-ce que tu aimes les réseaux sociaux ?

   F2: J'aime partager mes photos, mais je demande toujours la permission de mes amis avant de les mettre en ligne. S'ils ne sont pas d'accord, je ne les mets pas. Il faut accepter que les photos soient visibles à tous. En plus, on ne peut jamais vraiment effacer les choses qu'on a mises en ligne. Il me semble qu'elles restent sur Internet pour toujours.

Section Five — Customs and Festivals

Track 14 — p.49

E.g. **M1:** Je m'appelle Youssou et je viens du Sénégal, mais j'habite maintenant à Bordeaux avec mes parents, ma sœur et notre chien, Pépé. La semaine dernière, j'ai célébré mon seizième anniversaire.

1) **M1:** Mon anniversaire était jeudi. J'ai dû aller au lycée, donc j'ai décidé d'ouvrir mes cadeaux le soir. Je n'ai pas voulu me lever tôt pour le faire le matin ! On m'a offert des baskets, un jeu vidéo et un livre d'histoires mythologiques.

2) **M1:** J'ai fêté le jour de mon anniversaire avec ma famille. Mon père m'a cuisiné mon plat préféré et ma sœur m'a préparé un gâteau.

3) **M1:** Le week-end après mon anniversaire, j'ai retrouvé mes amis pour le célébrer encore. C'était la fête du travail donc il y avait des feux d'artifice. C'était bien de fêter ça avec ma famille et mes amis.

Track 15 — p.51

1) **M1:** L'Aïd est la fête qui marque la fin du ramadan. Pour le célébrer, les musulmans vont prier à la mosquée ensemble au petit matin. Tout le monde met ses plus beaux vêtements.

   Vers midi, on partage un repas festif avec la famille, les voisins et les amis. Ce qu'on mange dépend de la tradition du pays. Les invités font une grande fête — ils écoutent de la musique et dansent. Les gens offrent de petits cadeaux aux enfants. Selon la tradition, les enfants doivent porter de nouveaux vêtements.

Track 16 — p.51

2a) **M1:** Bonjour Madame Romero. Comment fête-t-on la Nouvelle Année en France ?

   F1: En général, le 31 décembre, les invités arrivent vers 20 heures et on prend l'apéritif pour fêter le réveillon de la Saint-Sylvestre.

2b) **M1:** C'est quoi le réveillon ?

   F1: Quand on fait le réveillon, on dîne avec les invités, mais on ne commence pas à manger avant 22 ou 23 heures. À minuit, on s'embrasse et on se souhaite la bonne année.

2c) **F1:** Ensuite, on continue à manger, à chanter et à danser en famille et avec nos amis. On fait la fête au moins jusqu'à 4 heures du matin avant de se coucher.

2d) **M1**: Et que font les gens le premier janvier ?

F1: On déjeune en famille vers 13 heures. C'est l'occasion de présenter nos meilleurs vœux à toute la famille. Les enfants reçoivent les étrennes. Les étrennes sont de petits cadeaux : des bonbons ou quelques euros pour fêter le nouvel an. Il est aussi coutume de donner des étrennes au facteur et aux pompiers.

Section Six — Where You Live

Track 17 — p.61

E.g. **F1**: À mon avis, faire des courses en ligne est plus facile que de les faire en magasin. On peut faire des courses à n'importe quelle heure du jour ou de la nuit. Et puis on ne perd pas de temps à aller aux magasins.

1) **F1**: Cependant, on ne peut pas demander conseil au vendeur — je n'aime pas ça, parce que parfois c'est utile de demander l'avis d'une autre personne.

2) **M1**: J'aime le fait qu'on ne fait pas la queue à la caisse, alors on gagne du temps. J'ai toujours beaucoup de choses à faire donc c'est un avantage important pour moi. Aussi, les supermarchés vous livrent vos courses quand vous le désirez.

Par contre, c'est difficile d'acheter des vêtements en ligne parce qu'on ne peut pas les essayer et qu'on n'est pas certain si la taille sera bonne.

Track 18 — p.62

E.g. **M1**: Après l'école, nous nous retrouverons au café de la Belle Époque. Pour y aller, prends l'autobus numéro 15. L'arrêt d'autobus se trouve près du lycée, de l'autre côté de la rue.

1) **M1**: Descends à la gare routière et change d'autobus. Prends le numéro 23 vers le centre-ville. Descends à la Grand-Place, à côté du marché.

2) **M1**: J'espère que tu vas te rappeler de tout ! Attends, malheureusement je n'ai pas fini les instructions, bon alors, puis tourne tout de suite à gauche et continue jusqu'à la bibliothèque.

3) **M1**: Traverse la rue aux feux et continue dans le même sens. Après environ cent mètres, tu trouveras la Belle Époque à gauche.

Track 19 — p.64

e.g. **F1**: Salut ! Je m'appelle Fatima et je gagne de l'argent quand j'aide à la maison. Je promène le chien tous les jours, ce qui me fait plaisir car j'aime faire de l'exercice et être dehors. Par contre, mon père veut que je l'aide à faire du jardinage et je déteste ça.

1a) **M1**: Bonjour ! Moi, je suis Ousmane. Souvent je fais la cuisine pour ma famille. Ça ne me gêne pas car je trouve cela relaxant. Le samedi, je dois laver la voiture, ce que je trouve très pénible.

1b) **F2**: Salut ! Je m'appelle Mai. J'aide ma mère à faire le ménage. Nous ne sommes que deux chez nous, donc je fais toujours la moitié du travail. Ce que j'aime le plus, c'est faire la lessive. Par contre, je déteste faire la vaisselle.

Track 20 — p.64

2a) **M1**: Je suis Frédéric et je suis allé au supermarché. J'avais l'intention d'acheter seulement du pain et du fromage, mais en fait je viens d'acheter pas seulement le pain et le fromage, mais aussi un gâteau aux fraises et une bouteille de vin rouge.

2b) **F1**: Je m'appelle Manon et je suis allée à la parfumerie. Ma mère adore le parfum et j'avais envie d'acheter un flacon de parfum spécial à lui donner. J'ai choisi un parfum chouette, mais quand j'ai voulu payer, j'ai découvert que j'avais oublié mon porte-monnaie. Quelle idiote !

2c) **M2**: Je suis Abdoul. Moi, je préfère faire du lèche-vitrine et je n'ai pas acheté grand-chose.

Section Seven — Lifestyle

Track 21 — p.72

1a) **M1**: Bien manger c'est très important. Ma mère m'a appris à cuisiner et ça m'aide à bien manger. En plus, je mange toujours au moins cinq fruits ou légumes par jour.

1b) **F1**: Pour être en bonne santé, il faut se coucher à une heure raisonnable — ni trop tôt ni trop tard. Il faut absolument bien dormir.

1c) **F2**: Mon médecin m'a recommandé la danse comme exercice. Pour rester en bonne santé, je dois danser trois fois par semaine.

Track 22 — p.72

2a) **F1**: Qu'est-ce que tu penses du tabagisme, Randa ?

F2: Je ne fume pas. Je pense que le tabagisme est dégoûtant. Je déteste quand les autres fument — je trouve l'odeur vraiment désagréable.

2b) **F1**: Et toi, Marcin, qu'est-ce que tu en penses ?

M1: Moi, je fume et j'aime fumer. Je sais que ce n'est pas sain, mais fumer m'aide à me détendre. Ma petite amie dit que je devrais essayer de fumer moins souvent.

2c) **F1**: Sophie, quel est ton avis ?

F2: Moi, j'étais fumeuse mais j'ai arrêté de fumer il y a un an. L'interdiction de fumer dans les lieux publics m'a fait comprendre que fumer, c'est vraiment antisocial.

Section Eight — Social and Global Issues

Track 23 — p.80

1) **F1**: Le gouvernement a annoncé que des réfugiés syriens seront accueillis en France. Plusieurs millions de réfugiés ont quitté la Syrie depuis le début de la guerre.

2) **M1**: À Lyon, trois personnes ont été tuées hier soir dans l'incendie d'une usine automobile. Il a fallu 12 heures pour éteindre les flammes.

3) **F2**: Grâce à un projet caritatif, tous les restaurants de la ville offriront un repas gratuit aux SDF aujourd'hui.

4) **M1**: On a déclaré un état d'urgence dans le sud de la France. En 24 heures il est tombé un mois de pluie.

Track 24 — p.82

1a) **M1**: Le recyclage est très important parce que nos réserves de ressources naturelles ne sont pas infinies.

1b) **M1**: Tout le monde peut aider à améliorer la situation. Chaque personne doit assumer la responsabilité de recycler ses propres ordures. Il faut aussi essayer d'acheter des produits aux emballages recyclables. Puis, on doit trouver le centre de recyclage le plus proche et recycler les emballages au lieu de les jeter dans la poubelle.

1c) **M1**: On peut recycler les boîtes en carton, les bouteilles en plastique et en verre et même les sacs en plastique.

Track 25 — p.82

2a) **M1**: Comme beaucoup d'entre vous le savent, la semaine dernière, les habitants de notre ville ont organisé une journée d'événements sportifs. Le but était de collecter des fonds pour les personnes atteintes du cancer du sein.

2b) **M1**: C'était l'idée de la mairesse de la ville. Sa mère est morte du cancer il y a deux ans et elle voulait faire quelque chose pour collecter de l'argent pour la recherche sur le cancer.

2c) **M1**: Il y avait beaucoup d'événements différents, y compris un tournoi de foot et une course autour de la ville. Beaucoup de participants se sont habillés en vêtements bizarres pour amuser les spectateurs.

Section Nine — Travel and Tourism

Track 26 — p.88

E.g. **M1**: Lorsque Passepartout est arrivé à International-Hôtel, il ne lui semblait pas qu'il avait quitté l'Angleterre.

1) **M1**: Le rez-de-chaussée de l'hôtel était occupé par un immense «bar», sorte de buffet ouvert gratis à tout passant. Viande sèche, soupe aux huîtres, des biscuits et du fromage, y sont apparus sans que le consommateur ait dû payer. Cela paraissait «très-américain» à Passepartout.

Le restaurant de l'hôtel était confortable. Mr. Fogg et Mrs. Aouda s'installaient devant une table et étaient abondamment servis.

Transcripts

Track 27 — p.92

1a) **F1**: Bonjour. Bienvenue à l'Hôtel de la Paix, Cannes. Pour faire une réservation pour les mois de mai, juin, juillet ou août, tapez un. Pour une réservation pour les mois de septembre jusqu'à avril, tapez deux.

1b) **F1**: Si vous désirez plus de renseignements sur les différents types de chambre qui sont disponibles, regardez notre site internet.

1c) **F1**: Pour parler avec un membre de notre équipe, laissez votre nom ainsi que votre numéro de téléphone et les dates du séjour prévu. Merci de votre appel.

Track 28 — p.92

2a) **M1**: Où aimes-tu rester pendant les vacances, Zamzam ?

F2: Moi, je suis fana de la nature. Chaque été je pars avec mes copains et on fait des randonnées à la montagne. Nous prenons tout ce dont nous aurons besoin — une tente, des provisions et des vêtements pratiques. Nous ne pouvons pas aller au supermarché pendant le séjour, donc il faut faire des préparations.

2b) **F2**: Et toi, Rayad ?

M1: Ce n'est pas pour moi, le camping. Je préfère un peu de luxe. Mes vacances idéales seraient au bord de la mer dans un grand hôtel avec une piscine chauffée, un gymnase et un bon restaurant, car je suis un peu gourmand. Heureusement, ce sont mes parents qui paient.

2c) **M1**: Et toi, Nathalie ?

F1: L'année dernière nous sommes allés dans une auberge de jeunesse en Belgique. Ce n'était pas du tout cher, c'est vrai, mais c'était affreux parce que les dortoirs étaient sales et les douches ne marchaient pas.

Section Ten — Current and Future Study and Employment

Track 29 — p.98

E.g. **M1**: Je m'appelle Nicolas. Ma matière préférée c'est la chimie parce que c'est vraiment intéressant, et je crois que cette matière me sera utile dans l'avenir.

1) **M1**: Je pense que l'école commence trop tôt — mon premier cours est à huit heures et demie ! En plus, je suis souvent en retard parce que j'y vais avec mon petit frère, et il marche trop lentement.

2) **M1**: J'étudie neuf matières à l'école. Je n'aime pas le mardi parce que j'ai deux heures de chimie et deux heures de physique et, en tout, ça fait quatre heures de science. Je trouve ça fatigant. Mais heureusement, nous n'avons pas d'école le mercredi.

3) **M1**: On prend le déjeuner chaque jour à midi. Je mange à l'école tous les jours avec mes amis. Après avoir mangé, nous jouons au football, sauf le jeudi quand je vais au club de tennis. Je ne m'intéresse pas au tennis, donc l'année prochaine je vais m'inscrire au cours de basket.

Track 30 — p.103

1a) **M1**: Salut Karine ! Est-ce que tu aimes les langues ?

F1: Pour moi les langues ne sont pas aussi utiles que les sciences. Je préfère la chimie mais je trouve que de nos jours, toutes les sciences sont indispensables. En plus, les langues sont plus difficiles pour moi.

1b) **F1**: Qu'en penses-tu, Nadia ?

F2: Je ne suis pas d'accord avec toi. Moi, j'adore communiquer avec les autres, donc savoir parler une autre langue, c'est important. Pourtant, pour moi, la matière la plus importante c'est l'informatique, car il faut comprendre la technologie pour survivre dans le monde. Heureusement, j'adore passer mon temps sur l'ordinateur parce que je pense que c'est l'avenir.

1c) **F2**: Tu n'es pas d'accord, Salim ?

M1: Si, mais je crois que les jeunes comptent trop sur les ordinateurs et passent trop de temps devant l'écran. Je trouve aussi qu'il est nécessaire d'être fort en maths, en sciences, en français et en anglais. Il ne faut pas toujours utiliser un ordinateur.

Track 31 — p.103

2a) **M1**: Nous cherchons des jeunes enthousiastes et motivés pour travailler avec nous dans notre hôtel l'été prochain. Il faut avoir un bon sens de l'humour et pouvoir travailler en équipe. Ce ne sont pas les qualifications qui comptent. Par contre, c'est votre personnalité et votre dynamisme qui sont importants.

2b) **F1**: Aimez-vous les enfants ? Et le contact avec le public ? Si votre réponse est oui, ce travail est parfait pour vous. Nous cherchons des jeunes qui ont déjà passé le bac pour travailler dans notre colonie de vacances. Logement et nourriture compris. Vous auriez un jour de congé par semaine. C'est un travail qui n'est pas toujours facile mais c'est très satisfaisant.

Practice Exam — Listening Paper

Track 32 — p.158-166

1) **F1**: 'Bistrot du Sommelier' vous propose un menu à prix fixe — trois plats pour 15 euros, chaque jour sauf le samedi.

2) **M1**: Venez vite voir le nouveau bistro 'Au Bon Marché'. Nous vous offrons un menu classique et des plats français. Notre service est rapide et nous avons aussi une terrasse à l'extérieur avec des vues superbes sur la mer.

3) **F2**: Un vrai goût de l'Italie à deux pas de Montmartre — nous vous invitons à découvrir les meilleurs plats de pâtes de toute la ville.

4) **F1**: Retrouvez les saveurs authentiques de l'Espagne dans notre bar à tapas ; ouvert tous les jours de 17h à 23h. Vous devez absolument réserver.

5) **M1**: Il y a beaucoup de matières que je trouve ennuyeuses — la géographie est la pire. Je préfère l'histoire parce que c'est vraiment intéressant, mais on doit trop lire.

6) **F2**: L'allemand ne me plaît pas parce que c'est trop compliqué. Pourtant, la matière qui me pose le plus de problèmes est la chimie, parce que je n'arrive pas à faire les calculs.

7) **F1**: Je fais de l'EPS — cela me permet de rester en bonne forme, mais ce n'est pas une matière très utile pour l'avenir. Je voudrais être informaticienne, donc l'informatique est la matière la plus pratique.

8) **F2**: Marc, est-ce que tu es sportif ?

M1: Oui, j'aime beaucoup le sport. Je joue au football deux fois par semaine et je fais partie de l'équipe de foot de mon collège.

9) **M1**: Je pratique différents sports selon la saison. En hiver, par exemple, je fais du patin à glace avec mon frère. Puis en été, quand nous allons à la plage, je fais du ski nautique.

10) **M1**: Et toi Sylvie, est-ce que tu fais du sport ?

F1: Oui, je suis membre d'un club de tennis. Je joue au tennis le week-end et aussi le mercredi soir.

11) **F1**: Pratiques-tu un sport, Lisa ?

F2: Moi non, je faisais du cyclisme il y a deux ans mais je me suis blessée et je ne peux plus en faire. Maintenant je préfère regarder le vélo à la télévision.

E.g. **F2**: Florian, mon amie m'a dit que tu avais choisi de travailler aux États-Unis avec une association caritative qui organise des colonies de vacances pour les enfants défavorisés. C'est vrai ?

M1: Oui, c'est vrai, j'y suis allé. Si on cherche une expérience unique, je recommande ces colonies de vacances. J'ai passé deux mois là-bas et j'ai l'intention d'y retourner l'année prochaine.

12) **M1**: Et toi, Sandrine, est-il vrai que tu as passé une année à Madagascar ?

F2: Oui, j'ai aidé une organisation environnementale et c'était incroyable. J'ai participé à beaucoup de projets — j'ai même passé neuf mois dans les forêts pour protéger les espèces en danger.

13) **F2**: Zayna, comment décrirais-tu ton expérience au cœur des Andes ?

F1: Quelle expérience ! C'était une expédition au Pérou qui avait pour but d'aider les villages pauvres dans les montagnes. Nous avons passé deux mois dans un petit village presque inaccessible. La communauté avait grand besoin d'un hôpital. Le travail m'a énormément plu mais c'était très fatigant !

14) **F1**: Et toi, Kassim, qu'est-ce que tu as fait ?

M1: Mon grand-père habite dans une maison de retraite dans ma ville, donc j'ai choisi d'y passer cinq semaines. J'ai aidé à cuisiner et à nettoyer, mais j'ai passé la plupart du temps avec les résidents parce que beaucoup d'entre eux se sentaient seuls.

E.g **F2**: Alors, Paul, comment expliques-tu la popularité des réseaux sociaux.

M1: De nos jours, presque tout le monde se sert des réseaux sociaux, donc c'est la façon la plus facile de contacter les gens — et ça ne coûte rien.

15) **F2**: Et tes amis ? Comment s'en servent-ils ?

M1: Normalement, mes amis postent des photos car on aime se tenir au courant de tout ce qui se passe dans nos vies. Quelquefois, ils organisent des fêtes sur les réseaux sociaux parce qu'il est possible de communiquer en groupe sans être ensemble.

16) **F2**: Quel moyen préfères-tu pour y accéder ?

M1: Si j'ai l'intention de lire des postes et regarder des vidéos, je préfère utiliser mon ordinateur. Cependant, j'utilise toujours mon portable pour envoyer des messages parce que c'est plus pratique et ça me permet de garder mes conversations privées.

17) **F2**: Est-ce que ta famille y accède ?

M1: Pour ma mère, les réseaux sociaux représentent la façon la plus facile de parler aux membres de sa famille qui habitent à l'étranger. Cependant, mon frère pense que les réseaux sociaux ne sont pas nécessaires.

18) **F2**: Tout le monde sait qu'il faut faire de l'exercice pour rester en bonne santé, mais beaucoup de gens disent qu'ils n'ont pas le temps. Si vous pensez que vous ne pouvez pas prendre le temps de faire de l'exercice, je vous conseille de réfléchir à votre routine quotidienne et d'envisager comment vous pourriez l'adapter.

19) **F2**: Par exemple, vous pourriez aller au travail à pied ou à vélo, au lieu de conduire. Si vous prenez l'autobus pour aller au travail, vous pourriez descendre un arrêt plus tôt pour marcher.

20) **F1**: J'aime mon collège, mais je pense que le collège pourrait faire plus d'effort pour améliorer l'expérience des étudiants en dehors des heures de classe.

21) **F1**: Il y a beaucoup d'équipes sportives, mais ce serait mieux si on pouvait aussi organiser des clubs pour les étudiants qui ne sont pas sportifs mais qui ont d'autres intérêts, comme la musique ou le théâtre.

22) **F2**: Les services de diffusion musicale en ligne sont accessibles en quelques clics et la popularité des services de musique en continu a augmenté. J'accueille le groupe musical suisse, *Les Moutardiers*, qui va nous donner leurs opinions. Alors, qu'en pensez-vous, Alain ?

M1: Il est facile de trouver la musique qu'on veut sur les services de diffusion musicale en ligne. Par contre, la qualité de son est inférieure aux CD.

23) **F2**: Et vous, Michelle, qu'est-ce que vous en pensez ?

F1: Il est possible d'écouter les chansons tout de suite et cela me convient parfaitement. Malgré tous les avantages, je crois que cette nouvelle manière d'écouter de la musique n'est pas très utile pour les nouveaux groupes, parce qu'ils ont besoin de vendre leurs albums afin de gagner de l'argent.

24) **F1**: J'adore Noël. Les villes sont pleines de lumières de Noël et tout le monde est heureux et gai. Ma tradition de Noël préférée est le sapin de Noël — mon frère et moi le décorerons la semaine prochaine après avoir rendu visite à notre tante.

25) **F1**: Cette année, je vais passer Noël avec ma famille dans le sud de la France. Normalement, c'est difficile d'organiser une réunion familiale parce que nous sommes très nombreux. Je dois acheter beaucoup de cadeaux. Je vais offrir un collier à ma belle-mère et j'ai une figurine d'un cheval pour ma cousine. Il me reste un cadeau de Noël à acheter — un train électrique pour mon petit frère.

26) **M1**: La maison de maître Baillehache était située rue Grouaise, à gauche, en allant à Châteaudun. C'était une petite maison blanche d'un seul étage. La large rue pavée était déserte en semaine mais animée le samedi du flot des paysans venant au marché. Derrière, un étroit jardin descendait jusqu'au Loir.

Ce samedi-là, dans la pièce qui servait d'étude et qui donnait sur la rue, à droite du vestibule, le petit clerc, un enfant de quinze ans, chétif et pâle, avait relevé l'un des rideaux, pour voir passer le monde.

27) **F2**: Jamil, as-tu des projets pour l'avenir ?

M1: Mon rêve, c'est d'être journaliste. Écrire est ma passion et je regarde les informations à la télévision tous les jours. Pour acquérir de l'expérience, j'écris des articles pour le journal scolaire et en été j'ai l'intention de passer quelques mois dans le bureau de mon cousin, parce qu'il travaille comme secrétaire pour un journal régional.

28) **M1**: Et toi Marie, quels sont tes projets pour l'avenir ?

F2: Moi, vraiment je ne sais pas. Quand j'étais plus jeune, je voulais être artiste parce que j'aimais peindre. Pourtant, mes parents pensaient que ce n'était pas un métier important comme avocat ou médecin. Alors, j'ai changé d'avis et maintenant je pense que je voudrais être agent de voyage car je suis forte en langues.

29) **M1**: Dans le nord du pays, surtout à Bruges, on prévoit des averses continues jusqu'à minuit. Après 2h, on s'attend à de la grêle dans les zones élevées et il y a un risque de neige.

30) **M1**: Alerte pour les citoyens de Bruxelles : des vents très forts en provenance du sud-est souffleront pendant toute la journée. On prévoit des températures plus basses et on conseille aux Bruxellois d'éviter les voyages superflus.

31) **M1**: Il fera froid dans le sud, surtout à Charleroi, où la température tombera en-dessous de zéro. On avertit tous les citoyens du temps brumeux qui réduira la visibilité dans un rayon de 50 mètres ou moins.

32) **F1**: La Bretagne est la destination idéale pour ceux qui aiment découvrir de nouvelles choses. Explorez les 2700 km de côtes et de nombreuses îles qui montrent la beauté de la région.
Visitez l'île d'Ouessant, le lieu le plus à l'ouest de toute la France, ou voyagez aux Sept-Îles pour observer les oiseaux.

33) **F1**: Découvrez la grande richesse historique de la Bretagne en visitant les châteaux médiévaux et les cités fortifiées. Plongez-vous dans la culture bretonne et assistez aux festivals tels que la 'Fête des Remparts' ou le 'Festival du Chant de Marin'.

34) **F1**: N'oubliez pas : aucun voyage en Bretagne n'est complet sans goûter ses fameuses soupes de poisson et sa bisque de homard. Si vous préférez quelque chose de sucré, essayez les kouign-amanns. Ces gâteaux datent du 19e siècle et ils se font avec de la pâte à pain, du beurre salé et du sucre.

Index

A

à, au, à la, à l', aux 2, 71, 87, 128
accents 16
accommodation 57, 88
adjectives 9, 18, 19, 57, 78, 110-113, 119
adverbs 33, 116-119
agreement
  of adjectives 4, 6, 7, 18, 28, 110, 113, 119
  of past participles 60, 136, 137, 142, 147, 148
alphabet 16
'après avoir' / 'après être' 147
articles 2, 17, 33, 61, 71, 102, 108-109, 128, 143

B

Bastille Day 48
blogs 41, 42
buildings 56, 57, 88, 91

C

careers 101, 102
ce, cet, cette, ces 10, 112
ceci, cela, ça 125
celui, celle, ceux, celles 125
'chaque' 112
charity 81
Christmas 49, 50
cinema 28
clothes 59, 60
comparatives 17, 113, 118, 123
conditional 7, 59, 144
conjunctions 42, 127
could (conditional) 144
countries 87

D

dates 3, 89
days of the week 2, 33
de, du, de la, de l', des 27, 42, 61, 89, 109, 128, 143
demonstrative adjectives 112
demonstrative pronouns 125
'depuis' 99, 129, 133, 139
describing people 18, 19
direct object pronouns 40, 121
direct objects 117, 121, 136
directions 62
'dont' 124

E

eating out 31
emphatic pronouns 123, 145
'en' 69, 87, 122, 123, 128, 147
environment 77, 78, 81
exam advice 152-156

F

false friends 19, 154
family and friends 17-21
festivals 48-50
films 9, 28
food 30, 31, 61, 69
free time 27-33, 41, 42, 48, 81
further education 101
future tenses 21, 135

G

gender 56, 108-112, 125
greetings 6

H

had done (pluperfect tense) 147
health 69-71
hobbies 27-29, 32, 33
holidays 87-91
home 56-58
homelessness 79, 80

I

'il faut' 39, 80, 149
imperatives 62, 123, 145
imperfect tense 19, 27, 138, 139
impersonal verbs 149
indefinite adjectives 112
indefinite pronouns 122
indirect object pronouns 121
indirect objects 121
infinitives 21, 39, 101, 102, 131, 133, 135, 149
instructions 62, 123, 145
intensifiers 119
Internet 40-42
interrogative
  adjectives 4
  adverbs 4
  pronouns 124
  verbs 5, 133
irregular
  adjectives 110, 111
  adverbs 116
  imperatives 145
  nouns 108
  verbs 41, 132, 135, 137, 138

J

je, tu, il, elle... 121
jobs 102

Index

L

le, la, l', les 108, 109, 121
listening exam 152, 157-166
literary texts 21, 56, 88, 154

M

marriage 21
may I... ? 6, 7
me, te, le, la... 121
me, te, lui... 121
me, te, se... 142
menus 31
mien, mienne... 125
mobile technology 39
moi, toi, lui, elle, soi... 123
mon, ma, mes 112
months of the year 3
music 27
myself, yourself... 123, 142

N

nationalities 16
natural disasters 79, 80
negatives 50, 123, 143, 145
nouns 108
numbers 1

O

'on' 49, 121, 148
opinions 8-10, 30, 117

P

'parce que' / 'car' 9
partnership 21
passive voice 148
past participles 91, 136, 137, 148
'pendant' 127, 129
perfect infinitives 147
perfect tense 136, 137
personalities 19
pluperfect tense 147

plurals 18, 108, 110
polite phrases 6, 7, 59
pollution 77, 78
possessive adjectives 112
possessive pronouns 125
poverty 79-81
prepositions 42, 87, 109, 128, 129, 133
present participles 69, 147
present tense 99, 131-133
pronouns 121-125

Q

quantifiers 119
quantities 61
quel, quelle, quels... 4
'quelque' 62
questions — how to ask them 4, 5, 124, 133
'qui' and 'que' 4, 29, 124

R

reading exam 154, 172-187
reflexive pronouns 58, 142
reflexive verbs 20, 33, 58, 81, 137, 142, 145
relationships 20, 21
relative pronouns 124
restaurants 31
rooms 57

S

school
  life 99
  pressures 100
  routines 98
  subjects 97
  types 99
  years 99, 101
seasons 3
shopping 59-61
should (conditional) 144
social media 41, 42
social problems 79-81
speaking exam 153, 167-171

special occasions 48-50
sport 32, 33
study 97, 101
subject pronouns 121
subjunctive 149
superlatives 113, 118

T

technology 39-42
tenses 131
times of day 2, 3
town 56, 62, 91
translations 17, 28, 40, 58, 71, 78, 90, 101, 102, 156
transport 56, 90, 98
'tu' / 'vous' 6, 62, 121
TV 29

U

'un', 'une' 102, 109
unemployment 79-81
used to (imperfect tense) 27, 138, 139

V

verbs 131
violence 79

W

was (imperfect tense) 138, 139
weather 63, 149
where is... ? 4, 62
would (conditional) 7, 59, 144
writing exam 155, 188-189

Y

'y' 122